Statistical Models
for the Social and
Behavioral Sciences

Statistical Models for the Social and Behavioral Sciences

---

*Multiple Regression
and Limited-Dependent
Variable Models*

WILLIAM H. CROWN

Westport, Connecticut
London

Library of Congress Cataloging-in-Publication Data

Crown, William H.
    Statistical models for the social and behavioral sciences :
    multiple regression and limited-dependent variable models / William
    H. Crown.
        p.   cm.
    Includes bibliographical references and index.
    ISBN 0–275–95316–5 (alk. paper)
    1. Regression analysis.   2. Social sciences—Statistical methods.
    I. Title.
    HA31.3.C76   1998
    519.5′36—dc21   97–5583

British Library Cataloguing in Publication Data is available.

Library of Congress Catalog Card Number: 97–5583
ISBN: 0–275–95316–5

First published in 1998

Praeger Publishers, 88 Post Road West, Westport, CT 06881
An imprint of Greenwood Publishing Group, Inc.

Printed in the United States of America

The paper used in this book complies with the
Permanent Paper Standard issued by the National
Information Standards Organization (Z39.48–1984).

10 9 8 7 6 5 4 3 2

Contents

Tables and Figures

TABLES

FIGURES

Acknowledgments

This book would not have been possible without the assistance of many people over the years. In particular, I would like to thank my classes in statistics, regression analysis, and econometrics at the Florence Heller Graduate School, Brandeis University who were the inspiration for the book. I would also like to thank Margaret Stubbs and Nan Kritzler who provided able manuscript preparation assistance, and who showed me the mysteries of equation editors in several word processing packages. In addition, I am indebted to my daughter Sarah for her assistance in preparing most of the graphics. The experience of working with Sarah was tremendously rewarding and, undoubtedly, the highlight of the entire writing and publication process. Finally, I would like to express my appreciation to Robin, my wife, who put up with me when I started this project while on vacation a decade ago and simply smiled whenever I spoke of finishing it.

1
Introduction to Multivariate Modeling

The public policy questions of today are extraordinarily complex. Consider, for example, the problem of the growing number of children in poverty. It is reasonable to argue that the growing number of children in poverty is related to the rise in the number of single, female-headed households. Yet it is not very likely that the rise in single, female-headed households is the *only* cause of the increase in child poverty. Rather, the increase in child poverty is a complicated function, not only of the rise in the number of single, female-headed households, but also of the work and marriage disincentives built into welfare programs, the lack of quality child care that restricts employment opportunities for parents, and many other factors. To understand the problems facing modern society, it is necessary to move beyond simple notions of bivariate associations to develop more-sophisticated theories of how such problems arise. Social scientists and policy makers hope that by understanding the causes of social and economic problems they will be in a better position to design policy remedies to reduce the incidence and/or the severity of these problems.

THEORY AND MODEL BUILDING

The process used by policy analysts to test theories concerning the causes of social problems and the policies developed to address them typically involves several steps. The first step is to develop a theory that expresses how a particular variable, such as the increase in child poverty, is related to other variables. Theory development usually takes place in the context of an existing literature. Researchers are constantly trying to identify and remedy knowledge gaps in various areas of social policy. Sometimes researchers identify variables that they believe are important to consider but which have been omitted in prior studies. In other instances, they may develop better measures of variables than those previously available (perhaps by conducting their own survey), or they may specify different relationships between a given set of explanatory variables and a policy variable of interest. In other instances, researchers may utilize alternative (more appropriate) statistical techniques than those previously used in the literature.

The theory is then tested by using data to estimate a statistical model that provides numerical estimates of the relationships between a policy variable (or variables) of interest and a set of explanatory variables. The estimated model may fully support, partially support, or contradict the theory. Of course, from the researcher's standpoint, it is nice to have the estimated model support the theory. This happens when the key variables have the expected signs and are statistically significant. All too frequently, though, key variables to one's theory turn out to be statistically insignificant or to have the "incorrect" sign. When this happens the theory must be reconsidered, the model respecified, or new data collected with which to test the original theory.

In any event, researchers usually attempt to revise the model by examining alternative functional relationships between the dependent and explanatory variables, by dropping insignificant variables, or by using an alternative statistical technique. If, at the end of this process, the model still provides statistical evidence that is partially or fully at odds with the theory, then two outcomes are possible: (1) the theory can be altered (or discarded altogether) or (2) additional data can be sought to carry out another test of the theory. Thus, theoretical plausibility is the first, and most important, criterion that is used to evaluate models.

ADDITIONAL CRITERIA FOR EVALUATING MODELS

In addition to theoretical plausibility, there are a number of other criteria that are commonly used to evaluate models. One frequently overlooked criterion is that of simplicity. When a researcher builds a model, the aim should be to represent the essence of the phenomenon as simply as possible. Yet there is no denying that the trend in most areas of social science research has been to build increasingly sophisticated models. Presumably these models replicate reality more closely than less sophisticated models, but they do so at a cost. As models become more realistic in terms of the variables included and the functional forms assumed, the essence of a problem may be obfuscated by detail. On the other hand, omitting important explanatory variables, misspecifying functional forms, ignoring simultaneous relationships between dependent and explanatory variables, and otherwise violating the assumptions that underlie the use of regression analysis and related techniques can result in seriously flawed estimates—limiting the ability to test theories. The tradeoffs involved in simplicity versus sophistication of approach will be discussed throughout the course of the book.

Computational cost is a criterion that is closely related to that of simplicity. There are often instances in which several estimation techniques can be applied to the same problem. Usually one of these techniques is superior to the others in terms of its statistical properties (discussed in Chapter 2). But often the theoretically preferred choice requires more computer time or is less widely available in statistical packages. A common example of this arises when estimating models with a binary dependent variable. Although it will be shown in Chapter 6 that it is preferable to use maximum likelihood techniques such as logit and probit when estimating models involving binary dependent variables, useful results can often be obtained by using regression analysis in such instances. A decade ago, it was difficult to find logit and probit routines in commercially available statistical packages, and such routines were comparatively expensive to use. Today, however, logit and probit are available in virtually all commercial statistical packages, and these routines are now computationally much more efficient than they were a few years ago. Thus, the cost and availability rationale for using regression analysis when one really ought to be using logit or probit is no longer very compelling. The commercial availability of statistical procedures always lags behind theoretical developments in the literature.

A final criterion for evaluating a model is "goodness of fit." In regression models the formal test for the significance of a model is the F-statistic, which tests whether at least one of the slope coefficients is statistically different from zero. Maximum likelihood models, such as logit and probit, use a Chi-Square test to accomplish the same thing. It is tempting to place considerable weight on goodness of fit in assessing a model's performance. It will be argued in Chapter 3, however, that goodness of fit is generally the *least* important criterion for evaluating model performance.

OVERVIEW OF THE BOOK

This is a book about building statistical models to analyze problems in social and behavioral research. Chapter 2 begins by reviewing concepts of probability and several important probability distributions. This discussion leads to a consideration of sampling distributions. Sampling distributions are central to hypothesis testing and to choosing the appropriate statistical technique for particular estimation problems. Chapter 2 also presents a brief discussion of expected value—an important statistical technique for determining the properties of alternative estimators or different ways to estimate population parameters. It is through the use of expected value that mathematical statisticians and econometricians are able to compare the properties of different estimators for various estimation problems. Finally, Chapter 2 discusses measures of bivariate associations among variables that are appropriate given the measurement level of the variables under consideration.

In Chapter 3, the regression model and its underlying assumptions are presented. The multiple regression model is derived and the interpretation of regression output is discussed. Multiple regression is an extraordinarily powerful statistical technique *provided that its underlying assumptions are met*. However, it is very important to know what kinds of problems may arise when these assumptions are violated.

One of the assumptions of multiple regression is that the estimated model is linear in the coefficients. In the real world, of course, relationships among variables are seldom linear. Fortunately, however, many types of nonlinearities are easily accommodated by regression models. Chapter 4 discusses a number of ways to handle nonlinearities in regression analysis and how these different approaches affect the interpretation of the results obtained.

It is also possible, using multiple regression, to examine the effects of qualitative variables on a dependent variable of interest. Chapter 4 discusses alternative ways that qualitative variables can be entered into regression models and the meaning of the resulting coefficients. The results of regression models with qualitative explanatory variables are compared to those of analysis of variance.

Collectively, Chapters 3 and 4 present the basic multiple regression model in some detail. Implicitly, however, the discussion in these chapters assumes that all of the assumptions of the regression model have been met. Chapter 5 considers these assumptions in more depth. One of the goals of this book is to present a discussion of the regression model's assumptions, diagnostic tests associated with these assumptions, and remedial techniques for dealing with violations of the regression model's assumptions that is accessible to researchers without extensive mathematical preparation.

In many cases, there are methods for dealing with violations of the regression model's assumptions. A notable exception is when the dependent variable is categorical or limited in some other manner. In such instances, alternative estimators based on maximum likelihood procedures are required. Chapter 6 presents the logic behind maximum likelihood estimators, as well as a detailed discussion of logit models. A thorough understanding of these models has been beyond the reach of many researchers because the discussion of maximum likelihood estimators is found mainly in econometrics texts and technical economics and statistics journals. Moreover, discussions of maximum likelihood estimators have tended to be highly technical with limited attention to practical empirical issues such as methods of interpreting and presenting results. Therefore, these practical aspects of logit models are given considerable attention in Chapter 6.

Chapter 7 extends the logit models considered in Chapter 6 to problems where the dependent variable has three or more categories. Chapter 7 also considers the often subtle issues of censoring, truncation, and sample selection bias. Using examples from different areas of social policy, it describes the various forms of sample selection and truncation and the effects that these may have on the statistical properties of estimators. Alternative methods to correct for these problems are then presented. Finally, Chapter 8 provides a summary of the various techniques discussed in the book.

2
Inferential Statistics and Measures of Association

ALTERNATIVE CONCEPTS OF PROBABILITY

Any statistical analysis, whether it be comparing the average incomes of two demographic groups or estimating the parameters of a complex multivariate model, is founded on basic concepts of probability. Two primary definitions of probability are widely used. The first is what is known as the "classical" definition of probability. The classical definition of probability is commonly used to calculate probabilities associated with distinct and identifiable events—for example, alternative outcomes in card games and in other games of chance, the rolling of a die, drawing balls of various colors from urns, and so forth.

The second definition of probability, and the one most widely used in social and behavioral research, is based on *relative frequencies*. This definition states that as the size of a sample approaches infinity, the relative frequencies calculated from the sample approach their corresponding probabilities in the population. In this sense, one can think of probabilities as being *population parameters* and relative frequencies as being *sample estimators*. Table 2.1 illustrates the calculation of relative frequencies using years of education as the variable of interest. The first column of Table 2.1 shows the *sample frequencies*, or number of people, age 18 and older having different education levels. For example, 539 people have less than a high school education, 2,009 have completed high school but gone no further, 1,064 have completed 4 or more years of college, and so on. The total sample size is 5,275. To calculate the percentage of people in the sample who have a particular education level, the frequency for that education level is simply divided by the total sample size. This is known as the *relative frequency* and is shown in column 2. Note that relative frequencies sum to one just as probabilities do. Probability distributions based on the notion of relative frequencies are commonly referred to as *density functions* in the statistics literature.

Sometimes researchers are interested in the probability that a variable takes on a value less than, or equal to, a certain amount. For example, a researcher might be

Table 2.1
Frequencies, Relative Frequencies, and Cumulative Frequencies

Years of Education	Frequency	Relative Frequency	Cumulative Frequency
<8 years	539	0.10	0.10
8–11 years	595	0.11	0.21
High school graduate	2,009	0.38	0.59
Some college	1,068	0.20	0.79
College graduate and higher	1,064	0.20	1.00[a]
	5,275	1.00[a]	

Source: Random sample of 1989 Current Population Survey.

[a] Table entries do not sum to 1.00 due to rounding.

interested in the probability that an individual has a high school education or less. Such probabilities are known as *cumulative probabilities* and are estimated by the *cumulative relative frequencies* shown in the third column of Table 2.1. For the lowest value of a variable, the cumulative frequency is equal to the relative frequency. For example, in Table 2.1, the cumulative frequency of having less than 8 years of education is 0.10—the same value as the relative frequency. The cumulative frequency of having a high school education or less, however, is equal to the sum of the relative frequencies associated with having less than 8 years (0.10), 8 to 11 years (0.11), and exactly 12 years (0.38) of education. These relative frequencies sum to 0.60, meaning that 60 percent of the population has a high school education or less. By definition, everyone has an education equal to the highest level or less. Consequently, the cumulative frequency associated with being educated past the college level or having *any* level of education less than that is 1.00.

Now suppose that education is cross tabulated with income level as in Table 2.2. The resulting frequencies refer to the number of people who are members of a particular income group *and* who have a particular education level. For instance, 210 people in Table 2.2 have incomes of less than $5,000 and less than 8 years of education, 345 persons have incomes of $10,000 to $14,999 and are high school graduates, 508 persons have incomes of $25,000 or more and have 4 years of college education or more, and so on. Cross tabulations such as those in Table 2.2 are known as *joint frequency distributions*. As with univariate distributions, joint frequency distributions can be converted to *joint relative frequency distributions* by dividing each table entry by the sample size. In the example, joint relative

Table 2.2
Joint Frequencies of Education and Income

Years of Education	<$5,000	5,000–9,999	10,000–14,999	15,000–19,999	20,000–24,999	25,000+
<8 years	210	150	85	42	23	29
8–11 years	230	135	89	58	28	55
HS grad	491	338	345	259	192	384
Some college	256	165	134	136	104	273
College grad & higher	123	94	111	112	116	508

Source: Random sample of 1989 Current Population Survey.

frequencies refer to the percentage of sample observations that are members of a particular income group and who have achieved a particular education level.

Dividing each entry in Table 2.2 by the total sample size (5,275) yields the joint relative frequency distribution shown in Table 2.3. For example, 4 percent of the sample has an education of less than 8 years and an income level of less than $5,000; 10 percent of the sample has 4 or more years of college and an income level of $25,000 or higher. Note that summing across the rows in Table 2.3 yields estimates of the probabilities associated with having a particular education level irrespective of income level. These estimates are exactly the same as the relative frequencies reported in Table 2.1. Conversely, summing down the columns of Table 2.3 results in an alternative relative frequency distribution that shows the probability of having a particular income level irrespective of education level. Such distributions, formed by consolidating the information in a joint relative frequency distribution, are known as *marginal relative frequency distributions* and provide estimates of *marginal probability distributions or density functions*.

In the example, the concept of joint relative frequencies has been illustrated by cross tabulating just two variables. This concept, however, is very general and is equally valid for cross tabulations involving any number of variables. Joint frequency distributions provide a fundamental measure of covariation among variables that is at the very core of model building and hypothesis testing in statistics.

USEFUL PROBABILITY DISTRIBUTIONS

The discussion thus far has considered some of the concepts of probability based on notions of relative frequency. However, a variety of different functions are useful for describing observed frequency distributions. In order to draw statistical inferences about population parameters from sample statistics it is necessary to make some assumptions about the functional form of probability distributions in different contexts. As in inferential statistics, several probability distributions are particularly useful for multivariate modeling. A knowledge of the relationships among these distributions is helpful for understanding hypothesis testing in regression and discrete-choice models.

The Normal Distribution

A good place to begin is with the normal distribution. For a normally distributed random variable X, the probability of observing a particular value of X is given by:

$$P(X_i) = \frac{1}{\sqrt{2\pi\sigma^2}} \, e^{-\frac{1}{2}\left(\frac{X_i - \mu_x}{\sigma_x}\right)^2}$$

The formula for the normal distribution is imposing but it is actually much simpler than it appears. All terms in the formula are constants except for the individual values of the random variable X. The terms π and e are mathematical constants equal to approximately 3.1416 and 2.718, respectively. Similarly μ_x is the population mean and σ_x^2 is the population variance for the random variable X.

The fact that the normal distribution varies with different values of μ_x and σ_x^2 makes it cumbersome to work with when conducting statistical tests because it is necessary to add up the area under the curve for each value of μ_x and σ_x^2. It is possible, however, to define a new variable $Z_i = (X_i - \mu_x)/\sigma$, which measures the standard deviation of each observation from the variable's mean. This new variable will have a standard deviation of one and a mean of zero and is known as a standardized normal random variable. Its probability distribution is a simplified version of that given above:

$$P(Z_i) = \frac{1}{\sqrt{2\pi}} e^{-\frac{1}{2}Z_i^2}$$

In most introductory statistics texts, the standardized normal distribution is given a great deal of attention as the appropriate probability distribution to use for testing hypotheses about population means using test statistics based on large samples. Ultimately, however, the usefulness of the normal distribution for testing hypotheses regarding means is limited because it is not valid for small samples. The t-distribution (discussed below) is valid in small samples, but has virtually identical probability values in large samples to those of the standardized normal distribution. Consequently, there is no appreciable advantage to using the normal distribution, even for testing hypotheses based on sample statistics from large samples. The main usefulness of the standardized normal distribution is that it serves as the building block for other probability distributions.

Table 2.3
Joint Relative Frequency Distribution of Education and Income

Years of Education	<$5,000	5,000–9,999	10,000–14,999	15,000–19,999	20,000–24,999	25,000+	f_i
<8 years	.04	.03	.01	.01	.00	.01	.10
8–11 years	.04	.03	.02	.01	.01	.01	.11
HS grad	.09	.06	.07	.05	.04	.07	.38
Some college	.05	.03	.03	.03	.02	.05	.20
College grad & higher	.02	.02	.02	.02	.02	.10	.20
f_j	.24	.17	.15	.12	.09	.24	1.00[a]

Source: Random sample of 1989 Current Population Survey.

[a] Table entries do not sum to 1.00 due to rounding.

On the other hand, in the regression and discrete-choice models discussed in this text, the standardized normal distribution will play a more important role than in elementary inferential statistics. For example, the errors associated with regression models are assumed to be normally distributed. Similarly, probit models assume that the probabilities associated with observing the values of a binary variable can be described by a cumulative normal distribution. Finally, just as in inferential statistics, the standardized normal distribution plays an important role as a building block for other probability distributions—in particular, the Chi-square, t-, and F-distributions—that are widely used in multivariate models.

The Chi-square Distribution

The Chi-square distribution is formed from the sum of squared independent standard normal variables:

$$\chi^2_{df} = \sum_{d=1}^{df} Z_d^2$$

The χ^2 distribution is highly skewed for low degrees of freedom and becomes more symmetric for higher degrees of freedom. Because they are formed from squared standard normal variables, χ^2 values are always positive. The χ^2 distribution is widely used for hypothesis testing in maximum likelihood models.

Like the standardized normal distribution, it plays an important role in defining other probability distributions.

The *t*-distribution

The *t*-distribution is defined by the ratio:

$$t = \frac{Z}{\sqrt{\chi^2/df}}$$

Like the χ^2 distribution, upon which it is partially based, the *t*-distribution varies with degrees of freedom. *t*-distributions are symmetric probability distributions that are "fatter in the tails" than the standardized normal distribution. As the number of degrees of freedom increases (with larger samples), the *t*-distribution approaches the normal distribution. *t*-statistics are used in regression and maximum likelihood models to test the statistical significance of individual coefficients.

The F-distribution

Ratios of χ^2 distributions, divided by their respective degrees of freedom, generate *F*-distributions. The *F*-distribution has a lower bound of zero like that of the χ^2 distribution and is positively skewed (also like the χ^2 distribution). The shape of the *F*-distribution varies with the degrees of freedom of each of the χ^2 distributions from which it is formed.

$$F_{v_1, v_2} = \frac{x_{v_1}^2/v_1}{x_{v_2}^2/v_2}$$

F-statistics are particularly useful for testing hypotheses about ratios of variances. *F*-tests play the same role in regression models as χ^2 tests do in maximum likelihood models.

SAMPLING DISTRIBUTIONS

Researchers are typically interested in testing hypotheses about population characteristics (or *parameters*) that are unobservable. To do this, sample data are used to generate estimates of these population parameters. Often, however, there are many different ways to generate such estimates. These different methods are called *estimators*. Some estimators are better than others. Statisticians evaluate alternative estimators by the characteristics of their *sampling distributions*. Sampling distributions are probability distributions of sample statistics such as means or variances.

All introductory courses in statistics discuss the sampling distribution of $\overline{X}$ at great length. Suppose that we had 1,000 samples of size N and we calculated $\overline{X}$ for each sample. The result would be a distribution of $\overline{X}$ values. Some of the sample means would be relatively high, some would be relatively low, and most would be somewhere in between. In other words, we would have a relative frequency distribution of sample means as shown in Figure 2.1. According to the Central Limit Theorem, if N is sufficiently large for each of the samples, this sampling distribution of $\bar{X}$ will be approximately normal with mean equal to μ (the population mean) and standard error equal to the sample standard deviation of X divided by the square root of the sample size. As the sample size N gets larger, the standard deviation of the sampling distribution gets smaller and smaller. If the sample included the entire population, the standard deviation of the sampling distribution would be zero because each $\bar{X}$ value would actually be the true population mean. The Central Limit Theorem is extremely powerful because it enables the researcher to assume that the sampling distribution of $\bar{X}$ is normally distributed *regardless of the shape of the original distribution of X*. For this reason, most hypothesis tests in inferential statistics are based on sampling distributions rather than the sample values themselves.

As mentioned above, however, sampling distributions are also helpful in deciding which methods of constructing sample estimates produce the "best" estimates of the corresponding population parameters. $\bar{X}$ is one sample estimator, or method for constructing an estimate of the population mean, but we could estimate the population mean in many other ways as well. For example, we could average the highest and lowest values of the sample, or we could simply make a wild guess. However, it turns out that the sample mean is the best estimator according to several specific statistical criteria. These criteria are very general and apply to all sample estimators.

PROPERTIES OF SAMPLING DISTRIBUTIONS

Multivariate models involve the estimation of coefficients that measure the effects of several factors on an outcome variable of interest. These coefficients are

Figure 2.1
Sampling Distribution of $\bar{X}$

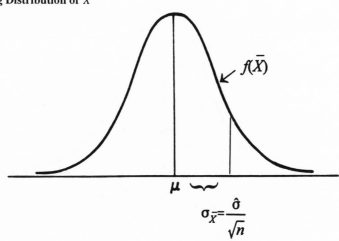

estimators of corresponding population parameters that cannot be observed, just as the sample mean is an estimator of the population mean. As with the estimation of the population mean, there are many ways to estimate the coefficients in multivariate models. Some of these estimators may be better than others —depending upon sample size, the units the variables are measured in, and other characteristics. To provide researchers with guidance in choosing among these various estimators, theoretical statisticians have derived the properties of many estimators under different conditions. These properties will be discussed at various points throughout the book.

Suppose a large number of coefficient estimates have been generated by estimating the same equation using a large number of different samples of the same size. The result would be the sampling distribution of $\hat{b}$ as shown in Figure 2.2. Some of the estimates might be very close to the true value, others might be considerably less than the true value, and still others might be considerably greater than the true value. If the mean value of the estimates produced by an estimation technique, or estimator, is exactly equal to the true population value, the estimator is said to be *unbiased*. If, as in Figure 2.3, the average value of the sampling distribution is not equal to the true population value, the estimator is said to be *biased* and the extent of the bias is equal to the difference between the mean of the sampling distribution and the true population value.

Unbiasedness is a desirable property but it is not much comfort in and of itself. This is because some of the $\hat{b}$ estimates produced by an unbiased estimator can be very different from the true population value. Consequently, researchers are also interested in the amount of variance in the sampling distribution of an estimator.

Suppose $\hat{b}^*$ is an unbiased estimator. If the variance of the sampling distribution of $\hat{b}^*$ is less than the sampling distribution of any other unbiased estimator $\hat{b}$, then

Figure 2.2
Sampling Distribution of Unbiased Estimator $\hat{b}$

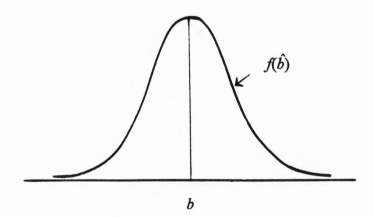

$f(\hat{b})$

b

Figure 2.3
Sampling Distribution of Biased Estimator $\hat{b}$

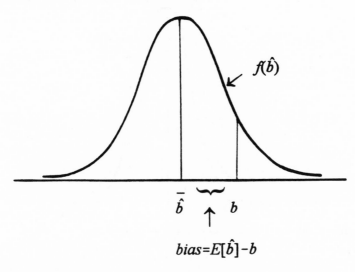

$$bias=E[\hat{b}]-b$$

$\hat{b}^{*}$ is said to be an *efficient* estimator of the true population parameter b. This is shown in Figure 2.4.

Note that the condition of efficiency requires that the estimator be unbiased. Minimum variance, in and of itself, is of little value. For example, one could repeatedly guess that the value of b was the same constant value. The resulting sampling distribution would have zero variance but the estimator is not likely to produce an unbiased estimate of b. Thus, efficient estimators are also known as best unbiased estimators.

It is, of course, possible that an estimator is only slightly biased and has a sampling distribution with a smaller variance than any unbiased estimator. This case is shown in Figure 2.5. Most researchers would prefer the estimator that generates $f(\hat{b}^{*})$ to that of $f(\hat{b})$. If one examines only unbiased estimators, however, the estimator that generates $f(\hat{b}^{*})$ is never considered. The tradeoff between bias and variance is formalized by the *mean square error (MSE) criterion*. The MSE criterion involves calculating a weighted average of the bias and variance of an estimator's sampling distribution. In practice, researchers do not usually examine the MSE of an estimator unless it is impossible to find an unbiased estimator with an acceptably small variance.

The properties of sampling distributions considered thus far are known as *small sample properties* because they hold for estimators regardless of the sample size. That is, an unbiased estimator is unbiased regardless of whether the sample is large or small. The same is true for efficient estimators and the MSE criterion. One reason for the great popularity of regression analysis is the desirability of its small sample properties.

Figure 2.4
Sampling Distribution of Efficient Estimator $\hat{b}^{*}$

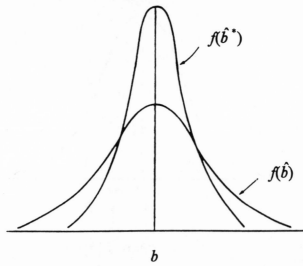

$$b$$

For many social and behavioral research problems, however, it is not possible to find estimators with these small sample properties. Regression analysis, for instance, is based on assumptions that are often violated in practice. When this is the case, the desirable small sample properties of regression may no longer hold.

When it is not possible to find an estimator with desirable small sample properties, researchers often justify the use of a particular estimator based upon its *asymptotic properties*—the properties of its sampling distribution in extremely large samples. The sampling distributions of most estimators change with increases or decreases in sample size. For example, the reader may recall that the variance of the sampling distribution of $\overline{X}$ decreases with increasing sample size. It is also often the case that biased estimators become less biased with increasing sample size. If the mean of the sampling distribution of $\hat{b}$ is equal to the true population value b as the sample size approaches infinity, the estimator is said to be *asymptotically unbiased*.

If the sampling distribution approaches a particular probability distribution as the size of the repeated samples approaches infinity, this probability distribution is known as the *limiting or asymptotic distribution*. Besides unbiasedness, two additional asymptotic properties are defined in terms of the limiting distribution. If the limiting distribution of $\hat{b}$ collapses on a particular value b^{*} as the sample size approaches infinity, b^{*} is called the *probability limit* of $\hat{b}$. If, in turn, b^{*} is equal to the true population value, then the estimator is said to be *consistent*.

The variance of the limiting distribution of $\hat{b}$ is known as the *asymptotic variance* of $\hat{b}$. If the estimator is consistent and its asymptotic variance is smaller than that of any other consistent estimator, $\hat{b}$ is said to be *asymptotically efficient*.[1]

Figure 2.5
Illustration of Mean Square Error (MSE) Criterion

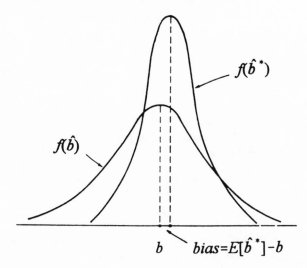

EXPECTED VALUE

Mathematical statisticians and econometricians spend a lot of time figuring out the properties of estimators so that applied researchers can choose appropriate estimators in different situations. But how can they relate different estimators that have been derived using sample data to population parameters when the population parameters are generally unobservable? The answer is by using a technique known as *expected value*.

A detailed treatment of expected value is beyond the scope of this text. But some insights into the technique can be gained through the aid of a simple example. Suppose we are interested in estimating the average years of educational attainment in the population. Table 2.4 reports a detailed frequency distribution of the educational data presented earlier in Table 2.1. Using this frequency distribution, we can calculate the average education level of the adult population using the following formula:

$$\bar{X} = \sum_i X_i f(X_i)$$

The above formula simply weights the education levels, X_i, by the relative frequencies of the sample members having these education levels, $f(X_i)$. In our example, the mean education level is 12.5 years.

Now suppose a random variable X has the following probability distribution:

$$X \quad f(X)$$
$$X_1 \quad f(X_1)$$
$$X_2 \quad f(X_2)$$
$$X_3 \quad f(X_3)$$
$$\vdots \quad \vdots$$
$$X_i \quad f(X_i)$$

where the $f(X_i)$ are the probabilities of observing a particular value for the random variable (e.g., the relative frequency of a particular education level in the population). The expected value of X is defined as:

$$E(X) = \sum X_i \; f(X_i)$$

$$= \mu_x$$

In this simple case, the expected value of X is nothing more than the weighted average of the values of X with the weights being given by $f(X_i)$

To see how expected value can be used to show the relationship between sample statistics and population parameters, consider the relationship between the sample mean and the population mean. The formula for calculating $\overline{X}$ is:

$$\overline{X} = \frac{1}{N}(\sum X_i)$$

Consequently, the expected value of $\overline{X}$ is given by:

$$E(\overline{X}) = E(\frac{1}{N}\sum X_i)$$

Because 1/N is a constant, it can be factored outside of the expected value operator:

$$= \frac{1}{N}E(\sum X_i)$$

This can be rewritten as:

$$= \frac{1}{N}[E(X_1) + E(X_2) + ... + E(X_i)]$$

Table 2.4
Detailed Relative Frequency Distribution of Educational Attainment

Years of Education	Frequency	Relative Frequency
0	34	.006
1	5	.001
2	14	.003
3	26	.005
4	31	.006
5	28	.005
6	86	.016
7	72	.014
8	243	.046
9	151	.029
10	228	.043
11	216	.041
12	2009	.381
13	393	.075
14	475	.090
15	200	.038
16	606	.115
17	135	.026
18	323	.061
	5275	1.00

But, by definition, the expected value of each X_i is μ, so:

$$= \frac{1}{N}(\mu + \mu + ... \mu]$$
$$= \frac{1}{N}(N\mu)$$
$$= \mu$$

In other words, we have proven that the expected value of the sample estimator X is the true population parameter μ; the sample mean is an unbiased estimator of the population mean. Expected value is much more powerful than this example suggests, however, because it can be applied to any estimator. Expected value is widely used by theoretical statisticians and econometricians to derive the statistical properties of estimators, such as their unbiasedness or efficiency. Knowledge of these properties helps researchers to evaluate the reliability of empirical estimates. An assessment of this reliability is crucial to the formulation of policy recommendations and hypothesis testing. In standard econometrics texts, a great deal of attention is devoted to deriving the properties of alternative estimators. In this text, the emphasis is placed on the *applications* of these findings from the econometrics literature. References are provided throughout the text for those interested in the derivations of estimators and/or additional empirical applications from the literature.

THE RESEARCH PROCESS AND HYPOTHESIS TESTING

Ultimately, statistical analysis is concerned with the formulation and testing of hypotheses. It is not the aim of this book to discuss the rudiments of hypothesis testing; several excellent texts cover this ground already. Nevertheless, it may be helpful to consider briefly the structure of a typical research project and how descriptive, bivariate, and multivariate statistical techniques are utilized to test hypotheses about a policy question of interest.

Assume that an analyst is interested in the relationships between income and education level. Generally, researchers begin with a descriptive analysis of the variables of interest. If the variables are measured on an interval level, this usually entails the calculation of means, medians, standard deviations, variance, kurtosis, and skewness. Descriptive analysis for categorical variables involves the calculation of frequency distributions, relative frequency distributions, and cross tabulations.

The motivations for the descriptive phase of the analysis are generally twofold: (1) to describe the characteristics of the sample and (2) to provide sample estimates of population parameters. These motivations are, of course, closely related but are usually not quite the same thing because of alternative sampling designs.

Sampling is necessary because it is rarely possible to collect information on all members of a population (or populations). Most statistics texts implicitly or explicitly assume that sampling is random because it is easiest to generate estimates of population parameters from random samples. In *random samples*, estimators such as means, medians, and relative frequencies provide unbiased estimates of the corresponding population parameters. Of course, to derive estimates of population frequencies (e.g., the number of people in the population who have specific education levels) it is necessary to weight the sample data to reflect population values. Again, this is very straightforward with random sampling; one simply multiplies the sample frequencies by the inverse of the sampling percentage. For example, to derive estimates of population frequencies with a 5 percent random sample, the sample frequencies are multiplied by 20 (the inverse of 5 percent).

Unfortunately, real-world samples are seldom random. This is because random samples need to be very large to generate sufficient numbers of cases for small population subgroups (e.g., racial minorities). Therefore, it is common to oversample (*stratify*) small subpopulations. As a consequence, members of different subgroups within the population typically have different *sample weights* and unweighted sample data will generate biased estimates of population parameters. Fortunately, it is usually an easy matter to weight the data in *stratified samples*. Such samples contain one or more weight variables that are applied to each case to correct for oversampling. Most statistical packages will accomplish the desired weighting with a simple command. In addition, specialized programs are available that adjust variance calculations to correct biases introduced by nonrandom sampling (or design effects).

The second stage of most policy analyses is to examine relationships among the variables. The test statistics used to measure such relationships, however, differ depending on the units of measurement for the variables. A wide variety of test statistics have been proposed to measure associations among categorical variables (both nominal and ordinal). It is always safe, however, to use a χ^2 statistic for this purpose. When one variable is measured on an interval basis and the other variable is a two-category variable, the appropriate statistical test is a *t*-test. When one variable is measured on an interval scale and the other variable is categorical (with more than two categories), the appropriate measure of association is one-way or two-way analysis of variance (ANOVA). Finally, when both variables are interval, the appropriate measure of association is the Pearson correlation coefficient.

The Chi-square Test

If the data on education and income are measured as categorical variables (as in Table 2.2) then the χ^2 statistic can be used to measure the association between them. The χ^2 test is a test of the null hypothesis that two categorical variables are independent from one another. The null hypothesis that the row and column variables in a table are independent is stated as:

$$H_0: f_{ij} = f_i \, f_j$$
$$H_a: f_{ij} \neq f_i \, f_j$$

You may recall from elementary statistics that two variables are independent if their joint probability is equal to the product of their marginal probabilities. Put differently, there is no relationship between two variables if their joint probability distribution (relative frequencies) can be produced using only the information in the marginal probability distributions. The above null hypothesis can be tested with the χ^2 statistic:

$$X^2 = \sum \frac{(f_o - f_e)^2}{f_e}$$

where f_o is the observed frequency in a cell of a crosstab (or contingency) table and f_e is the expected frequency if the variables were independent.

The expected frequency, f_e, is found by multiplying the product of the marginal distributions by the sample size:

$$f_e = n\, f_i\, f_j$$

Using these definitions, the calculated value for the χ^2 statistic associated with Table 2.2 is 737. The χ^2 statistic has degrees of freedom equal to the number of rows minus one (r-1) times the number of columns minus one (c-1). In our example, the degrees of freedom = (5-1) (6-1) or 20. The tabulated value for χ^2 with 20 degrees of freedom at the 95 percent confidence level is 10.85. Since the calculated value of the χ^2 statistic (737) is greater than the tabulated value, the null hypothesis of independence between income and education is rejected. Stated differently, there is a statistically significant relationship between income and education.

Testing Differences in Two Sample Means

When one variable is interval and the other is a two-category nominal variable, it is often of interest to test if the mean value of the interval variable differs between the two categories. For example, suppose we were interested in testing whether the mean education level of people above and below the median income level differed. The null hypothesis in such a case is generally that the two means are equal:

$$H_0: \bar{X}_1 - \bar{X}_2 = 0$$
$$H_a: \bar{X}_1 - \bar{X}_2 \neq 0$$

There are two major variants of the t-test for the difference in two sample means. These are the pooled variance and separate variance t-tests. One should use the pooled variance t-test when the variances of the two samples are not significantly different. Otherwise, one should use the separate variance t-test. The formulas for the two types of t-tests are given below.

Pooled Variance

$$t = \frac{\overline{X}_1 - \overline{X}_2}{s\sqrt{\dfrac{1}{N_1} + \dfrac{1}{N_2}}} \qquad d.f. = (N_1 + N_2 - 2)$$

where

$$s = \sqrt{\frac{(N_1 - 1)s_1^2 + (N_2 - 1)s_2^2}{N_1 + N_2 - 2}}$$

Separate Variance

$$t = \frac{\overline{X}_1 - \overline{X}_2}{\sqrt{\dfrac{s_1^2}{N_1} + \dfrac{s_2^2}{N_2}}} \qquad d.f. = (N_1 + N_2 - 2)$$

To choose the appropriate *t*-test, an *F*-test is first used to determine if the sample variances are significantly different. The *F*-statistic is computed by dividing the larger sample variance by the smaller sample variance:

$$F = \frac{larger\ sample\ variance}{smaller\ sample\ variance}$$

The numerator of the *F*-statistic has degrees of freedom equal to the size of the sample associated with the larger variance minus one; the denominator has degrees of freedom equal to the size of the sample associated with the smaller variance minus one. If the calculated value of the *F*-statistic is greater than the tabulated value for a given confidence level, the null hypothesis that the two sample variances are equal is rejected and a separate variance *t*-test is used. Conversely, if the calculated *F*-statistic is insignificant we use a pooled variance *t*-test.

In our example, mean years of education is 11.6 for those with incomes below the median income value of $12,533 and 13.4 for those with incomes above the median. The ratio of the two sample variances is 1.26. The *F*-statistic has degrees of freedom equal to 2,636 for both the numerator and denominator. At the 95 percent confidence level, the tabulated *F*-value corresponding to these degrees of freedom is 1.00. Since the calculated value for the *F*-statistic is greater than the tabulated value, the null hypothesis of equal variances is rejected and the separate variance *t*-test is used.

The calculated value for the separate variance *t*-test is -22.69. The tabulated *t*-value for the 95 percent confidence level and 5,273 degrees of freedom is 1.96. Since the absolute value of the calculated *t*-statistic is greater than the tabulated value, the null hypothesis of no difference in the mean education levels of those with incomes above and below the median income level is rejected. In other words, there is a difference in the average education levels of the two income groups. This is the same conclusion reached using the χ^2 statistic.

One-Way Analysis of Variance

When one variable is measured on an interval scale and the other variable is *categorical (with three or more categories)*, researchers are often interested in testing whether the mean value of the interval variable differs by category. Tests of differences between pairs of means could, of course, be carried out using *t*-tests. This has a drawback, however. Suppose the categorical variable has 5 categories. Then it would be necessary to test the following 10 null hypotheses:

$$\mu_1 = \mu_2 \quad \mu_2 = \mu_3 \quad \mu_3 = \mu_4 \quad \mu_4 = \mu_5$$

$$\mu_1 = \mu_3 \quad \mu_2 = \mu_4 \quad \mu_3 = \mu_5$$

$$\mu_1 = \mu_4 \quad \mu_2 = \mu_5$$

$$\mu_1 = \mu_5$$

This is problematic because we run the risk of rejecting some of these null hypotheses when, in fact, we should not (i.e., of committing a Type I error). At a 95 percent confidence level, for example, there is a 5 percent probability with each test that we will identify a statistically significant difference in means that is completely due to chance. These 5 percent probabilities accumulate as more tests are conducted. By the time 10 such tests are conducted the chances of incorrectly rejecting at least one of the null hypotheses may be as high as 50 percent. ANOVA overcomes this problem by testing the null hypothesis that all of the means are equal:

$$H_o \quad \mu_1 = \mu_2 = \mu_3 = \mu_4 = \mu_5$$

$$H_a \quad \mu_1 \neq \mu_2 \neq \mu_3 \neq \mu_4 \neq \mu_5$$

Since ANOVA involves the testing of only one null hypothesis, the probability of committing a Type I error is just one minus the confidence level chosen by the researcher. Of course, in controlling the multiple comparison error rate with ANOVA, the researcher is also giving up the ability to test *which* means are different from one another.[2]

ANOVA utilizes a measure of variation between the samples that is based on the differences between the individual sample means and the grand mean for all of the samples pooled together. This is known as the *between variance*:

$$\hat{\sigma}_\beta^2 = \sum_{i=1}^{m} N_i (\overline{X}_i - \overline{X})^2 / (M-1)$$

where the $\overline{X}_i$ are the means for each of the samples, $\overline{X}$ is the overall mean for all of the samples pooled together, N_i is the number of observations in each sample, and M is the number of samples.

The *within sample* measure of variation is based on the deviation of the sample observations from their respective means. This is known as the within sample variance:

$$\hat{\sigma}_w^2 = \sum_m \sum_i (X_{im} - \overline{X}_m)^2 / (N - M)$$

The within sample variance can also be written as:

$$\hat{\sigma}_w^2 = \frac{(N_1 - 1)s_1^2 + (N_2 - 1)s_2^2 + ... + (N_m - 1)s_m^2}{N - M}$$

which is just a generalization of pooled variance for the two-sample t-test.

The ratio of the between variance to the within variance has an F-distribution with M-1 degrees of freedom in the numerator and N-M degrees of freedom in the denominator:

$$F_{m-1, n-m} = \frac{\hat{\sigma}_\beta^2}{\hat{\sigma}_w^2}$$

If the calculated value of the F-statistic is greater than the tabulated value, the null hypothesis that all of the means are jointly equal to the same population mean is rejected.

The calculated F-statistic for the difference in mean education levels across the six income categories shown in Table 2.2 is 149.64. The F-statistic has 5 degrees of freedom for the numerator and 5,269 degrees of freedom for the denominator. At the 95 percent confidence level the tabulated F-value for these degrees of freedom is 2.21. Since the calculated F-statistic of 149.64 exceeds the tabulated value of 2.21 we reject the null hypothesis of no difference in the mean education levels by income category. In other words, average education levels do differ by income level. Again, the findings are consistent with those from the χ^2 and t-statistics.

Correlation

It is reasonable to hypothesize that there is a positive association between income and education levels. That is, individuals with higher than average education levels tend to have higher than average income levels. The strength of this association can be measured by calculating the covariation between the two variables:

$$Cov(X, Y) = \frac{1}{N - 1} \sum_i (X_i - \overline{X})(Y_i - \overline{Y})$$

A large negative value for $Cov(X,Y)$ indicates that, on balance, the association between X and Y is a negative one. This means that as the values of X increase, the corresponding values for Y tend to decrease and vice versa. A large positive value for $Cov(X,Y)$ indicates that as the values of X increase, the values of Y also tend to increase and vice versa. Small values for $Cov(X,Y)$, whether positive or negative, indicate a weak linear relationship between X and Y; if $Cov(X,Y) = 0$ there is no linear relationship between X and Y.

The problem with covariance as a measure of association is that the computed value of the covariation between two variables is dependent upon the units that the variables are measured in. Clearly, it would be preferable to have a measure of the strength of association between two interval variables that is independent of the measurement units. One such measure is the correlation coefficient, which is the covariance divided by the standard deviations of the two variables. This simplifies to:

$$r_{XY} = \frac{\sum (X_i - \overline{X})(Y_i - \overline{Y})}{\sqrt{\sum (X_i - \overline{X})^2 \sum (Y_i - \overline{Y})^2}} \quad or \quad \frac{Cov(X,Y)}{\sqrt{var(X)\,var(Y)}}$$

The correlation coefficient varies between -1.0 and 1.0. Values of -1.0 indicate a perfect negative linear association between X and Y; values of 0.0 indicate no linear association; and values of 1.0 indicate a perfect positive association between X and Y. In our sample, the calculated value for the correlation between education and income is 0.34. This value is statistically different from zero at better than a 99 percent confidence level.

Although a useful statistic, r_{xy} is limited in several ways. First, it is a measure of linear association only. Figure 2.6 illustrates that it is possible for $r_{xy} = 0.0$ when there is, in fact, a perfect nonlinear association between X and Y. More important, correlation is a measure of association only; it says nothing about the direction of causation between two variables.

Suppose, for example, that data were available on the number of households in poverty and the number of single, female-headed households over the past 20 years. Suppose also that the correlation between these variables was positive. The correlation statistic does not indicate whether the number of households in poverty is caused by the number of single, female-headed households or vice versa. Perhaps both variables tend to increase over time because of some common factor such as national welfare policy. Perhaps the observed correlation is simply due to chance. Or (most likely) perhaps both variables are jointly determined by a complex set of social, economic, and institutional factors.

To examine these possibilities, a multivariate model is often used as a third stage in the analysis. Multivariate models enable the researcher to examine the strength of a statistical relationship between an explanatory variable and a policy

Figure 2.6
Scatterplots and Pearson Correlations

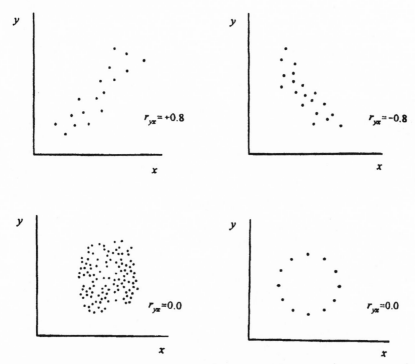

outcome variable of interest, controlling for the effects of other variables. It is often the case that strong bivariate relationships among variables disappear when they are analyzed in a multivariate model because other variables may measure similar underlying factors. For example, a strong relationship between education and income may disappear once the effects of marital status, race, age, and gender are controlled. Multiple regression, discussed in Chapters 3 through 5, is a useful tool for examining such relationships when the dependent variable of interest is measured on an interval scale. Maximum likelihood techniques, discussed in Chapters 6 and 7, are useful for estimating multivariate models when the dependent variable is measured on a categorical scale or is limited in some other way.

NOTES

1. Some readers may be puzzled by this last statement. After all, isn't the variance of a consistent estimator zero? If so, aren't the variances of all consistent estimators equal? The answer to this apparent paradox lies in understanding that the asymptotic distribution of a consistent estimator is its distribution *just before* it collapses.

2. A variety of other methods have been proposed for dealing with the multiple comparison problem. See, for example, Neter, Wasserman, and Kutner (1990, pp. 876–877).

3
Regression Analysis

CONCEPTUAL BASIS FOR REGRESSION ANALYSIS

Regression analysis is a technique that enables researchers to test hypotheses about relationships between variables in a much more powerful way than is possible with the bivariate methods used in the previous chapter. Regression analysis predicts the value for a "dependent" variable given the values for one or more "explanatory" or "independent" variables. The use of regression analysis, however, requires having a theory about the nature of the relationships among the variables. Policy analysts and social scientists often work with samples containing a thousand or more variables and tens of thousands of cases or observations. Researchers wading into data bases of this magnitude without the aid of a theory soon find themselves awash in printouts and hopelessly confused.

Figure 3.1 illustrates the basic concept of regression analysis for the simplest case, involving only one explanatory variable. In the case of one explanatory variable two regression coefficients must be estimated. The constant term of the regression line, $\hat{b}_1$, measures the expected value for the dependent variable when the value of the explanatory variable is zero. The slope coefficient, $\hat{b}_1$, measures the change in the dependent variable resulting from a one-unit increase in the explanatory variable. Regression analysis estimates the line that best describes the linear association between the dependent variable Y and the explanatory variable X. This line is completely described by the two coefficients $\hat{b}_0$ and $\hat{b}_1$.

DERIVATION OF THE REGRESSION MODEL

Assume for the moment that we have somehow estimated the line in Figure 3.1. This line enables us to predict a Y value corresponding to each X value. However, the predictions will seldom be perfect. Sometimes the regression line will underpredict the actual value of Y given a particular value for X; other times, it

Figure 3.1
Illustration of Simple Regression

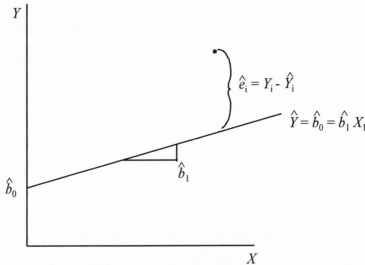

will overpredict Y. The differences between the actual values for Y and the predicted values $\hat{Y}$ are known as the errors or residuals $\hat{e}$.

It would clearly be desirable if regression analysis found values for $\hat{b}_0$ and $\hat{b}_1$ that minimize these errors in some way. For example, one possibility would be to find the values of $\hat{b}_0$ and $\hat{b}_1$ that minimize the sum of the errors around the regression line. But if one uses this approach, any regression line passing through the middle of the scatterplot would produce positive and negative errors that would exactly cancel each other out. There are an infinite number of such lines, so minimizing the sum of the errors is not a very helpful criterion in estimating values for $\hat{b}_0$ and $\hat{b}_1$.

An alternative criterion would be to find the values for $\hat{b}_0$ and $\hat{b}_1$ that minimize the sum of the absolute value of the errors. This solves the problem of the positive and negative errors canceling each other out but it is difficult mathematically to find the values of $\hat{b}_0$ and $\hat{b}_1$ that minimize the sum of the absolute errors. This is because calculus cannot be used to solve for the maximum and minimum points of absolute value functions.

On the other hand, it is a straightforward matter to find the values of $\hat{b}_0$ and $\hat{b}_1$ that minimize the sum of the squared errors around the regression line. Squaring the errors has several advantages. First, the negative errors squared no longer cancel the positive errors, so they contribute to the total sum of squared errors as desired. Second, squaring the errors increases the effect of large errors on the slope coefficients of the regression line; this highlights outliers or extreme cases. Finally, squaring the errors enables differential calculus to be used for finding the coefficient values that minimize the sum of squared errors. (For interested readers, a very brief summary of differential calculus is provided in Appendix A.)

Recall that the regression residuals or errors are equal to the difference between the actual and predicted values for Y:

$$\hat{e}_i = (Y_i - \hat{Y}_i)$$
$$= (Y_i - \hat{b}_0 - \hat{b}_1 X_i)$$

Squaring these errors and summing over all of the observations results in the sum of the squared errors:

$$\sum \hat{e}_i^2 = \sum (Y_i - \hat{b}_0 - \hat{b}_1 X_i)^2 \tag{1}$$

The values for $\hat{b}_0$ and $\hat{b}_1$ that minimize equation (1) can be found by taking the partial derivative of (1) with respect to $\hat{b}_0$ and $\hat{b}_1$ and setting the results equal to zero:

$$\frac{\partial \sum \hat{e}_i^2}{\partial \hat{b}_0} = -2 \sum (Y_i - \hat{b}_0 - \hat{b}_1 X_i) = 0$$

$$\frac{\partial \sum \hat{e}_i^2}{\partial \hat{b}_1} = -2 \sum (Y_i - \hat{b}_0 - \hat{b}_1 X_i)(X_i) = 0$$

This results in two equations with two unknown values, $\hat{b}_0$ and $\hat{b}_1$. These equations can be solved[1] for the computational formulas that will yield estimates of $\hat{b}_0$ and $\hat{b}_1$:

$$\hat{b}_0 = \overline{Y} - \hat{b}_1 \overline{X} \tag{2}$$

$$\hat{b}_1 = \frac{\sum X_i Y_i - N \overline{X} \overline{Y}}{\sum X_i^2 - N \overline{X}^2} \tag{3}$$

Since $\hat{b}_0$ and $\hat{b}_1$ are estimated with sample data, they have sampling distributions just like any other sample statistic (such as $\overline{X}$). That is, given 1,000 different samples, it would be possible to estimate $\hat{b}_0$ and $\hat{b}_1$ for each of these samples. The result would be sampling distributions for $\hat{b}_0$ and $\hat{b}_1$. As with inferential statistics, the statistical significance of $\hat{b}_0$ and $\hat{b}_1$ depends upon the sizes of these coefficients relative to the standard errors of their respective sampling distributions. The formulas for the standard errors of $\hat{b}_0$ and $\hat{b}_1$ are tedious to derive without matrix algebra, but it can be shown that they are given by the following:

$$S_{\hat{b}_0} = \sqrt{\frac{\left(\dfrac{\sum \hat{e}_i^2}{N-2} \right) \sum X_i^2}{N \sum (X_i - \overline{X})^2}} \tag{4}$$

$$S_{\hat{b}_1} = \sqrt{\frac{\sum \hat{e}_i^2}{(N-2)\sum (X_i - \bar{X})^2}} \tag{5}$$

Note that the standard errors for $\hat{b}_0$ and $\hat{b}_1$ are both a function of the sum of squared errors for the regression.

STATISTICAL SIGNIFICANCE OF COEFFICIENT ESTIMATES

Given a set of estimates for the regression coefficients and their standard errors, the null hypotheses that $\hat{b}_0$ equals a particular value b_0^* and that $\hat{b}_1$ equals b_1^* can be tested with:

$$t_{\hat{b}_0} = \frac{\hat{b}_0 - b_0^*}{s_{\hat{b}_0}} \tag{6}$$

$$t_{\hat{b}_1} = \frac{\hat{b}_1 - b_1^*}{s_{\hat{b}_1}} \tag{7}$$

Equations (6) and (7) each have a t-distribution with $N - k + 1$ degrees of freedom, where N is the sample size and k is the number of explanatory variables in the regression. In a regression that includes a constant term and one explanatory variable, $k + 1$ is equal to 2.

Researchers are often more interested in the signs and statistical significance of the estimated coefficients than in their specific numerical values. The reasons for this will be discussed in detail later. For now, it is sufficient to note that the values of the estimated coefficients are frequently sensitive to the other variables included in (or excluded from) the model, as well as the functional form used in specifying the model. In any event, when researchers wish to test the statistical significance of an estimated coefficient, it is common practice to test whether the coefficient is significantly different from zero. This is because a zero slope coefficient implies that there is no linear relationship between the explanatory variable and the dependent variable.

Thus, the usual t-tests for the statistical significance of estimated coefficients in the simple regression model are:

$$t_{\hat{b}_0} = \frac{\hat{b}_0}{s_{\hat{b}_0}}$$

$$t_{\hat{b}_1} = \frac{\hat{b}_1}{s_{\hat{b}_1}}$$

To determine if the calculated t-ratios are statistically significant, they are compared to the tabulated value of t for the selected alpha level (e.g., 0.05); if the calculated value exceeds the tabulated value, the coefficient is considered to be statistically significant. Note that it is perfectly possible (and indeed likely in larger models) that some coefficients will be statistically significant and others will not.

If there is no expectation about the sign of the coefficient, the researcher compares the calculated value to the tabulated value for t, assuming one-half of the alpha region in each tail. The p-values produced by most statistical packages assume such two-tailed tests. On the other hand, it is often the case that the researcher will have a theoretical expectation about the sign of an estimated coefficient. If this is the case, the entire alpha region should be concentrated in one tail. Concentrating alpha region in one tail lowers the critical value of the t-statistic that must be exceeded in order to reject the null hypothesis that the coefficient is significantly different from zero. For example, in a very large sample, the critical t-value for a two-tailed test at the 95 percent confidence level is 1.96; for the one-tailed test it is 1.67.

GOODNESS-OF-FIT MEASURES

At this point in the discussion, formulas have been presented for obtaining numerical estimates of the regression coefficients, as well as tests of the statistical significance of these coefficients. It would be useful, however, to also have a measure for how well the model as a whole describes the variation in the dependent variable.

The total deviation of a particular point from its mean is given by $(Y_i - \bar{Y})$. The difference between the observed value for Y_i and the predicted value from the regression is given by $(Y_i - \hat{Y}_i)$. Because this is the error for a single sample point, it is reasonable to consider this to be the portion of the total deviation that is not explained by the model. The remaining portion of the total deviation $(\hat{Y}_i - \bar{Y})$ is, therefore, the portion that *is* explained by the model. Thus, the total deviation of a particular observation of the dependent variable from its mean can be decomposed into two pieces—the piece explained by the regression model and the piece that is not explained by the model:

$$(Y_i - \bar{Y}) = (\hat{Y}_i - \bar{Y}) + (Y_i - \hat{Y}_i) \tag{8}$$

Squaring each deviation and summing over all values of the dependent variable yields an expression for the total variation of Y around its mean:

$$\sum (Y_i - \bar{Y})^2 = \sum (\hat{Y}_i - \bar{Y})^2 + \sum (Y_i - \hat{Y}_i)^2 + 2\sum (\hat{Y}_i \ \bar{Y})(Y_i \ \hat{Y}_i) \tag{9}$$

Note that the terms $2\sum (\hat{Y}_i - \bar{Y}) (Y_i - \hat{Y}_i)$ arise because of the cross products between $(Y_i - \hat{Y}_i)$ and $(\hat{Y}_i - \bar{Y})$ that occur when one squares the right-hand side of equation (8). It was mentioned earlier that regression analysis is based on many assumptions. One of these assumptions is that the expected value of the errors is zero. This, in turn, implies that the sum of the cross product terms in equation (9) is zero. Therefore, the total variation of the dependent variable around its mean is equal to the unexplained variation plus the explained variation:

$$\sum (Y_i - \bar{Y})^2 = \sum (\hat{Y}_i - \bar{Y})^2 + \sum (Y_i - \hat{Y}_i)^2 \tag{10}$$

Phrased somewhat differently, the total sum of squares (TSS) of the dependent variable is equal to the regression sum of squares (RSS) plus the sum of squared errors (SSE):

$$TSS = RSS + SSE \tag{11}$$

Dividing both sides of equation (11) by TSS yields:

$$1 = \frac{RSS}{TSS} + \frac{SSE}{TSS}$$

This expresses the TSS in terms of two *proportions*—the proportion explained by the regression and the proportion that is not explained by the regression.

The proportion of the total variation of Y around its mean that is explained by the regression model is known as R^2 and is found by:

$$R^2 = \frac{RSS}{TSS} = 1 - \frac{SSE}{TSS}$$
$$= 1 - \frac{\sum \hat{e}_i^2}{\sum (Y_i - \bar{Y})^2} \tag{12}$$

R^2 varies between 0 and 1. High values for R^2 indicate that the model explains a high proportion of the total variation in Y around its mean. For example, a value of 0.90 would mean that the regression model explained 90 percent of the total variation in Y.

Intuitively, it might seem that high R^2 values would be indicative of a good model. Yet this is not always true. For one thing, R^2 values tend to be higher for some types of data than for others. Regression models estimated using time-series data (data collected on variables over time) tend to have higher R^2s than regression models estimated using cross-sectional data. For example, a time-series regression model of a macroeconomic variable, such as the Gross National Product, could easily have an R^2 value greater than 90 percent. In contrast, a cross-sectional model of the determinants of personal earnings might have an R^2 of only 20 percent.

Correlation values for regression models also tend to vary systematically with the aggregation level of the data—models based on aggregate data tend to have higher R^2s than models based on micro data (data for individuals, families, households, etc.). Of course, the level of data aggregation is often related to whether the data are time-series or cross-sectional in nature. Macroeconomic time-series data are also aggregate data. In contrast, individual-level earnings data are often measured with cross-sectional surveys such as the Dicennial Census or the Current Population Survey. But there are many exceptions. Longitudinal studies of individuals, households, or families (such as the Retirement History Survey or the Panel Study of Income Dynamics) collect cross-sectional data on a panel of respondents at several points in time—thereby combining the characteristics of time-series, cross-sectional, and micro data.

AN EXAMPLE OF SIMPLE REGRESSION

Suppose that you are a federal budget analyst and your job is to figure out what is creating the persistent federal deficits. Like everyone else in Washington, you read the newspapers which seem to be saying that the elderly are "busting" the budget. To see if this is the case, you collect information on the size of the population age 65 and over and on the federal budget deficit over the years from 1976 to 1985. This information is displayed in the first two columns of Table 3.1.

The first task in estimating the equation is to calculate the coefficients of the regression line. Recall from equation (3) that

$$\hat{b}_1 = \frac{\sum X_i Y_i - N\bar{X}\bar{Y}}{\sum X_i^2 - N\bar{X}^2}$$

where Y_i are the values for the dependent variable (federal deficits) and X_i are the values for the explanatory variable (elderly population size). To use this formula to estimate the slope coefficient $\hat{b}_1$ it is first necessary to calculate the mean of the explanatory variable $\bar{X}$, the mean of the dependent variable $\bar{Y}$, the sum of the squared values of X_i, and the sum of the product of each X_i value times each Y_i value, $\sum X_i Y_i$. N refers to the sample size—in this case, 10.

The calculation of $\bar{Y}$ and $\bar{X}$ is carried out in the usual fashion and is shown at the bottom of columns 1 and 2 in Table 3.1. The calculation of $\sum X_i Y_i$ is shown in column 3 of Table 3.1. The entries in column 3 are found by multiplying the corresponding Y_i and X_i values in columns 1 and 2. Summing these products results in $\sum X_i Y_i$ shown at the bottom of column 3. Finally, to generate the $\sum X_i^2$, the X_i values in column 2 are squared and all of these squared values are summed. The results are shown in column 4 of Table 3.1. Substituting all of these values into equation (3) yields:

$$\hat{b}_1 = \frac{29781.9 - (10)(25.94)(111.27)}{6756.54 - (10)(25.94)^2}$$

$$= 33.16$$

This coefficient indicates that for each one-million-person increase in the population age 65 and over, the federal deficit increases by 33.16 billion dollars.

Table 3.1
Calculations for Simple Regression of Federal Deficits

Year	Deficits ($billions) y (1)	Population 65+ (millions) x (2)	xy (3)	x^2 (4)	$\hat{y}_i = -748.9 + 33.16X_i$ (5)	$\hat{e}_i = y - \hat{y}$ (6)	$\hat{e}^2$ (7)	$(x_i - \bar{x})^2$ (8)	$(y_i - \bar{y})^2$ (9)
1976	73.7	23.3	1717.21	542.89	23.72	49.98	2498	6.97	1411.5
1977	53.6	23.9	1281.04	571.21	46.62	6.98	48.72	4.16	3325.83
1978	59.2	24.5	1450.04	600.25	63.52	-4.32	18.66	2.07	2711.28
1979	40.2	25.1	1009.02	630.01	83.42	-43.22	1867.97	0.71	5050.94
1980	73.8	25.7	1896.66	660.49	103.31	-29.51	870.84	0.06	1404.00
1981	78.9	26.2	2067.18	686.44	119.89	-40.99	1680.18	0.07	1047.82
1982	127.9	26.8	3427.72	718.24	139.79	-11.89	141.37	0.74	276.56
1983	207.8	27.4	5693.72	750.76	159.68	48.12	2315.53	2.13	9318.04
1984	185.3	28.0	5188.40	784.00	179.58	5.72	32.72	4.24	5480.44
1985	212.3	28.5	6050.55	812.25	196.16	16.14	260.50	6.55	10207.06

$$\bar{y} = \frac{1112.7}{10} = 111.27 \qquad \bar{x} = \frac{259.4}{10} = 25.94 \qquad \sum xy = 29781.9 \qquad \sum x^2 = 6756.54$$

$$\sum \hat{e}_i^2 = 9734.49 \qquad \sum(x_i - \bar{x})^2 = 27.70 \qquad \sum(y_i - \bar{y})^2 = 40233.47$$

Source: Economic Report of the President (1988). Washington, DC: U.S. Government Printing Office.

Once the slope coefficient $\hat{b}_1$ has been estimated, the estimation of the constant term is easy. From equation (2) the coefficient for the constant term is:

$$\hat{b}_0 = 111.27 - (33.16)(25.94)$$

$$= -748.90$$

The estimated value for $\hat{b}_0$ means that if the elderly population were equal to zero, we would expect the federal deficit to be -748.90 billion dollars—in other words, a surplus of $748.9 billion!

Of course, these estimates will have no policy importance unless they are statistically significant. To test if the coefficients are statistically different from zero, the coefficient values are divided by their standard errors. The resulting ratios are *t*-statistics that can be used for hypotheses testing.

To calculate the standard errors for $\hat{b}_0$ and $\hat{b}_1$ two additional pieces of information are needed—the sum of the squared errors from the regression equation $\sum e_i^2$ and the sum of squared deviations of the explanatory variable (elderly population) from its mean, $\sum(X_i - \overline{X})^2$.

Calculation of $\sum e_i^2$ is shown in columns 5 and 6 of Table 3.1. To estimate the residuals from the regression equation, the predicted values for the dependent variable $\hat{Y}_i$ generated by the model are first calculated. These are shown in column 5.

To calculate the predicted values, each of the X_i values is substituted into the estimated equation. For example, in 1976 the elderly population was 23.3 million. The value 23.3 is multiplied by the slope coefficient 33.16, and the result is added to the constant of -748.9. This yields a $\hat{Y}$ estimate for 1976 of 23.72:

$$23.72 = -748.9 + 33.16(23.3)$$

In this manner, a predicted value for $\hat{Y}_i$ is generated for each year in the sample. The errors shown in column 6 of Table 3.1 are calculated as the difference between the actual value of Y(column 1) and the predicted value (column 5). Squaring each of the errors in column 6 yields the squared errors in column 7. Finally, summing the values in column 7 yields the sum of the squared errors, $\sum e_i^2$.

The squared deviations of the explanatory variable around its mean, shown in column 8 of Table 3.1, are found simply by subtracting the mean elderly population for the sample as a whole from the elderly population in each year and squaring the results. Summing all of the entries in column 8 yields the sum of the squared deviations, $\sum(X_i - \overline{X})^2$.

It is now possible to calculate the standard errors for $\hat{b}_0$ and $\hat{b}_1$. Substituting the appropriate values in the equations for the standard errors of $\hat{b}_0$ and $\hat{b}_1$ yields

$$s_{b_0} = \sqrt{\frac{\left(\dfrac{\sum \hat{e}_i^2}{N-2}\right) \sum X_i^2}{N \sum (X_i - \bar{X})^2}}$$

$$= \sqrt{\frac{\left(\dfrac{9734.49}{8}\right)(6756.54)}{(10)(27.70)}}$$

$$= 172.28$$

$$s_{b_1} = \sqrt{\frac{\sum e_i^2}{(N-2) \sum (X_i - \bar{X})^2}}$$

$$= \sqrt{\frac{9734.49}{(8)(27.70)}}$$

$$= 6.63$$

The *t*-statistics can now be calculated by taking the ratio of each coefficient to its standard error:

$$t_{b_0} = \frac{\hat{b}_0}{s_{b_0}}$$

$$= \frac{-748.9}{172.28}$$

$$= -4.35$$

$$t_{b_1} = \frac{\hat{b}_1}{s_{b_1}}$$

$$= \frac{33.16}{6.63}$$

$$= 5.00$$

Both of these *t*-statistics have 8 degrees of freedom ($N - 2$). One degree of freedom is used up in estimating the slope coefficient; another is used up in estimating the constant term. At a 95 percent confidence level, the tabulated *t*-value for 8 degrees of freedom is 2.306. The calculated *t*-statistics for both coefficients are greater in *absolute value* than the critical value of the *t*-statistic from the table. This means that the null hypotheses that the constant term and slope coefficient are equal to zero are rejected.

Thus far, we have calculated the coefficients of the regression model and determined that they are statistically different from zero. But we still do not have a sense of how much of the variation in federal budget deficits is explained by elderly population size. This measure is provided by the R^2 of the model.

From equation (12) it can be seen that the R^2 is a function of the sum of the squared errors from the regression $\sum \hat{e}_i^2$ and the sum of the squared deviations of Y around its mean $\sum (Y_i - \bar{Y})^2$. Calculation of $\sum (Y_i - \bar{Y})^2$ is shown in column 9 of Table 3.1.

Substituting into equation (12), we can calculate the R^2 as follows:

$$R^2 = 1 - \frac{\sum \hat{e}_i^2}{\sum (Y_i - \bar{Y})^2}$$

$$= 1 - \left(\frac{9734.49}{40233.47} \right)$$

$$= .76$$

Thus, according to the model, elderly population size explains 76 percent of the variation in federal budget deficits.

In short, the model indicates that elderly population size does a very respectable job of predicting the size of the federal budget deficit. The t-statistic for elderly population size is highly significant and the model explains 76 percent of the variation in the federal budget deficit. There are, however, at least three major reasons why we should be dubious about the conclusion that elderly population size is such a significant predictor of the federal deficit.

First, the use of data collected over time (time series) will tend to generate models with high R^2s and inflated t-statistics—a problem known as autocorrelation. Autocorrelation is discussed briefly later in this chapter and, in more detail, in Chapter 5.

Second, the R^2 of the model is probably overstated because of the aggregate nature of the data. As noted earlier, regression models based on highly aggregated data tend to have higher R^2s than models based on less highly aggregated data. In the current example, the high aggregation level of the data interacts with the autocorrelation problem to overstate the R^2.

A third major problem with the simple model discussed above is that it contains only one explanatory variable. It is possible that the size of the older population *does* contribute to the size of federal deficits, but it is likely that other factors such as unemployment, wars, and the size of the child population also contribute to federal spending. Moreover, to properly model deficits, it is necessary to include not only variables that affect federal spending, but also variables that affect tax revenues such as income levels. It is likely that, after we account for all of these other influences, the size of the older population would play a much smaller role in "explaining" federal deficits.

MULTIPLE REGRESSION

Extending the model to include two or more explanatory variables is straightforward. The sum of squared errors (SSE) from a multiple regression equation with K variables is minimized by taking the partial derivative of the SSE expression with respect to each variable and the constant term:

$$SSE = \sum (Y_i - \hat{b}_0 - \hat{b}_1 X_{i1} - \hat{b}_2 X_{i2} - ... - \hat{b}_k X_{ik})^2$$

$$\frac{\partial SSE}{\partial \hat{b}_0} = -2\sum (Y_i - \hat{b}_0 - \hat{b}_1 X_{i1} - \hat{b}_2 X_{i2} - ... - \hat{b}_k X_{ik})$$

$$\frac{\partial SSE}{\partial \hat{b}_1} = -2\sum (Y_i - \hat{b}_0 - \hat{b}_1 X_{il} - \hat{b}_2 X_{i2} - ... - \hat{b}_k X_{ik})(X_{i1})$$

$$\vdots$$

$$\frac{\partial SSE}{\partial \hat{b}_k} = -2\sum (Y_i - \hat{b}_0 - \hat{b}_1 X_{i1} - \hat{b}_2 X_{i2} - ... - \hat{b}_k X_{ik})(X_{ik})$$

This results in $K+1$ equations with $K+1$ unknown coefficients. If the derivatives are set equal to zero, these $K+1$ equations can be solved to generate computational formulas for each of the coefficients in terms of the sample variables. Unfortunately, the formulas for the slope coefficients become very unwieldy for models with two or more explanatory variables unless matrix algebra is used. This is why, in the interest of generalizability, advanced statistics texts make heavy use of matrix algebra. In matrix notation, the formula for the constant term and slope coefficients is always:

$$B = (X'X)^{-1}X'Y$$

where B is a column vector of coefficients, X is a table or matrix of data for the explanatory variables, and Y is a column vector containing the observations for the dependent variable. The beauty of matrix notation is that this formula is always the same, whether the model has 1 explanatory variable or 30. Moreover, the same generalizability pertains to other results, such as the formulas for standard errors.

As in the case of simple regression, the constant term in a multiple regression model represents the expected value for the dependent variable when all of the explanatory variables are equal to zero. The slope coefficient for each variable represents the change in the dependent variable with respect to a one-unit increase in that particular explanatory variable *controlling for the effects of the other variables included in the equation.*

Also as in the case of simple regression, the statistical significance of each variable in a multiple regression can be assessed with a *t*-test based on the ratio of each estimated coefficient to its standard error. In multiple regression, it is very possible, indeed likely, that some variables will be statistically significant and others will not. In a model with K variables, the *t*-statistics have $N - (K + 1)$ degrees of freedom.

BETA COEFFICIENTS

Having estimated coefficients for several variables, one is often tempted to compare the magnitudes of the coefficients as a measure of the relative strength of the relationship between particular explanatory variables and the dependent variable. This is not valid because the sizes of the coefficients for the different explanatory variables are a function of the units that the explanatory variables are measured in. To be able to compare the relative size of the impacts of different explanatory variables on the dependent variable, it is necessary to first standardize the units that these variables are measured in.

One way to do this is to construct a new set of variables that are expressed in terms of standard deviations from their means:

$$\frac{(Y_i-\bar{Y})}{S_Y} = B_1\frac{(X_{1i}-\bar{X}_1)}{S_{X_1}} + B_2\frac{(X_{2i}-\bar{X}_2)}{S_{X_2}} + \ldots \; B_k\frac{(X_{ki}-\bar{X}_k)}{S_{X_k}}$$

These new variables are z-scores corresponding to the original variables. Using these z-scores, it is possible to estimate a regression model where the slope coefficients represent the standard deviation change in the dependent variable associated with a standard deviation increase in an explanatory variable, controlling for all of the other variables in the equation. These slope coefficients are known as beta coefficients to distinguish them from ordinary regression coefficients. Note that no constant term is included in this equation because it makes no sense to talk about an expected standard deviation change in the dependent variable when the variation in all of the explanatory variables is set to zero.

It turns out that there is an easier way to estimate beta coefficients than the method just described. Beta coefficients can be easily calculated by multiplying each ordinary *slope* coefficient of the regression model by the ratio of the standard deviation of that variable to the standard deviation of the dependent variable:

$$\hat{B}_k = \hat{b}_k\frac{S_x}{S_y}$$

Easier still, most statistical packages produce beta coefficients as part of the standard multiple regression output or offer them as an option. Because beta coefficients measure standard deviation changes, the beta coefficients for different variables *can* be directly compared. The variable with the largest absolute beta coefficient (either positive or negative) has the greatest impact on the dependent variable; the variable with the next largest beta coefficient has the next largest impact; and so on.

It is usually the case that the largest beta coefficients in an equation also have the highest t-statistics. But this need not be the case. The beta coefficients are just the regression coefficients multiplied by the standard deviations of the explanatory variables and divided by the standard deviation of the dependent variable. If estimated regression coefficients are large, and/or the standard deviations of the explanatory variables are large relative to the dependent variable, beta coefficients can be large even if the corresponding explanatory variables are not statistically significant. The statistical significance of beta coefficients is the same as that of the regression coefficients upon which they are based. If the regression coefficients are not statistically significant, neither are the beta coefficients—no matter how large they are.

ADJUSTED R^2

In the discussion of the simple regression model, it was noted that the R^2 measure is sensitive to the aggregation level of the data, whether the data are time-series or cross-sectional, and other factors. Another difficulty with the R^2 measure is that its value approaches one as the number of variables in the regression approaches the sample size—irrespective of the explanatory power of the variables. An alternative measure, known as the adjusted R^2 (or $\bar{R}^2$), corrects for this tendency by assessing a degrees-of-freedom penalty to the R^2 measure for each explanatory variable included in the model:

$$\bar{R}^2 = 1 - (1 - R^2)(\frac{N-1}{N-k})$$ (13)

The addition of a variable to a regression equation only increases the adjusted R^2 if the variable's explanatory power is greater than the degrees-of-freedom correction. Note from equation (13) that the adjusted R^2 equals R^2 in the case of simple regression. In models involving more than one explanatory variable, however, the adjusted R^2 will always be less than the unadjusted R^2. In fact, the adjusted R^2 can be negative! In this last instance, the researcher would do well to rethink the theoretical model underlying the regression or reexamine the data used to estimate the model. Sometimes, when an estimated model performs so poorly, it is the result of a data-processing problem such as incorrectly reading variables from a dataset. Data quality issues can be assessed by examining the descriptive statistics for all variables before the model is estimated.

It should be clear from the preceding discussion that the model with the highest R^2, or even the highest adjusted R^2, is not necessarily the best. The signs and statistical significance of the independent variables are much more important criteria for evaluating a model than the proportion of variation in the dependent variable that the model explains. We have already discussed the individual t-tests of significance for each variable. A more general test of the model is to evaluate the null hypothesis that all of the *slope* coefficients of the explanatory variables are jointly equal to zero:

$$H_o : b_1 = b_2 = b_3 = ... = b_k = 0$$

$$H_a : b_1 \neq b_2 \neq b_3 \neq ... \neq b_k \neq 0$$

This null hypothesis can be evaluated by using the *F*-statistic. As one might expect, the *F*-statistic is a function of the model's R^2:

$$F_{k,N-(k+1)} = \frac{R^2}{(1-R^2)} \left(\frac{N-(k+1)}{k} \right)$$

If none of the slope coefficients are statistically different from zero then there is no systematic variation of the dependent variable with any of the explanatory variables. In this instance, the *F*-statistic will indicate that the model is not statistically significant. A model with no significant variables will also tend to have a low R^2 (except in the case where the number of variables approaches the sample size). Consequently, models with low R^2s tend to have low *F*-statistics. Conversely, models with high R^2s tend to have large *F*-statistics. The magnitude of the *F*-statistic needed to reject the null hypothesis that all of the slope coefficients are jointly equal to zero varies with the number of variables in the equation, the number of observations in the sample, and the level of statistical significance at which the test is carried out. Moreover, if just one variable is statistically significant, the null hypothesis that all of the slope coefficients are equal to zero is rejected. Usually, at least one variable will be statistically significant so the standard *F*-test for the significance of a regression is not very interesting—it almost always indicates that the model is statistically significant.

A MULTIPLE REGRESSION EXAMPLE

Table 3.2 reports the multiple regression results for a very simple model of hours worked as a function of a person's education level, age, wages, and other income.[2] Regression coefficients must be carefully interpreted because they are sensitive to the units that the dependent and independent variables are measured in. For example, it is *not* safe to assume that years of education have the biggest effect on hours worked just because this variable has the largest slope coefficient. To properly interpret the coefficient magnitudes, it is necessary to take account of how the variables are measured. In Table 3.2, the dependent variable is the number of hours per week an individual usually worked in 1989. Education level and age are measured in years, wages are measured in dollars per hour, and other income is measured in dollars per year. Thus, a one-unit (one-year) increase in education level would increase average hours worked by 0.51 hours (or about 30 minutes). Similarly, a one-year increase in age would increase individual labor supply by 0.09 hours; a one-dollar-per-hour increase in wages would increase labor supply by 0.12 hours; and each dollar of additional other income would *decrease* hours

Table 3.2
A Multiple Regression Model of Individual Hours Worked

Variable	Regression Coefficient	Standard Error	t	Beta Coefficient
Education	0.5090	0.0772	6.590	0.1095
Age	0.0887	0.0161	5.505	0.0954
Wages	0.1218	0.0259	4.708	0.0795
Other Income	−0.0004	0.00004	−9.461	−0.1613
Constant	27.5372	1.1915	23.112	

$\underline{R}^2 = 0.042$
$\overline{R}^2 = 0.041$
$F_{4,3818} = 42.1618$

supplied by 0.0004 hours. Setting the effects of education, age, wages, and other income to zero, we would expect individuals to supply an average of 27.5 hours of work per week.

The second column in Table 3.2 reports the standard errors for the coefficients in the model. Recall that the standard error for each coefficient is the hypothetical standard deviation of the sampling distribution calculated from a large number of parameter estimates based upon many different samples of a fixed size. Some of these samples would generate relatively low parameter estimates; others would generate relatively high estimates. Most would be somewhere in between.

The estimated regression coefficients divided by their standard errors will have *t*-distributions. Except for very small sample sizes the *t*-distribution is a close approximation of the normal distribution. This suggests that *t*-values greater than 1.96 will usually be statistically significant at the 95 percent confidence level, assuming a two-tailed test. Put somewhat differently, when the *t*-value is greater than 1.96, we can be 95 percent sure that the coefficient is not equal to zero. This implies that there is a relationship between the explanatory variable and the dependent variable. Based on this rule of thumb, it is apparent that education level, age, hourly wage, and other income are all statistically significant predictors of individual labor supply.

Note, in this example, that all of the explanatory variables are statistically significant. This need not be the case, however. Most models will contain a mixture of variables—some of which will have coefficients significantly different from zero and some of which will not. In such cases, researchers will sometimes make the error of saying that the variable "had the expected sign but was not statistically significant." Such an inference really makes no sense because the fact that the coefficient is statistically insignificant at a given confidence level means that that the null hypothesis that the coefficient is equal to zero cannot be rejected.

The final column in Table 3.2 reports the beta coefficients for the model. These are the coefficients that one would get if the dependent and explanatory variables were all converted to z-scores prior to running the regression and the regression was then estimated without a constant term. The advantage of the beta coefficients relative to the regular regression coefficients is that the beta coefficients are unitless—they represent the standard deviation change in the dependent variable with respect to a one-standard-deviation increase in an explanatory variable, controlling for the other variables in the model. Beta coefficients can be directly compared. The largest beta coefficient (in absolute value) has the biggest effect on the variation of the dependent variable, the next largest beta coefficient has the second biggest effect, and so on.

Most statistical packages produce the beta coefficients as part of the standard output or offer them as an option. In the event that a particular package does not offer beta coefficients as part of the output, however, they are easy to calculate. One simply takes the estimated regression coefficient, multiplies it by the standard deviation (*not* the standard error) of the explanatory variable, and divides the result by the standard deviation of the dependent variable.

In the current example, the standard deviation of the dependent variable was 12.81; it was 2.76 for education level, 13.79 for age, 8.36 for wages, and 4905.56 for other income. Using these standard deviations, in conjunction with the regression coefficients in Table 3.2, we can find the beta coefficients for the explanatory variables as follows:

$$Education \quad 0.1095 = 0.5090\left(\frac{2.756}{12.811}\right)$$

$$Age \quad 0.0954 = 0.0887\left(\frac{13.786}{12.811}\right)$$

$$Wages \quad 0.0795 = 0.1218\left(\frac{8.357}{12.811}\right)$$

$$Other\ Income \quad -0.1613 = -0.00042\left(\frac{4905.559}{12.811}\right)$$

Table 3.2 reports three measures of the overall goodness of fit of the model. The R^2 value of 0.042 indicates that the model explains 4.2 percent of the variation of the dependent variable around its mean. As discussed earlier in this chapter, however, the R^2 measure can be a misleading indicator of goodness of fit. Its value will approach 1.0 (indicating a perfect fit) as the number of explanatory variables approaches the sample size—even if none of the explanatory variables are statistically significant! This situation tends to occur when working with aggregate data, such as national macroeconomic statistics or state-level data, where the number of observations is limited.

On the other hand, micro data on individuals, families, or households tend to have low R^2s because there is so much variation in individual behavior. Low R^2s do not necessarily mean that the model is poor. This is because micro level models tend to produce more efficient parameter estimates than models based on aggregate data.

In either event, it is best to calculate the adjusted R^2 because it corrects for the tendency of R^2 to approach one as the number of explanatory variables increases (even though this effect is of little practical importance in large samples). The adjusted R^2 does this by assessing a degrees-of-freedom penalty for each variable added to the equation. It is always lower than the R^2 except in the case where only one variable is included in the model; then the two measures are equal. In Table 3.2 the adjusted R^2 is 0.041—only slightly smaller than the unadjusted R^2 of 0.042. The adjusted R^2 indicates that the model explains 4.1 percent of the *variance* in individual labor supply.

Finally, the formal measure of goodness of fit is given by the F-statistic. The F-statistic tests the null hypothesis that all of the slope coefficients are jointly equal to zero. Unless the model is very poor (has no statistically significant variables), the F-statistic is nearly always statistically significant, enabling the null hypothesis to be rejected. The model reported in Table 3.2 is no exception. The F-statistic of 42.16 greatly exceeds the tabulated value of 2.37 (4 degrees of freedom in the numerator, 3818 degrees of freedom in the denominator, 95 percent confidence level).

SPECIALIZED F-TESTS

There are a variety of statistical tests that a researcher may wish to carry out besides assessing the significance of individual coefficients or the entire regression equation. For example, a researcher may be interested in determining the collective contribution of a set of variables to an equation or in testing whether two regression equations are significantly different. Both of these statistical tests can be carried out using an F-statistic.

Testing the Contribution of a Subset of Variables

Suppose that a researcher estimated a model of a person's income as a function of labor force variables, demographic variables, and health variables. For reasons that will become apparent in a moment, call this model the *unrestricted* model. Now suppose that the researcher would like to test whether the health variables collectively contribute to the regression equation. To conduct this test, the health variables are dropped from the model and the model is reestimated including only the labor force variables and the demographic variables. In essence, because the health variables have been dropped from the equation, their coefficients have been set to zero. Because of this, the second regression is called the *restricted* model.

It is always the case that dropping variables will cause the R^2 to fall and the sum of squared errors (SSE) to increase. Consequently, it is possible to test whether the health variables contribute to the regression by testing whether the difference in the

R^2s for the unrestricted and restricted models is statistically significant. If the unrestricted model contains k variables and we drop g variables, the appropriate F-statistic is as follows:

$$F_{g,\ N-(k+1)} = \frac{(R_{UR}^2 - R_R^2)/g}{(1 - R_{UR}^2)/[N-(k+1)]}$$

This F-statistic has degrees of freedom equal to g and $N - (k + 1)$. If the calculated value of the F-statistic is greater than the tabulated value, the null hypothesis of no difference between the restricted and unrestricted models is rejected—that is, the subset of variables *does* contribute to the regression equation.[3]

Table 3.3 reports two models of total personal income. The unrestricted model includes age, education level, work status, two health-status variables (poor health status and the number of prior hospital stays in the previous year), and dummy indicator variables for marital status, gender, and race. All of these variables except hospital stay are statistically significant at the 95 percent confidence level or better. The restricted model contains the same variables, except that the health status variables are dropped. Using the R^2s for the two models, it is possible to test if the health variables explain a statistically significant portion of the variation in total personal income.

The unrestricted R^2 reported in Table 3.3 is 42.3 percent and the restricted R^2 is 42.1 percent. The Unrestricted R^2 is the R^2 associated with the original model (with all of the variables in Table 3.3). Because two variables were dropped, g is equal to 2. N is the sample size of 5,000 and k is the number of explanatory variables (8) in the full (unrestricted) model. Thus, the calculated F-statistic is given by:

$$F_{2,4991} = \frac{(0.4228-0.4208)/2}{(1-0.4228)/4991}$$

$$= 8.647$$

The tabulated value for the F-statistic with df = 2,4991 at a 95 percent confidence level is 3.00. Since 8.647 is greater than 3.00, the null hypothesis that there is no difference between the unrestricted and restricted models is rejected. In other words, the health variables make a statistically significant contribution to the original model in Table 3.3. Of course, this should come as no surprise in the present example because the poor-health variable was statistically significant in the unrestricted model. Consequently, removing the poor-health variable, along with the prior-hospitalization variable, would be expected to result in a statistically significant drop in the model's R^2. In some instances, however, the collective contribution of a group of variables might not be so obvious. For example, one could imagine having several health variables in the model, each of which was significant at around the 90 percent confidence level. It is possible in such cases,

Table 3.3
Income Level Regression with, and without, Health-Status Variables

Variable	Unrestricted Model		Restricted Model	
	Coefficient	t	Coefficient	t
Age	10.72	13.72	9.39	13.23
White	111.68	3.09	121.56	3.37
Education	17.99	8.80	19.26	9.51
Female	−472.36	−16.66	−472.02	−16.66
Married	137.41	4.59	138.96	4.64
Poor Health	−209.51	−4.18	—	—
Hospital Stay	39.63	0.76	—	—
Work	1147.90	34.66	1157.40	35.01
Constant	−124.56	−3.30	−129.79	−3.44
R^2	0.4228		0.4208	
N	5,000		5,000	

Source: Calculations based on the 1984 Panel (Waves 3&4) of the Survey of Income and Program
Participation (SIPP).

where none of the variables in question is statistically significant individually, for these variables to be statistically significant collectively.

Testing the Equality of Regression Equations

Another important use of the F-statistic is to test the equality of regression equations based on different subsamples. For example, we might be interested in testing whether the determinants of personal income differ by gender. One way to test such a hypothesis is to construct dummy variables (variables which have values of only zero and one) to capture the effects of gender. Dummy variables were used in the models reported in Table 3.3; the interpretation of such variables is discussed in Chapter 4. Another method, however, is to split the sample into the groups defined by the dummy variable (i.e., gender), run separate regressions for each of the subsamples, and test the null hypothesis that the two regressions are equivalent.[4]

To illustrate this approach, consider a simple model hypothesizing that income levels are a function of marital status, age, education level, race, poor health, and work status. The first step is to estimate the model of income level using all of the observations for both men and women. From this model, obtain the sum of squared errors (SSE_c).

Next the sample is split by gender, the same model is estimated (with the same variables as the full model) for both men and women, and the sum of squared errors SSE_a and SSE_b is obtained for each model. If the sample of women contained N observations, that for men contained M observations, and each of the equations contained k explanatory variables, the relevant F-test would be:

$$F_{(k+1),N+M-2(k+1)} = \frac{SSE_c-(SSE_a+SSE_b)/(k+1)}{(SSE_a+SSE_b)/[N+M-2(k+1)]}$$

This F-statistic is distributed with $k+1$ and $N + M - 2 (k+1)$ degrees of freedom. If the calculated value of the F-statistic is greater than the tabulated value for a given level of statistical significance, the null hypothesis that the determinants of hours worked are the same for men and women is rejected.[5]

Table 3.4 reports the regression results to carry out this F-test using a sample of 5,000 observations from the 1984 Panel of the Survey of Income and Program Participation. The first two columns of Table 3.4 contain the estimated coefficients and t-statistics for the pooled sample of men and women. Columns 3 and 4 present the model for men and columns 5 and 6 present the model for women. From visual inspection of the coefficient estimates and t-statistics, it appears that the income models for men and women are different. This can be tested using the SSE values reported at the bottom of the table for each model. The SSE_c for the pooled model is 4.985 x 10^9; the SSE_a is 7.527 x 10^8; and the SSE_b is 3.626 x 10^9. The number of explanatory variables, k, is 6.

Substituting these values into the above formula for the F-test yields:

$$F_{7,4986} = \frac{[4.985x10^9-(7.527x10^8+3.626x10^9)]/7}{(7.527x10^8+3.626x10^9)/4986}$$

$$= 98.63$$

The critical value for the F-statistic with df = 7,4986 is 2.01 at the 95 percent confidence level. Therefore, the calculated value of F exceeds the tabulated value and the null hypothesis that there is no difference in the regression equations of income levels for men and women is rejected. In short, the determinants of male and female income levels, as indicated by the regression equations, are different.

ASSUMPTIONS UNDERLYING REGRESSION MODELS

It is very important to recognize that regression models are based on a number of assumptions that have implications for the interpretation and validity of the

Table 3.4
Income Level Regressions for Male, Female, and Pooled Samples

Variable	Pooled Sample Coefficient	t	Male Coefficient	t	Female Coefficient	t
Age	9.46	11.85	7.69	12.98	11.06	7.48
White	80.37	2.17	7.91	0.26	214.50	3.40
Education	15.15	7.25	14.57	8.81	22.58	6.29
Married	191.28	6.27	−159.92	−6.55	498.41	9.27
Poor Health	−207.86	−4.15	−84.49	−2.32	−426.83	−4.60
Work	1228.60	36.53	854.79	32.64	1325.90	22.19
Constant	−317.74	−8.62	−142.23	−4.34	−514.52	−8.74
$\bar{R}^2$	0.39		0.45		0.44	
F	533.64		343.22		325.89	
SSE	4.985×10^9		7.527×10^8		3.626×10^9	
N	5,000		2,476		2,524	

Source: Calculations based on the 1984 Panel of the Survey of Income and Program Participation (SIPP).

results obtained. When these assumptions are met, the estimates produced by ordinary least squares (OLS) regression have a number of desirable statistical properties. On the other hand, when the assumptions are not met, the OLS estimators no longer have these desirable statistical properties. Before we proceed further, therefore, these assumptions and their implications need to be identified.

No Specification Error

Actually, this is not one assumption but several. Unfortunately, there are many possible categories of specification error. Regression analysis assumes that the relationship between the dependent variable and the explanatory variables is linear in the coefficients. At first glance, this appears to be an extremely restrictive assumption. However, in Chapter 4 it will be shown that, with suitable transformations to the data, regression analysis can be used to estimate a broad range of nonlinear relationships. Failure to take account of nonlinear relationships between the explanatory and dependent variables results in biased coefficient estimates.

Another type of specification error is the omission of relevant explanatory variables. Like the failure to estimate the proper functional form, excluded variables result in biased coefficient estimates. In truth, this assumption is nearly always violated to some degree. After all, the basic rationale for building a model in the first place is to simplify reality so that it can be better understood. The practical issue then, is whether all of the *important* variables have been included in the model so as to minimize the bias introduced by excluded variables.

Relevant variables are excluded from analysis for a variety of reasons. Sometimes a researcher knows that a particular variable should be included in the model (i.e., the variable is part of the theoretical model) but data on the variable are unavailable. In this instance, the researcher is at least aware that the variable is missing and that some bias has probably been introduced into the coefficients that have been estimated. Usually, in such a case, the researcher will try to minimize the bias by including a variable in the model that is a proxy for the one that is missing. A more serious problem is the omission of a variable because the researcher does not realize that it belongs in the theoretical model. In such a case, the researcher may unknowingly place confidence in an estimated model that has misleading policy implications because the coefficients are biased.

The inclusion of irrelevant variables is less serious than the problem of excluded variables. In models containing irrelevant variables, it can be shown that the coefficient estimates are unbiased but not efficient. The estimated standard errors are also unbiased. Consequently, *t*-tests of the statistical significance of the coefficients remain valid in such models.

No Measurement Error

Measurement errors are assumed to be small in magnitude and random. One would expect systematic measurement errors to result in biased estimates of regression coefficients and standard errors. However, even random measurement errors can lead to biased estimates when such errors occur in measuring the explanatory variables. It is extremely difficult to decipher the direction and magnitude of the bias introduced by measurement error in multivariate regression models. Much of the work in modern survey design is focused on reducing measurement error at its source by improving the quality of data collected.

No Perfect Multicollinearity

It is also assumed that there is no perfect correlation among the explanatory variables. High correlations among two or more of the explanatory variables create a problem known as multicollinearity. Multicollinearity makes it impossible for the regression model to decompose the variation of the dependent variable that is due to one variable versus another. As a consequence, one gets highly unstable coefficients and *t*-statistics that fluctuate widely in magnitude (and even sign) depending upon which variables are included in the equation.

Assumptions about the Error Term

Most of the assumptions underlying the use of the regression model concern the distribution of the error term. As discussed earlier in reference to Figure 3.1, the estimated regression line will not be a perfect predictor of the actual values of the dependent variable. Sometimes the regression will overpredict the actual value; other times it will underpredict. There are several possible reasons for these errors—improper functional form, measurement errors, and excluded variables. To this list we might add the unpredictability of human behavior.

The regression residuals are assumed to be normally distributed with mean zero and constant variance. The assumption of normality is not needed to derive the formulas for the regression coefficients and standard errors. Consequently, even if the residuals are not normally distributed, the regression coefficients are still the best linear unbiased estimators (BLUE). On the other hand, the *t*-tests for the significance of the coefficients *do* depend on the assumption of normality. Fortunately, it can be shown that the sampling distribution for the least squares estimators approaches the normal distribution for large sample sizes.[6] Even in small samples the least squares estimates may not be too seriously affected if the distribution of the residuals is not too different from the normal distribution.[7]

A second assumption concerning the residuals is that they have an expected value of zero. Violating the assumption that the expected value of the residuals is equal to zero affects only the constant term—shifting it by the (nonzero) mean of the errors. This is often not a major concern because the slope coefficients are usually the main focus of interest in policy models. In fact, one of the virtues of the constant term is that it tends to absorb the effects of various violations of assumptions, thereby helping to reduce the bias that would otherwise be introduced into the slope coefficients.

Third, the error terms are assumed to have a constant variance or to be *homoscedastic*. For a given set of values for the explanatory variables, a regression model will predict one value for the dependent variable. However, corresponding to this prediction, there is a distribution of actual values for the dependent variable and, therefore, a distribution of errors. The assumption of homoscedasticity says that the variance of these errors for different values of the explanatory variables should be constant. If the variance of the residuals is not constant, the errors are said to be heteroscedastic. In the presence of heteroscedasticity the regression coefficients are still unbiased, but the *t*-statistics are unreliable.

Fourth, it is assumed that there is no correlation among the residuals. The presence of such an association, known as *autocorrelation*, is primarily a problem that occurs with time-series data. In cross-sectional data, however, the presence of autocorrelation can indicate excluded variables or other specification problems. As in the case of heteroscedasticity, the regression coefficients are unbiased in the presence of autocorrelation, but the *t*-statistics are unreliable.

Fifth, the residuals are assumed to be uncorrelated with the independent variables. Correlation of the error term with the explanatory variables introduces bias in the coefficient estimates.

The overarching assumption of the regression model is that the errors are random. It is assumed, for example, that the number of excluded variables is numerous so that the individual effects of any particular omitted variable are negligible. Similarly, measurement errors are assumed to be negligible and unpredictable. And, of course, human behavior is assumed to have a random component that cannot be systematically described by a regression model. To the extent that the assumption of randomness is not met, it implies that other violations of assumptions may be present. The statistical implications will depend upon which of the other assumptions is violated. For example, a systematic pattern in the errors that was due to the choice of an improper functional form or omitted variables will result in biased coefficient estimates. On the other hand, autocorrelation of residuals due to the use of time-series data suggests that the *t*-statistics associated with the variables cannot be trusted.

Subsequent chapters will examine how to test for violations of these assumptions. Given the long list of assumptions just outlined, it would seem impossible to conduct a regression analysis without violating at least one of the assumptions—and this is the case. Yet in many instances it is possible to correct these violations and still continue to use regression analysis. When such corrections are not possible, however, more advanced statistical techniques must be used.

There is disagreement in the literature about how serious violations of the regression assumptions actually are. This is not a meaningful discussion in the abstract. In any particular application, violation of one or more of the assumptions may introduce substantial bias or seriously undermine the validity of statistical tests. The same types of violations in another application might have comparatively mild repercussions. There has been considerable recent work on robust estimators, which are less sensitive to violations of assumptions.[8]

NOTES

1. Further details on the procedure used to solve for the regression coefficient formulas (as well as the other results presented in this chapter) can be found in any econometrics text and most specialized texts on regression. See, for example, Maddala (1977), Pindyck and Rubinfeld (1991), Ghosh (1991), Hamilton (1992), and Greene (1993).

2. For an excellent reference of the estimation of labor supply equations, see Killingsworth (1983).

3. There are equivalent versions of this *F*-test based on the regression sum of squares (RSS) and the sum of squared errors (SSE). For example, see Johnson, Johnson, and Buse (1987). Godfrey (1988) notes that this test amounts to a test for omitted variables if one assumes that the full model is correct.

4. This test was suggested by Chow (1960).

5. The reader will note that the form of the *F*-test in each of the above applications is very similar. There are, in fact, many such tests. A good introductory discussion is given in Johnson, Johnson, and Buse (1987).

6. See Malinvaud (1966, pp. 195–197).
7. Malinvaud (1966, pp. 251–254).
8. See Hamilton (1992) for a useful introduction to robust methods in regression.

4
Nonlinearities and
Categorical Explanatory Variables

THE MEANING OF LINEARITY

Provided that the assumptions discussed at the end of the preceding chapter are met, the OLS estimators are best linear unbiased estimators (BLUE). This means that of all the unbiased linear estimators, the OLS estimators have the smallest variance. Linearity implies that the estimators are of the general form:

$$y = b_0 + \hat{b}_1 x_1 + \hat{b}_2 x_2 + ... + \hat{b}_k x_k + \hat{e}$$

This form appears to be extremely restrictive. Clearly, many problems would not have such a convenient linear form. Figure 4.1, for example, illustrates two hypothetical nonlinear relationships between dependent and independent variables. Figure 4.1a shows the relationship between income and age. At lower ages, income levels increase rapidly as young workers gain experience. In middle age, however, income increases much less rapidly and eventually peaks. Finally, at later ages, income actually declines, dropping sharply at retirement, and staying fairly level thereafter.

Figure 4.1b illustrates a simple production function relationship between output and labor. Suppose output is measured in terms of the number of patients served by a mental health clinic and labor is the number of counselors on the staff. When few counselors are present, the addition of another staff member increases considerably the number of patients who can be served. Gradually, however, the addition of more counselors increases the number of patients served by smaller and smaller amounts. Eventually, there comes a point when the addition of one more counselor actually causes the number of patients served to drop. This could occur because of limitations on office space, overloading of the support staff, or other constraints on growth.

Figure 4.1
Illustration of Nonlinearities

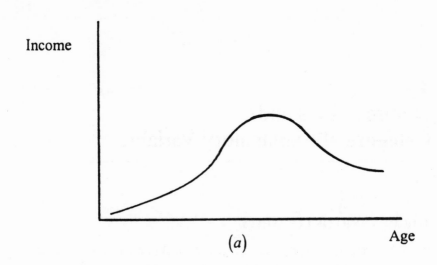

(a)

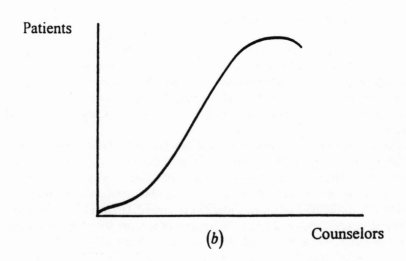

(b)

To the extent that the dependent variable is a nonlinear function of one or more explanatory variables and this nonlinearity is ignored, a specification error will be committed and the regression estimates will be biased. Fortunately, there are two basic approaches to modeling nonlinearities that will often enable regression analysis to be used despite its assumption of linearity. These two approaches are polynomial regression and logarithmic transformations.

POLYNOMIAL REGRESSION

A nonlinear relationship, such as that in Figure 4.1a that involves only one bend in the curve can always be modeled by adding a squared term to the equation. This can be done quite simply by creating a new explanatory variable that is equal to the square of the original variable prior to running the regression. Both variables are then entered into the regression. From the standpoint of the statistical software, another explanatory variable has simply been added to the model. This new variable will have a linear relationship with the dependent variable, but the overall relationship between the original explanatory variable and the dependent variable will now be nonlinear.

The approach just described can be extended to model more complex functional forms. Theoretically, a function with k bends can be modeled by introducing terms with powers of $k + 1$. For example, the curve in Figure 4.1a contained one bend, so age plus age squared was introduced into the equation. The production function in Figure 4.1b contains two bends, so it would be necessary to include explanatory variables of labor, labor squared, and labor cubed to estimate such a curve.

There are some potential problems with the polynomial regression approach, however. One problem is the degrees of freedom that are used up when higher-order terms are added to the model. In the case of Figure 4.1a this was not a major issue because the model contained just one explanatory variable and the function had only one bend. But one might easily imagine a model with several explanatory variables, each of which involved higher-order terms. If the sample size was not large relative to the number of variables added to the equation, the degrees of freedom lost could reduce the statistical significance of the model.

Moreover, there is another, more serious problem—that of multicollinearity. It is often the case that the original variable and its higher-order terms will be highly correlated with one another. As discussed in Chapter 5, multicollinearity can have serious effects on the statistical significance of the coefficient estimates. Nevertheless, multicollinearity is not always a problem with polynomial regression. For this reason, higher-order terms— especially squared variables—are common in applied research.

EXPONENTIAL FUNCTIONS

The regression equations considered thus far have all been linear functions of the explanatory variables or linear functions of these explanatory variables raised to some power. The following are some examples of these types of functions:

$$y = x^2$$
$$y = x^2 + 2x + 5$$

But there is another class of functions that involve a number raised to some power such as:

$$y = a^x$$

where a could be any number. These functions are known as exponential functions. In high school mathematics the reader probably encountered functions like this where a was equal to 10. There are some straightforward rules for manipulating exponential functions:

$$a^x . a^y = a^{x+y} \qquad\qquad a^0 = 1$$

$$(a^x)^y = a^{xy} \qquad\qquad \frac{a^x}{a^y} = a^{x-y}$$

$$(ab)^x = a^x b^x \qquad\qquad a^{-x} = \frac{1}{a^x}$$

$$\left(\frac{a}{b}\right)^x = \frac{a^x}{b^x}$$

Figure 4.2 shows the graphs for three simple exponential equations. These graphs illustrate that exponential equations are capable of describing a wide variety of functional forms. The equations generating Figures 4.2a and 4.2b appear to be very similar but the graphs of these functions are quite different. Figure 4.2c is particularly interesting because it provides a close approximation to the normal distribution.[1]

The e in the equation for Figure 4.2c should not be confused with the residuals $\hat{e}_i$ in a regression model. The e in the equation for Figure 4.2c is a compact notation for the special number 2.71828 . . . , which commonly appears in functions ranging from population and economic growth to probability distributions. Some insight may be gained by considering the function that gives rise to e:

$$f(m) = \left(1 + \frac{1}{m}\right)^m \qquad\qquad (1)$$

Suppose this function is evaluated for different values of m. The number e is defined by the value that equation (1) approaches for very large values of m (i.e., as m approaches infinity):

$$f(1) = \left(1+\frac{1}{1}\right)^1 = 2$$

$$f(2) = \left(1+\frac{1}{2}\right)^2 = 2.25$$

$$f(3) = \left(1+\frac{1}{3}\right)^3 = 2.37$$

$$\underset{m\to\infty}{Lim} \left(1+\frac{1}{m}\right)^m = 2.71828...$$
$$= e$$

Although a wide variety of functions are characterized by exponential relationships (e.g., population growth rates and the compounding of interest), these relationships are inherently nonlinear. This makes exponential functions difficult to handle mathematically and precludes their estimation by regression analysis.

LOGARITHMIC FUNCTIONS

Fortunately, there is another type of function that is the inverse of exponential functions. These are logarithmic functions and they are very helpful in transforming exponential functions into a linear form. As with exponential functions, there are a series of rules that govern the use of logarithmic functions:

Rule 1 $\log_a(xy) = \log_a x + \log_a y$

Rule 2 $\log_a(x/y) = \log_a x + \log_a y$

Rule 3 $\log_a x^r = r\log_a x$

Rule 4 $\log_a a = 1$

Rule 5 $\log_a 1 = 0$

The a in the above equations refers to the base of the logarithms, and there are two common choices—base 10 and base e. In the natural sciences, economics, mathematics, and statistics, functions involving e are so common that logarithms to the base e have a special name—natural logarithms (also sometimes known as Naperian logarithms). Along with the special name there is a special notation. Natural logs are referred to by the notation *ln* rather than $\log_a$ or $\log_e$.

To see how natural logs can be used to help estimate a linear regression equation corresponding to an underlying nonlinear model, consider the following migration model:

$$m = \frac{\hat{b}_0 p_1^{\hat{b}_1} p_2^{\hat{b}_2}}{DIST^{\hat{b}_3}}\,\hat{e} \tag{2}$$

Figure 4.2
Some Simple Exponential Functions

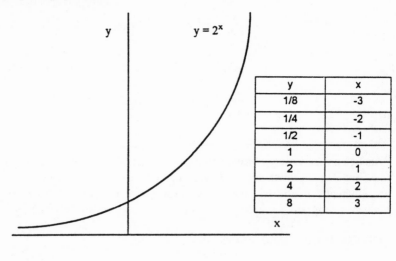

$y = 2^x$

y	x
1/8	-3
1/4	-2
1/2	-1
1	0
2	1
4	2
8	3

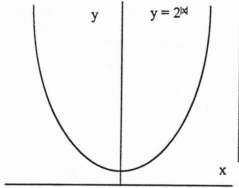

$y = 2^{|x|}$

y	x
8	-3
4	-2
2	-1
1	0
2	1
4	2
8	3

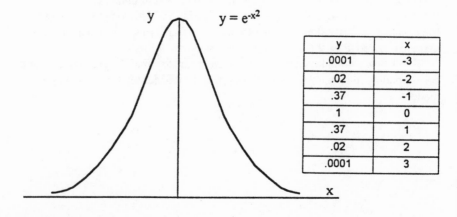

$y = e^{-x^2}$

y	x
.0001	-3
.02	-2
.37	-1
1	0
.37	1
.02	2
.0001	3

where

$$m = \text{migration between areas}$$
$$p_1 = \text{population in origin area}$$
$$p_2 = \text{population in destination area}$$
$$DIST = \text{distance between areas}$$

This is a so-called gravity model of migration. It posits that the migration between two areas is positively related to the size of the population in the origin area and the destination area, but is inversely related to the distance between the two areas. This highly nonlinear relationship can be transformed into a linear one by applying a series of logarithmic transformations using the rules listed above. Begin by applying rule 2, treating the numerator in equation (2) as though it were x and the denominator as though it were y. This results in:

$$\ln m = \ln \left[\hat{b}_0 p_1^{\hat{b}_1} p_2^{\hat{b}_2} \hat{e} \right] - \ln \left[DIST^{\hat{b}_3} \right]$$

Using rule 1, $\ln \left[\hat{b}_0 p_1^{\hat{b}_1} p_2^{\hat{b}_2} \hat{e} \right]$ can be rewritten as the sum of the logarithms of the product terms. This leads to:

$$\ln m = \ln \hat{b}_0 + \ln(p_1^{\hat{b}_1}) + \ln(p_2^{\hat{b}_2}) + \ln \hat{e} - \ln(DIST^{\hat{b}_3})$$

Finally, using rule 3 yields:

$$\ln m = \ln \hat{b}_0 + \hat{b}_1 \ln p_1 + \hat{b}_2 \ln p_2 - \hat{b}_3 \ln DIST + \ln \hat{e}$$

Using the logged variables in the model, rather than the original unlogged values, results in an equation that is linear in the coefficients:

$$m^* = \hat{b}_0^* + \hat{b}_1 p_1^* + \hat{b}_2 p_2^* - \hat{b}_3 DIST^* + \hat{e} \tag{3}$$

From the standpoint of the regression software this is a linear equation. Yet the estimated slope coefficients are the power terms in the highly nonlinear equation (2).

There are several points worth noting about the interpretation of statistical estimates from models such as the migration model just discussed. First, as mentioned above, the slope coefficients in the logged version of the model correspond directly to the power terms in the underlying nonlinear model. However, this is not the case with respect to the constant term. The constant term is the natural log of the $\hat{b}_0$ coefficient in the underlying model. Thus, i˜ one wanted to substitute the estimated coefficients into the nonlinear model, it wou'ʼᴊ be necessary to first exponentiate $\ln \hat{b}_0$:

$$\hat{b}_0 = e^{\ln \hat{b}_0}$$

Researchers, however, seldom substitute the estimated coefficients back into the underlying functional form. For a variety of reasons, it is generally the signs and statistical significance of the slope coefficients that are of greatest interest. One reason is that the specific numerical values of coefficient estimates are sometimes very sensitive to the other variables included in the model. This sensitivity may be due to multicollinearity (see Chapter 5) or bias introduced by the omission of important explanatory variables. In addition, the constant term often ends up absorbing the effects of specification errors.

In fact, an example of this is provided by the migration model that we have been considering. Notice that in taking the logs of equation (2), the error term was also logged implicitly. Since ordinary least squares regression assumes that the expected value (mean) of the errors is equal to zero, in the estimated equation (3) the expected value of the *log of the errors* is assumed equal to zero. But from rule 5 the natural log of one is equal to zero. This implies that the expected value of the residuals themselves is equal to one. A nonzero expected value for the errors biases the constant term. Consequently, the estimated constant term in a double log model is biased. This does not usually concern researchers because there are many other factors that also limit the reliability of the constant term.

A more serious practical problem with using logarithms arises from the fact that logarithms of numbers less than or equal to one are undefined. It is often the case that the dependent or independent variables take on zero or negative values. For example, this is often a problem in studies involving income because income can easily be zero or even negative (e.g., due to business losses).

One common approach to this problem is to arbitrarily set the zero and negative values to some small positive number before taking logs. The definition of "small" is arbitrary but researchers often choose a value depending on the units that the variable is measured in. For example, consider a model with census tract poverty rates as an explanatory variable. Poverty rates can range in value from zero to one. It is possible that some census tracts would have poverty rates of zero, so all zero values may be set equal to a small value, say, 0.0001.

In the case of an income variable measured in dollars, on the other hand, one might set all of the nonpositive values to one because one is not very different from zero. If many of the observations for income, however, had large negative values, then setting these negative values to zero might introduce substantial bias into the model. Assume, for the moment, that only the explanatory variables have zero or negative values; then the following exponential model could be estimated:

$$y = e^{\hat{b}_0 + \hat{b}_1 x + \hat{e}}$$

The exponential model is estimated by taking logs only of the dependent variable:

$$ln\,y = \hat{b}_0 + \hat{b}_1 x + \hat{e}$$

This formulation has the advantage of eliminating the need to take logs of the explanatory variables. However, if it is not the correct specification, the estimated coefficients will be biased. What criteria can be used for choosing between alternative specifications of the model?

COMPARING ALTERNATIVE MODEL SPECIFICATIONS

Researchers typically use several criteria for choosing among alternative functional forms. Sometimes a particular functional form is assumed because of theoretical considerations. This is common in economics, where econometricians may assume a particular form for a production function or a consumption function. In most instances, however, the functional form is not known and must be determined (or approximated) through a limited amount of experimentation.

A common approach is to estimate linear, log-log (for double log), and exponential versions of the model and then to choose the "best" one.[2] Table 4.1 reports estimates for these three types of functional forms using the migration example discussed above. The log-log model is model 1, model 2 is an exponential model, and model 3 is the basic linear model.

To select the appropriate functional form, one usually begins by comparing the signs and statistical significance of the variables in the different models. Researchers look favorably upon models that have statistically significant coefficients with the expected signs.

All three of the models reported in Table 4.1 meet this criterion. According to the gravity model theory, migration flows are expected to be large between pairs of origin and destination regions that have large populations but, everything else being equal, to be smaller between origin and destination regions that are far from one another. The gravity model theory, therefore, would predict positive coefficients for both the origin and destination region population variables and a negative coefficient for the distance variable. Each of the estimated models satisfies these expectations.

Another important set of criteria, however, is how well each of the models satisfies the assumptions underlying the regression model. This topic will be dealt with at considerable length in Chapter 5. One simple criterion that can serve as the basis for comparison, however, is the normality of the error distributions of the models. Most statistical packages enable the researcher to print a histogram of a model's residuals. Recall from Chapter 3 that regression analysis requires the distribution of errors to be normal in order for the significance tests to be valid. Thus, models with normal (or nearly normal) error distributions are preferred to those whose error distributions are not normal, everything else being equal.

All three of the migration models in Table 4.1, however, have fairly normal error distributions (not shown) and coefficient estimates that conform to theoretical expectations. What other criteria can we use to choose among the models?

In this instance many researchers would select the double log model because its functional form fits the theory associated with the gravity model. Another useful property of double log models is that the coefficients for continuous variables can be interpreted as elasticities. This is a property that is particularly attractive to economists. For example, the coefficient for the log of the destination population indicates that each 1 percent increase in the destination population leads to a 0.47 percent increase in interstate migration. The coefficients in the exponential model have a closely related interpretation. In the exponential model the coefficients for the continuous variables represent the percentage change in the dependent variable with respect to each one-unit increase in the explanatory variable.

Often, however, researchers do not have a theory that suggests the functional form to be estimated. They may have a pretty good idea of the variables that belong in the model, as well as an expectation about the signs of the estimated coefficients, but that is about it. In the event that we estimate several different regression models representing alternative functional forms and the results are very similar in terms of the estimated signs of the coefficients and the normality of the residuals, it is generally best to choose the model that requires the fewest additional assumptions. For example, suppose the choice were between a simple linear model and a log-log model. Suppose further that in estimating the log-log model it had been necessary to set some of the values of a particular variable (e.g., income) equal to a small constant in order to avoid the undefined logarithm problem. In this instance, it would probably be better to select the simple linear model because it avoids the potential bias introduced by constraining the values of the income variable to be greater than zero.

It is tempting to also use the adjusted R^2 of the different models as a basis for comparison. It is invalid, however, to compare the adjusted R^2 from a simple linear model to that of a log-log or exponential model because in the latter two types of models the dependent variable is the log of Y, whereas in the linear model it is simply Y. Comparing the adjusted R^2s of these models amounts to comparing apples and oranges.

Table 4.1
Comparison of Three Regression Models of Interregional Migration

	(1) LNMIG		(2) LNMIG		(3) MIG	
Variable	Coef.	t	Coef.	t	Coef	t
LNPOPD	0.4668	2.890	—	—	—	—
LNPOPO	0.8426	5.217	—	—	—	—
LNDIST	−0.6340	−4.853	—	—	—	—
POPD	—	—	0.00002	2.676	4.6505	2.308
POPO	—	—	0.00004	5.168	8.6422	4.288
DIST	—	—	−0.00048	−3.723	−118.0411	−3.496
CONSTANT	3.3627	1.312	11.1617	34.210	75305.5187	0.880
$\bar{R}^2$	0.45		0.39		0.32	

Source: Author's estimates using 1975–1980 migration and population data from U.S. Census Bureau and distance data from Crown (1991).

Nevertheless, it is possible to compare the adjusted R^2s of different models if the estimated parameters are substituted back into the original functional form. The predicted values for the observations can then be calculated, along with the errors or residuals of these predicted values from the actual values for the dependent variable. Finally, the adjusted R^2 can then be calculated for each model. These adjusted R^2s are comparable because the dependent variables of the models are consistent with one another.

In fact, Box-Cox regression is a technique that searches for the transformation of the dependent variable that maximizes the R^2 of the model. The technique involves estimating a series of regression models, each of which uses Y raised to a different power. The R^2s of these models are calculated as just discussed to ensure that they are comparable, and the method identifies the transformation that yields the highest R^2. The basic linear model and logged dependent variables are special cases of Box-Cox regression.

CATEGORICAL EXPLANATORY VARIABLES IN REGRESSION

Often the explanatory variables to be included in a regression model are qualitative in nature. Common examples are variables such as marital status, race, and gender. Qualitative variables such as these are handled in regression by creating dummy variables which have values of either zero or one (e.g., gender might be coded as equal to one if a survey respondent was female and zero if the respondent was male).

To see how dummy variables are interpreted, consider the following simple example. Suppose that hourly wages are hypothesized to be a function of experience and gender. Including only experience as the explanatory variable results in the following regression:

$$w\hat{a}ges = \hat{c}_0 + \hat{c}_1 experience \tag{4}$$

Assuming that both men and women are in the sample, the regression coefficients in equation (4) will be some function of the coefficients for men measuring the relationship between experience and wages and the coefficients for women measuring the same relationship. Equation (4), however, provides no way to test for the effects of gender on wages. In fact, equation (4) restricts the coefficients for the experience variable to being equal for men and women.

The simplest way to test the effect of gender on wages is to add a dummy variable for gender to equation (4). Assume that the coefficient for gender is negative (i.e., that being female reduces wage levels). Then adding gender to equation (4) results in the following:

$$w\hat{a}ges = \hat{b}_0 + \hat{b}_1 experience - \hat{b}_2 gender \tag{5}$$

Notice that gender is like a switch; it is either on or off. If a particular survey respondent is a female, the value of gender is equal to one. Multiplying this value by the coefficient for gender ($-\hat{b}_2$) results in a constant effect on wages of ($-\hat{b}_2$) for all females. Consequently, equation (5) could be rewritten for female respondents as:

$$wa\hat{g}es = (\hat{b}_0 - \hat{b}_2) + \hat{b}_1 experience$$

On the other hand, if a survey respondent is male, the value of gender will be zero. Multiplying zero by the coefficient for gender causes it to drop out of equation (5) altogether. Thus, equation (5) could be rewritten for the male respondents as:

$$wa\hat{g}es = \hat{b}_0 + \hat{b}_1 experience$$

These results are shown graphically in Figure 4.3a. The upper regression line is that for men; the lower line is for women. Simply adding gender as an explanatory variable has distinguished the two lines for men and women, but the lines differ only by a constant amount ($-\hat{b}_2$); the slope coefficients are the same.

It might be more realistic to hypothesize that gender has an interactive effect with experience in determining wage levels. For example, because of their caregiving roles, women frequently have interrupted work histories. Consequently, one would expect that being female would influence experience levels. Equation (6) shows a regression equation with the gender dummy variable interacted with experience:

$$wa\hat{g}es = \hat{b}_0 + \hat{b}_1 experience - \hat{b}_2(gender * experience) \tag{6}$$

Again, the $\hat{b}_2$ coefficient is assumed to be negative because being female is assumed to be negatively associated with wages. For the female respondents gender is equal to one so the interaction term is equal to $\hat{b}_2 * experience$. This means that the equation contains two different slope coefficients for the experience variable. These can be factored out and combined to yield the following wage equation for women:

$$wa\hat{g}es = \hat{b}_0 + (\hat{b}_1 - \hat{b}_2)experience$$

In the case of men, however, the value of gender will be equal to zero, so the entire interaction term in equation (6) will drop out. Consequently, the wage equation for men is:

$$wa\hat{g}es = \hat{b}_0 + \hat{b}_1 experience$$

The resulting wage equations for men and women when the gender dummy is entered in an interactive fashion are shown in Figure 4.3b. In this case the implied equations for men and women have the same constant term, but the slope coefficient for females will be smaller. This suggests that a year's increase in experience will raise the wages of women less than those of men.

The obvious extension is to enter gender in both an additive and an interactive fashion. This results in the following:

Figure 4.3
Interpretation of Dummy Variables

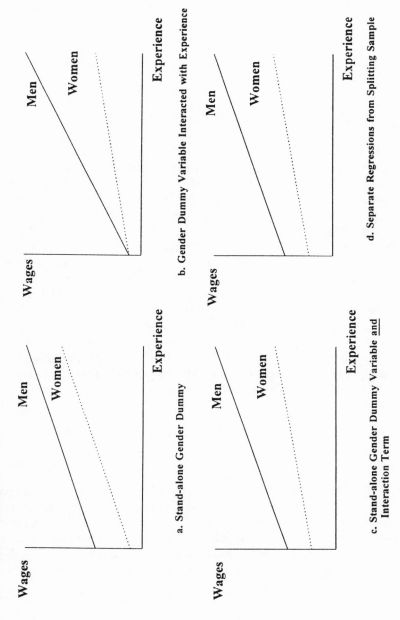

$$wa\hat{g}es = \hat{b}_0 + \hat{b}_1 experience - \hat{b}_2(gender * experience) \quad \hat{b}_3 gender \qquad (7)$$

As above, the coefficients on the variables involving gender are assumed to be negative. For females, gender is equal to one and equation (7) simplifies to:

$$wa\hat{g}es = (\hat{b}_0 - \hat{b}_3) + (\hat{b}_1 - \hat{b}_2) experience$$

For males, gender is equal to zero and equation (7) simplifies to:

$$wa\hat{g}es = \hat{b}_0 + \hat{b}_1 experience$$

The resulting regression lines are shown in Figure 4.3c. The top line is the regression for men; the bottom line is that for women. In the regression for women both the constant term and the slope are lower than that for men.

Of course, in the dummy variable model considered in equation (7), only one regression model is actually estimated. Theoretically, the coefficients for the dummy variables can be used to decompose the regression into separate regressions for men and women, but this is seldom done in practice. Researchers are usually content to make statements about the sign and statistical significance of the dummy variable coefficients. One reason for this is that the interpretation of the dummy variable coefficients becomes much more complex when the categorical variable has more than two categories. And when the model includes more than one categorical variable (which is usually the case), the interpretation becomes more complicated yet.

Shifting both the constant term and the slope would seem to be the most general formulation possible for examining the effects of gender on wages. But there is an approach that is even more general. This involves splitting the sample into men and women (assuming the sample size is sufficiently large to allow this) and running a separate regression for wages as a function of experience for both men and women:

$$wa\hat{g}es = \hat{b}_0 + \hat{b}_1 experience \qquad \text{(men)}$$

$$wa\hat{g}es = \hat{c}_0 + \hat{c}_1 experience \qquad \text{(women)}$$

Figure 4.3d shows the resulting regression lines. Graphically, this approach appears identical to the dummy variable approach just considered. It is more general, however, because there is a separate set of regression residuals for each equation. These separate sets of residuals mean that there are separate t-statistics for the variables in each model. An F-test such as that discussed in Chapter 3 can then be used to test the null hypothesis that the relationship between experience and wages is the same for men and women.

DUMMY VARIABLES WITH MULTIPLE CATEGORIES

Suppose an analyst wished to test the simple hypothesis that household income differs by region of the country. Assume also that the region variable takes on four values (1 = North, 2 = South, 3 = Midwest, and 4 = West). To enter region into a regression model, the original region variable must first be recoded into a series of four dummy variables. For example, North would be coded as one if region = 1 and zero otherwise. Similarly, South would be coded as one if region = 2 and zero otherwise, and so on. These four dummy variables are mutually exclusive. However, a careful inspection of these dummy variables illustrates an important point. Adding these dummy variables together results in a new variable where every value is equal to one. Since there is no variation in this new variable, there can be no possible covariation of this new variable with the dependent variable. This is known as the dummy variable trap. To avoid the dummy variable trap it is necessary to always exclude at least one of the dummy variable categories from the regression. For instance, in the region example, a maximum of three regional dummy variables can be entered in the regression.

The omitted dummy variable category or categories have implications for the interpretation of the dummy variable coefficients. Suppose that, to avoid the dummy variable trap, the Midwest region is excluded and the following regression is estimated:

$$Y = \hat{b}_0 + \hat{b}_1 North + \hat{b}_2 South + \hat{b}_3 West + \hat{e}$$

$$Y = \hat{b}_0 + \hat{b}_1 North + \hat{b}_2 South + \hat{b}_3 West + \hat{e}$$

Table 4.2 shows the possible values that each dummy variable can take on and the implications for the expected value of Y, $E(Y)$, given a particular regional location. If someone is living in the North, the value for North is one and the values for South and West are zero. These zero values for South and West cause them to drop out of the equation. By assumption, the expected value of the residuals in the regression model is equal to zero. Thus, the expected value of household income $E(Y)$ for someone living in the North is $\hat{b}_0 + \hat{b}_1$. Let's call this average income u_1. Following the same logic, the expected value of household income for someone living in the South is $u_2 = \hat{b}_0 + \hat{b}_2$ and that for someone living in the West is $u_3 = \hat{b}_0 + \hat{b}_3$.

What about the excluded Midwest region? For someone living in the Midwest, the values of North, South, and West are all equal to zero, leaving only the constant term. Thus, the expected value of the household income for someone living in the Midwest is $u_4 = \hat{b}_0$

The relationships shown in Table 4.2 provide an interpretation of dummy variable regression coefficients when more than one category is involved. From Table 4.2 the dummy variable coefficients can be rewritten as:

$$\hat{b}_1 = u_1 - \hat{b}_0$$
$$\hat{b}_2 = u_2 - \hat{b}_0$$
$$\hat{b}_3 = u_3 - \hat{b}_0$$

Substituting u_4 for $\hat{b}_0$:

$$\hat{b}_1 = u_1 - u_4$$
$$\hat{b}_2 = u_2 - u_4$$
$$\hat{b}_3 = u_3 - u_4$$

This implies that the dummy variable coefficient for a particular region represents the difference between the mean of household income in that region and household income in the excluded region. This result suggests that there is a relationship between regression models with dummy variables and ANOVA. In fact, the *F*-statistics for one-way ANOVA and regression with dummy variables are identical. The between sum of squares and within sum of squares in one-way ANOVA are equivalent to the regression sum of squares and error sum of squares in regression.

REGRESSION AND TWO-WAY ANOVA

Now suppose the analyst would like to test for differences in average income by region and race of the household head. Assume that race is defined as white or nonwhite. Then the possible mean income values are as follows:

	North	South	Midwest	West
White	u_{11}	u_{12}	u_{13}	u_{14}
Nonwhite	u_{21}	u_{22}	u_{23}	u_{24}

In each row of the above table the effects of race are controlled. In other words, it is possible to test the null hypothesis that the mean incomes of white households are equal in all regions or the null hypothesis that the mean incomes of nonwhite households are equal in all regions. Similarly, in each column of the table the

Table 4.2
Expected Value of Income by Region

Region	Dummy Variable			E(Y)
	North	South	West	
North	1	0	0	$u_1 = b_0 + b_1$
South	0	1	0	$u_2 = b_0 + b_2$
West	0	0	1	$u_3 = b_0 + b_3$
Midwest	0	0	0	$u_4 = b_0$

effects of region are controlled. Consequently, it is possible to test the null hypothesis that the mean incomes of white and nonwhite households are equal in each region.

The relationship between two-way ANOVA and regression analysis is a straightforward extension of the one-way ANOVA relationship. To see this, first define a new dummy variable for race, R, which is equal to one for nonwhite household heads and zero for white household heads. Using the regional dummy variables defined above, the regression model is:

$$Y = \hat{b}_0 + \hat{b}_1 D_1 + \hat{b}_2 D_2 + \hat{b}_3 D_3 + \hat{b}_4 R + \hat{e}$$

The relationships of the average incomes by region and race with the coefficients of the regression model are summarized in Table 4.3.

INTERACTION TERMS

There is a possible complication, however. As soon as there is more than one categorical explanatory variable, there is the possibility of interactions among these variables. In other words, racial differences in average incomes may be wider in some regions than in others.

To test for such interactions using regression analysis, it would be necessary to construct all of the possible combinations of the dummy variable for race with the three regional dummy variables. If there was another categorical variable such as gender in the model, the number of possible combinations to be explored would quickly become unmanageable.

Table 4.3
Expected Value of Income by Race and Region

| Race | Region | Dummy Variable | | | | E(Y) |
		North	South	West	Race	
White	North	1	0	0	1	$u_{11} = b_0 + b_1 + b_4$
White	South	0	1	0	1	$u_{12} = b_0 + b_2 + b_4$
White	Midwest	0	0	1	1	$u_{13} = b_0 + b_3 + b_4$
White	West	0	0	0	1	$u_{14} = b_0 + b_4$
Nonwhite	North	1	0	0	0	$u_{21} = b_0 + b_1$
Nonwhite	South	0	1	0	0	$u_{22} = b_0 + b_2$
Nonwhite	Midwest	0	0	1	0	$u_{23} = b_0 + b_3$
Nonwhite	West	0	0	0	0	$u_{24} = b_0$

Fortunately, two-way ANOVA provides a way to check for the presence of interactions in a relatively painless and systematic way. If the two-way ANOVA indicates that only the main effects variables are statistically significant, there is no need to explore possible interactions in the regression model. On the other hand, if some interactions do exist, the two-way ANOVA will identify which variables are involved. The researcher can then create the necessary interaction terms by computing the product of the relevant dummy variables. These interaction terms are then entered into the regression model as additional variables.

For example, suppose a two-way ANOVA indicates that the main effects for region, race, and gender are all statistically significant. In addition, however, there is a statistically significant two-way interaction between gender and race. To include this effect in the model it is necessary to compute a new variable that is equal to the product of the gender and race dummy variables. This new variable will have values of one only if the household head is a nonwhite female. Finally, the new variable is entered into the regression along with the original dummy variables for region, race, and gender.

The procedure just described for incorporating interaction effects into regression models is straightforward but is not always trouble-free. In particular, it is frequently the case that interaction terms will be highly correlated with the main effects variables—introducing the problem of multicollinearity. The problem of multicollinearity, methods for detecting its presence, and some approaches for dealing with it are discussed in the next chapter. In addition to multicollinearity, Chapter 5 discusses the detection of other violations of the assumptions of the ordinary least squares model—as well as estimation techniques for dealing with these violations.

NOTES

1. Compare the equation for Figure 4.2c with the actual equation for the normal distribution:

$$y = \frac{1}{\sqrt{2\pi\sigma_x^2}} \, e^{-\frac{1}{2}\left(\frac{x_i-\mu}{\sigma_x}\right)^2}$$

2. Of course, there are many other functional forms in addition to these three. For a useful review of functional forms used in econometric research, see Ghosh (1991).

5
Violations of Regression Assumptions

At the conclusion of Chapter 3 the assumptions that underlie the regression model and the implications of violating those assumptions were considered briefly. In this chapter, tests for violations of the assumptions, and approaches for remedying, when possible, these violations, are considered in greater detail. A good place to begin is with the normality of the regression residuals, because violations of regression assumptions are often reflected in a non-normal distribution of residuals.

NORMALITY OF RESIDUALS

Estimates of the model coefficients obtained by using ordinary least squares (OLS) regression are BLUE (best linear unbiased estimators) regardless of whether the residuals from the model are normally distributed. But tests of the statistical significance of the coefficients (t-statistics) and the overall model goodness of fit (F-statistic) depend upon the normality of the residuals for their validity. In other words, if the residuals are not normally distributed, statistical inferences based on the t-statistics or the F-statistic cannot be trusted.

Although White and MacDonald (1980) find that the consequences of violating the normality assumption vary from one study to another, Godfrey (1988, pp. 143–145) notes that normality is not generally tested. The easiest way to "test" for normality is simply to plot a histogram of the residuals, superimposed on the normal distribution. Unless one is very fortunate, this generally indicates that the distribution of residuals is quite different from the normal distribution. That is, the plotted distribution may have fatter tails (more cases than one would expect in the tails of the distribution than if it were normal), it might be more tightly concentrated around zero than the normal distribution would predict, or it might be skewed in one direction or the other. To deal with this problem, one usually experiments with transformations of the dependent variable and/or the explanatory variables to identify the functional form for the model that generates the distribution of errors that is most nearly normal (see Chapter 4).

Kiefer and Salmon (1983) suggest a Wald statistic which measures the deviation of the residuals from normality in terms of skewness and kurtosis:

$$W = N_1[\frac{S}{6} + \frac{(k-3)^2}{24}]$$

where S is the skewness coefficient squared, K is the measure of kurtosis, and N_1 is the sample size. W has a χ^2 distribution with 2 degrees of freedom.

MULTICOLLINEARITY

One of the most serious and pervasive problems with using regression analysis is that of multicollinearity. Multicollinearity arises when two or more of the explanatory variables in a multiple regression equation are highly correlated. To see why this is a problem, consider a simple regression in which there are two explanatory variables:

$$Y = \hat{b}_0 + \hat{b}_1 x_1 + \hat{b}_2 x_2 + \hat{e}$$

In this case, it can be shown[1] that the standard errors of the slope coefficients are as follows:

$$S_{\hat{b}_1} = \sqrt{\frac{S^2}{\sum x_{1i}(1-r^2)}}$$

$$S_{\hat{b}_2} = \sqrt{\frac{S^2}{\sum X_{2i}(1-r^2)}}$$

where:

$$S^2 = \sum \frac{\hat{e}_i^2}{n-k}$$

r = simple correlation between X_1 and X_2

It is apparent from the formulas for the standard errors that as the correlation between X_1 and X_2 approaches one, $(1-r^2)$ will approach zero, and the standard error will "explode"—making the t-statistics for these variables insignificant. Of course, this does not mean that every insignificant t-statistic is due to multicollinearity.

An obvious test for multicollinearity is to examine the correlations among the explanatory variables. In multiple regressions involving only two explanatory variables this is a useful diagnostic tool. It is often suggested that correlations above 0.85 are likely to lead to multicollinearity problems. This rule of thumb, however, is arbitrary and breaks down altogether if the regression equation contains more than two explanatory variables. The reason for this can be seen by considering the generalized formula for the standard error of a regression coefficient:

$$S_{b_k} = \sqrt{\frac{S^2}{(1-R_k^2)(N-1)S_k^2}}$$

where R_k^2 is the R^2 for the model which regresses explanatory variable k on all of the other explanatory variables in the original model. S^2 is the error variance from the original model and S_k^2 is the error variance from the regression of variable k on all of the other explanatory variables. Each R_k^2 (there is one for each explanatory variable in the original model) shows the strength of the linear relationship between that explanatory variable and *all* of the other variables in the model. For this reason, it is a much more general indicator of multicollinearity than the simple correlations among the explanatory variables.

One can see that as R_k^2 gets close to one, the standard error for the variable will become very large, just as in the simple case described above. Note that $(1-R_k^2)$ is the proportion of the variation in X_k *not* explained by the other variables. This quantity is often referred to as the tolerance. The tolerance ranges between zero and one; researchers would like the tolerance for each variable to be high (close to one) rather than low. The inverse of the tolerance, $1/(1-R_k^2)$, is known as the variance inflation factor (VIF); the VIF is unbounded at the upper end.

Example

Table 5.1 reports the results of a regression to examine the determinants of 1950–87 growth in state per-capita income. The estimated model reflects hypotheses that state per-capita income growth is a function of growth in manufacturing wages, growth in the percentage of the population employed, urban population growth in the South, the decline of farming, and growth in education levels of the labor force. The results indicate that growth in the employment percentage, urban population percentage in the South, and median years of schooling have positive and statistically significant effects on state per-capita income growth. This is indicated by the positive regression coefficients for these variables, in combination with *t*-statistics that are statistically significant at the 95 percent confidence level or better.

At first glance, manufacturing wages and farming also seem to have the expected relationship with state per-capita income growth. For example, it is plausible that increases in manufacturing wages would positively affect state per-capita income growth; conversely, increases in the farming population would be expected to decrease per-capita income. Although the signs of the estimated coefficients conform to the hypothesized relationships, the coefficients are not statistically significant at the 95 percent confidence level or better. Therefore, at a

Table 5.1
Tolerance and VIF Diagnostics for Multicollinearity in a Model of State Per-Capita Income Growth

Variable	Coefficient	t-statistic	Tolerance	VIF
Wage	0.4118	1.419	.5826	1.716
EMPLOY/POP	1.1607	3.050	.6071	1.647
South Urban %	0.6189	2.496	.4066	2.460
Farm %	−0.4873	−1.315	.5421	1.845
Years School	0.8681	2.616	.4314	2.318
Constant	0.1268	0.394	—	

R^2 = 0.719
Adjusted R^2 = 0.685
F = 21.469

95 percent confidence level, they are not statistically different from zero, and the signs of the estimated coefficients are not reliable.

The preceding discussion highlights a common error made in the interpretation of regression results. Sometimes researchers will state that a parameter "had the expected sign but was not statistically significant." There is no statistical basis for making such a statement because a coefficient that is not statistically significant at a given confidence level is not significantly different from zero in either a positive or a negative direction.

Given the theoretical importance of manufacturing wage growth and farming as explanatory factors in per-capita income growth, it would be important to rule out multicollinearity among the explanatory variables as the reason for the lack of significance of these variables. As discussed above, it is possible to check for the presence of multicollinearity by calculating the tolerance and VIF statistics (also reported in Table 5.1).

For example, the regression of manufacturing wages on the remaining explanatory variables (population employment percentage, Southern urban population percentage, farm population percentage, and median years of schooling) yields an R^2 of 42 percent. The tolerance for manufacturing wages is therefore 58 percent (1 - 0.42). The higher a variable's R^2, the greater is its linear association with the other explanatory variables and, consequently, the greater is the problem of multicollinearity.

If we look at the tolerances for the variables, it is apparent that the lowest tolerances are for the percentage growth in Southern urban population percentage and median years of schooling. Yet both of these variables are statistically significant and have their theoretically expected signs. Clearly, multicollinearity has not inflated the standard errors of these variables to the point where they are no longer statistically significant. In contrast, the two insignificant variables, manufacturing wage growth and farming population percentage, have considerably higher tolerances. Therefore, it *does not* seem likely that the statistical insignificance of these variables is due to multicollinearity. Not surprisingly, the variance inflation factors (VIF), which are simply the inverse of the tolerances, tell exactly the same story.

REMEDIES FOR MULTICOLLINEARITY

There are several approaches to dealing with the problem of multicollinearity if it is present in the model. Theoretically, the most attractive of these approaches is to increase the sample size. In some cases, increasing the sample size may reduce the standard errors of the affected variables enough so that they become statistically significant. This is a theoretically desirable approach because it preserves the original specification of the model, which presumably was based on theoretical grounds.

Unfortunately, it is not generally possible to increase the sample size in most studies without considerable expense and additional time. Moreover, there is no guarantee that increasing the sample size will enable statistically significant estimates of the coefficients to be obtained. In the example considered above, for instance, it would not be possible to increase the sample size because the units of observation are the states, and all of the states were already included in the model.

Consequently, a common approach taken by researchers is to omit variables from the model until the multicollinearity problem is solved. This can be done by using the tolerances to identify the variables contributing to the multicollinearity. The obvious problem with this approach is that it violates the original specification of the model. If the researcher really believed in the original specification, then dropping one or more variables to solve a multicollinearity problem would introduce specification error into the model (discussed below).[2] The latter is potentially more serious than multicollinearity because specification error may introduce bias into the model.

It is not always a problem to drop highly correlated explanatory variables, however. For example, a model of labor force hours might include several different measures of health status as explanatory variables. It is important to the theoretical model to have a measure of health status as an explanatory variable, but multiple measures may add little to the explanation of labor supply. Moreover, the multiple indicators of health status are likely to be highly correlated with one another. In such an instance, the risk of incurring substantial specification bias from dropping some of the health-status indicators is probably small.

A third approach for dealing with multicollinearity is to create new variables that are some combination of the multicollinear ones. Although this approach alters the functional form of the model, it has the merit of retaining the variables that were in the original theoretical model. Sometimes a logical way of combining the correlated variables suggests itself. For example, researchers might hypothesize that household expenditures are a function of household income and household size. Upon estimating the model, however, the researchers may find that household income and household size are highly correlated with one another. If they use per-capita income instead of household income and household size in the model, the specification still contains the elements of household income and household size, but the multicollinearity problem is eliminated.

Another method for creating combinations of the explanatory variables is to use principal components or factor analysis.[3] These approaches reduce the original number of variables to a smaller number of new variables that are linear combinations of the original ones. The new variables can be constructed so that they are completely uncorrelated with one another. Moreover, this approach reduces the number of coefficients that must be estimated in the regression.

Unfortunately, although the use of principal components or factor analysis may lead to good statistical models, the resulting models may be less useful for analysis purposes. This is because the specific influence of explanatory variables may be obscured by the more general factors of which they are a part. The interpretation of factors, especially if they are composed of seemingly unrelated original variables, may be difficult. On the other hand, the selective use of principal components or factor analysis for problems such as the multiple health-status indicators example above can facilitate the construction of aggregate variables that can be entered into a regression along with other original variables.

A fifth approach to the multicollinearity problem is the use of estimates from other research. Suppose, once again, that a researcher is trying to estimate a household expenditure equation. It is hypothesized that household expenditures are a linear function of household income, household size, age of household head, race, regional location, and gender of household head:

$$Expend_i = \hat{b}_0 + \hat{b}_1 Income + \hat{b}_2 Size + \hat{b}_3 Age + \hat{b}_4 Race + \hat{b}_5 Region + \hat{b}_6 Gender + \hat{e}_i$$

In this equation, it is very likely that household size and age of household head would be highly correlated. Now assume that a reliable estimate of the coefficient for household age composition is available from a previous study. This estimate could be used to obtain unbiased estimates for the remaining variables by adjusting the dependent variable in the following way:

$$(Expend_i - \hat{b}_3 Age_i) = \hat{b}_0 + \hat{b}_1 Income + \hat{b}_2 Size + \hat{b}_4 Race + \hat{b}_5 Region + \hat{b}_6 Gender + \hat{e}_i$$

The adjusted estimates would be obtained by subtracting from each value of Expend the corresponding value of $\hat{b}_3$ x Age. The resulting variable would be used to estimate a regression on all of the remaining variables other than Age. The practical problem with this approach is that it requires exogenous, or outside, information on the coefficient value for at least one of the correlated explanatory variables. Sometimes, reliable estimates are available (e.g., time-series estimates of the marginal propensity to consume out of income are consistently about 0.95), but often such estimates are not available—especially in new areas of research lacking an established empirical literature. Moreover, if the coefficient taken from prior research was not estimated in a model with the same specification as the model being estimated, then the coefficient may be biased (assuming the current specification is correct). On the other hand, if the specifications are the same, there may be little point in repeating the estimation.

Finally, a technique known as ridge regression (Hoerl and Kennard, 1970) generates biased estimates but with smaller standard errors than those provided by ordinary least squares (OLS) regression in the presence of multicollinearity. On the basis of the Mean Square Error criterion (recall Figure 2.5), therefore, ridge regression estimators are sometimes preferred to those of OLS regression when there is multicollinearity among the explanatory variables.

The standardized regression model can be expressed in terms of a matrix of the simple correlations among the explanatory variables R_{xx} the beta coefficients B, and the correlations of the explanatory variables with the dependent variable R_{yx}:

$$R_{xx}B=R_{yx}$$

If one adds a constant to the diagonal of the correlation matrix R_{xx}, the standardized model becomes:

$$(R_{xx}+cI)B=R_{yx}$$

where I is a diagonal matrix of the same size as R_{xx}. Solving for the standardized beta coefficients yields the ridge regression estimators:

$$B=(R_{xx}+cI)^{-1}R_{yx}$$

The resulting coefficients are biased but tend to be more stable than the OLS beta coefficients.

The trick with ridge regression is to pick the smallest possible value for c possible, so as to minimize the amount of bias introduced into the coefficient estimates (when $c = 0$ the ridge regression estimators equal the OLS estimators). One way to do this is to plot the estimated coefficients against incremental values for c. Figure 5.1 shows a hypothetical example with three variables. For increasing values of c less than 0.3 the coefficient estimates for b_2 and b_3 increase; the estimates for b_3 decrease. However, the coefficient values for all of the coefficients seem to stop changing for values of c greater than 0.3. Therefore, the ridge regression estimator would pick c equal to 0.3 because this would be the value that would generate stable estimates of the coefficients with the least amount of bias.

HETEROSCEDASTICITY

A major assumption of the regression model is the assumption of homoscedasticity:

$$\text{Var}(e_i) = \sigma^2$$

Figure 5.1
Choice of *c* in Ridge Regression

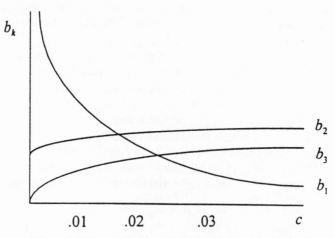

Homoscedasticity means that the variance of the error terms is constant for different levels of the explanatory variables. Figure 5.2 illustrates that for each value of X there is a distribution of Y values. For example, one would expect to find a distribution of expenditures among families with incomes of $30,000. Some families with incomes of $30,000 will save a substantial amount. Most will spend nearly all of the $30,000, and others may spend more than $30,000 by borrowing or consuming out of past savings. As shown in Figure 5.2, however, the regression model will predict only one expenditure level for families with incomes of $30,000. As a result, the distribution of actual expenditures around the regression line implies that there must also be a distribution of errors. Theoretically, there is a distribution of such errors for each level of the explanatory variable (income). The assumption of homoscedasticity is that the variance of each of these error distributions is equal to the same value, σ^2. If this is not the case, the errors are said to be heteroscedastic. Regression models with heteroscedastic errors will have unbiased coefficient estimates but the t-tests of significance will be unreliable.

Heteroscedasticity can have a variety of different forms; three possible forms are shown in Figures 5.3a through 5.3c. The most common form empirically is the increasing variance of the error terms shown in Figure 5.3a. This is fortunate because increasing variance of the error term tends to lead to underestimated t-statistics. As will be shown shortly, it is often possible to correct for the problem of heteroscedasticity using a technique known as weighted least squares. However, if the estimated coefficients are statistically significant despite the presence of heteroscedasticity, there may not be much need to correct for it. In fact, an improper correction for heteroscedasticity may introduce a problem of bias that is more serious than the original understating of the t-statistics. On the other hand, if the t-statistics are not statistically significant, or if the heteroscedasticity is not the increasing variance type, corrective measures may be called for.

Figure 5.2
Homoscedasticity

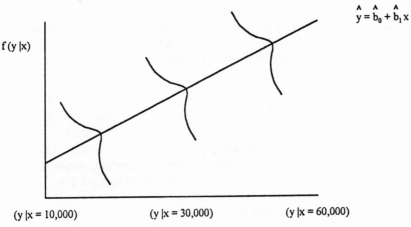

$(y \,|x = 10{,}000)$ $(y \,|x = 30{,}000)$ $(y \,|x = 60{,}000)$

WEIGHTED LEAST SQUARES

To correct heteroscedasticity it is necessary to transform the original model so that the error term in the transformed model has a constant variance. This is known as weighted least squares (WLS). To illustrate how weighted least squares works, assume that the variance of the errors differs systematically with the level of the explanatory variable X:

$$\text{Var}\,(\hat{e}_i^2) = CX_i^2$$

This implies:

$$e_i = \sqrt{C}X_i$$

Suppose the original model was

$$\hat{Y} = \hat{b}_0 + \hat{b}_1 X_{1i} + \hat{e}_i$$

Dividing the equation by X_i yields:

$$\frac{Y_i}{X_1} = \hat{b}_0 \frac{1}{X_1} + \hat{b}_1 \frac{X_1}{X_1} + \frac{\hat{e}}{X_1}$$

Substituting $\sqrt{C}X_i$ for e_i, the variance of the transformed equation is

$$Var(\frac{\hat{e}_i}{X_1}) = \frac{1}{X^2_1} Var(\hat{e}_i)$$

$$= C$$

In other words, the variance of the transformed equation is now the constant value C—thereby solving the heteroscedasticity problem. However, the resulting equation must be interpreted with caution. In the transformed equation, $\hat{b}_1$ becomes the constant term because X_i/X_i is a vector of ones. Thus the constant term in the transformed equation corresponds to the slope coefficient in the original equation. Similarly, the slope coefficient in the transformed equation corresponds to the constant in the original equation.

HETEROSCEDASTICITY TESTS

Application of the WLS procedure as discussed above requires knowledge of at least two things. First, it is necessary to know whether a heteroscedasticity problem exists. Second, if there is evidence of heteroscedasticity, it is necessary to know its form so that the appropriate transformation can be carried out.[4]

Visual Inspection of Residuals

A simple "test" for heteroscedasticity is to plot the standardized residuals (on the vertical axis) against the dependent variable (on the horizontal axis). If no heteroscedasticity is present, the plot will appear to be a random cloud. If a pattern is evident in the scatterplot (e.g., as in Figure 5.3a), then a formal statistical test for heteroscedasticity is warranted. It is a good idea to always run this simple diagnostic check for heteroscedasticity since it is so easily accomplished and can be very helpful in interpreting the statistical significance of coefficient estimates.

Rank Correlation Test

There is a large literature dealing with the diagnosis and correction of heteroscedasticity.[5] Many of these tests assume at least some knowledge on the part of the researcher of the functional form of the nonconstant error variance. The simplest test for heteroscedasticity is probably the rank correlation test proposed by Johnson (1972). In this test, the absolute values of the regression residuals are ranked, as are the values of each of the explanatory variables. The rank correlation of each explanatory variable with the residuals is calculated using the standard rank correlation formula:

$$r = 6\sum \frac{D^2}{n(n^2-1)}$$

where D is the difference between the ranks of the absolute value of the residuals and the values of the explanatory variable, and n is the sample size.

Example

It has been observed for several decades that regression equations of family expenditures tend to have heteroscedastic error variances (e.g., Prais and Houthakker,

Figure 5.3
Alternative Forms of Heteroscedasticity

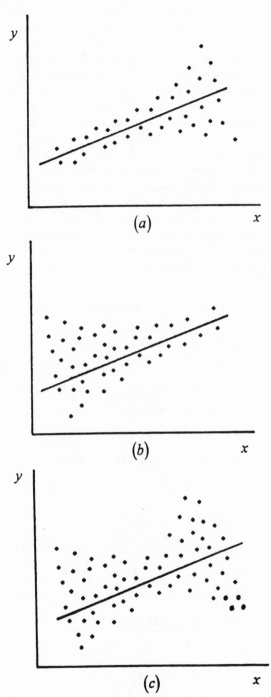

1955). Table 5.2 shows the regression results for a model of total household expenditures estimated using the 1984 Consumer Expenditure Survey. Household expenditures are modeled as a function of the education level, age and gender of household head, household income, and regional location. All of the explanatory variables are statistically significant except for the dummy variable measuring location in the Northeast. The model has an adjusted R^2 of about 12 percent. The signs and statistical significance of the coefficients seem to make theoretical sense, but a plot of the standardized residuals, superimposed on the normal distribution (Figure 5.4a), indicates that there is a group of cases with very large standardized residuals (greater than 10 standard deviations) and the residuals are more tightly clustered about zero than the normal distribution. These findings suggest caution in trusting the t-statistics that are reported for the model in Table 5.2.

Figure 5.4b is a plot of the standardized residuals and household expenditures. It indicates that most of the observations are for relatively low expenditure levels and that the corresponding residuals for these low expenditure levels are also low. The standardized residuals tend to be larger for higher expenditure levels—especially for a small group of observations that have particularly high expenditure levels and large residuals. This gives a "fan shape" to the overall pattern of the plot, suggesting the presence of heteroscedasticity.

Table 5.2
Initial Regression Model of Total Household Expenditures, 1984

Variable	B	SE B	Beta	T	Sig T
West	141.906316	48.322144	.022174	2.937	.0033
Female	−244.971457	39.153220	−.043446	−6.257	.0000
High School	338.425402	48.627802	.058201	6.960	.0000
White	333.125571	51.185548	.043917	6.508	.0000
Age	3.045042	1.043899	.020634	2.917	.0035
Family Income before Tax	.030891	9.2945E-04	.239594	33.235	.0000
Northeast	73.153332	49.400053	.010935	1.481	.1387
Family Size	188.494393	11.987225	.111874	15.725	.0000
South	155.381021	46.406509	.025246	3.348	.0008
College	658.743194	47.517059	.123513	13.863	.0000
(Constant)	−166.713740	94.631956		−1.762	.0781

Adjusted R^2 = 0.12

Source: Estimates based on 1984 Consumer Expenditure Survey.

Figure 5.4
Diagnostic Plots of Residuals

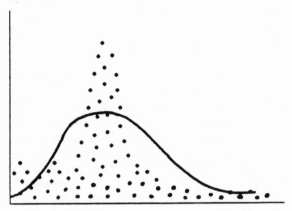

(a) Standard Residuals Versus Normal Distribution

z resid

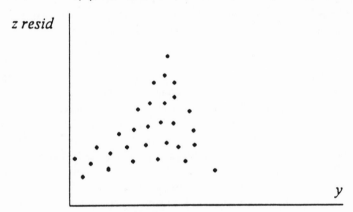

y

(*b*) Diagnostic Plot for Heteroscedasticity

As an initial statistical test for the presence of heteroscedasticity, the rank correlation statistic was computed. To do this, the residuals from the regression in Table 5.2 were saved and the absolute values of these residuals were computed. The rank correlation of the absolute residuals with before-tax income was 0.35; it was 0.26 with family size, 0.21 with college, and -0.06 with the age of the household head. All of these correlations are statistically significant at better than the 99 percent confidence level. Thus, heteroscedasticity was indicated with respect to several explanatory variables.

Goldfeld-Quandt Test

Goldfeld and Quandt (1965) presented a test for heteroscedasticity that is also fairly straightforward and, perhaps for this reason, widely used. However, application of this test assumes that the researcher knows the variable that is the source of the heteroscedasticity. The test has four steps:

1. The observations are ordered by the values of the variable, X_k, hypothesized to be the source of the heteroscedasticity.
2. An arbitrary number, p, of the central observations are dropped from the sample to partition it into two groups.
3. SSE_1 and SSE_2, the sums of squared residuals from these two regressions, are calculated.
4. An F-statistic is calculated from the ratio SSE_2/SSE_1 where $SSE_2 > SSE_1$. This F-statistic has $(N-p-2k)/2$ degrees of freedom for both the numerator and denominator.

If the calculated value for the F-statistic is greater than the tabulated value for the given numbers of degrees of freedom and a particular confidence level, a heteroscedasticity problem is indicated. The power of this F-test, however, is influenced by the choice of p. The usual rule of thumb is to choose p equal to one-third (i.e., leave out the middle third of the cases).[6]

Example

Theoretically, one would expect that low-income families would spend virtually all of their income to meet their consumption needs. If this were true, there would not be much room for variation in behavior and one would expect the residuals for low-income households to be relatively small. On the other hand, one would expect a great deal of variation in expenditure levels among high-income families. High incomes permit much greater latitude in spending and saving behavior. Consequently, one would expect the variance of the residuals for high-income families to be larger than those for low-income families. This theoretical expectation is supported by the large and statistically significant rank correlation of the absolute residuals with before-tax income discussed above.

To see if the same conclusion would be reached using the Goldfeld-Quandt test, the before-tax income levels corresponding to the 33rd and 67th percentiles were identified by constructing a relative frequency distribution of income. The original sample was then split into two subsamples. The first subsample consisted of all households having incomes less than $8,990 (33rd percentile); the second subsample consisted of all households having incomes greater than $24,763 (67th percentile).

The model specification shown in Table 5.2 was then estimated for each of the subsamples. For the purposes of the Goldfeld-Quandt test, the only information needed from these regression results is the sum of squared errors for each of the models. The sum of the squared errors for the high-income households was $SSE_2 = 73{,}302{,}527{,}410$; for the low-income households $SSE_1 = 26{,}078{,}792{,}021$. The ratio $SSE_2/SSE_1 = 2.81$. To calculate the degrees of freedom for F, start with the total sample size of 20,600. The number of excluded cases, p, is equal to 6,867, and the number of explanatory variables, k, is equal to 10. Therefore, the degrees of freedom equals (20,600 - 6,867 - 20)/2 or 6,857.

The tabulated F-value for 6,857 degrees of freedom in the numerator and denominator is equal to one at either the 95 or 99 percent confidence level. Therefore, because the calculated F-statistic of 2.81 exceeds the tabulated value of 1.00, the null hypothesis of homoscedasticity (no heteroscedasticity) with respect to income is rejected. In other words, the regression error variance differs by household income level.

Breusch-Pagan Test

The Goldfeld-Quandt test is useful for diagnosing heteroscedasticity when a particular variable is suspected to be the source of the problem. It is possible, however, that heteroscedasticity may arise from more than one variable or from other sources such as grouping of the data. In such cases, the tests for hetero-scedasticity and the WLS adjustments that must be made are more involved than the simple one-variable model discussed above. Moreover, the Goldfeld-Quandt and rank correlation tests reveal nothing about the specific functional form of the heteroscedasticity, so neither is very useful for specifying a WLS model to correct the problem.

Breusch and Pagan (1979) presented a test for heteroscedasticity that can identify a broad range of functional forms for nonconstant error variance. In addition, their approach leads to a WLS specification for correcting hetero-scedasticity with a broad range of functional forms.

The first step in the Breusch-Pagan test is to estimate the original regression:

$$\hat{Y} = \hat{b}_0 + \hat{b}_1 X_{i1} + \hat{b}_2 X_{i2} + ... + \hat{b}_k X_{ik} + \hat{e}_i$$

The residuals from the original regression are used to calculate the standardized squared residuals:

$$\hat{g}_i = \hat{e}_i^2 / (\Sigma \hat{e}_i^2 / N)$$

Using $\hat{g}_i$ as the dependent variable, one then estimates the regression:

$$\hat{g}_i = \hat{c}_0 + \hat{c}_1 Z_{i1} + \hat{c}_2 Z_{i2} + ... + \hat{c}_p Z_{ip}$$

where the Z_{ip} are variables thought to be generating the heteroscedasticity. Using the regression sum of squares, RSS, from the second regression (with $\hat{g}_i$, the standardized squared residuals, as the dependent variable), one can calculate a χ^2 statistic as follows:

$$\chi^2 = RSS/2$$

The χ^2 has p-1 degrees of freedom. If the calculated value for the χ^2 exceeds the tabulated value for the relevant number of degrees of freedom and confidence level, then the null hypothesis of homoscedasticity (constant error variance) is rejected and a heteroscedasticity problem is indicated.

If the null hypothesis of homoscedasticity is rejected, Breusch and Pagan suggest a straightforward weighted least squares approach to correct for the non constant error variance. The residuals from the original regression are first squared and then used to estimate an equation of the form:

$$\hat{e}_i^2 = \hat{c}_0 + \hat{c}_1 Z_{i1} + \hat{c}_2 Z_{i2} + \dots + \hat{c}_p Z_{ip}$$

The above equation[7] is used to generate estimates of $\hat{e}_i^2$. The square root of each $\hat{e}_i^2$ is then taken to create $\hat{e}_i$. Finally, the dependent and explanatory variables are divided by $\hat{e}_i$ and the original equation is reestimated using the transformed variables:

$$Y_i/\hat{e}_i = \hat{b}_0(1/\hat{e}_i) + \hat{b}_1(X_{i1}/\hat{e}_i) + \hat{b}_2(X_{i2}/\hat{e}_i) + \dots + \hat{b}_k(X_{ki}/\hat{e}_i)$$

The resulting equation will have a constant error variance and the coefficients are interpreted as though no transformation had been necessary.

Example

In considering the rank correlation test for heteroscedasticity, several variables were found to be correlated with the absolute residuals. The Breusch-Pagan test provides a check for heteroscedasticity stemming from one or more variables at the same time. To begin, the regression in Table 5.2 was estimated, saving the residuals as before. The residuals were then squared and divided by 6,188,072—the sum of squared errors divided by N (127,474,276,673/20,600). The standardized squared residuals were then regressed on household income, family size, college education, and the age of the respondent. The only output that is used from this regression is the regression sum of squares, RSS. The RSS divided by 2 has a χ^2 distribution with p-1 degrees of freedom. In this example, p is equal to 4 (the number of variables in the regression of the standardized residuals). The test statistic RSS/2 is equal to 5,118. The tabulated value for χ^2 at the 99 percent confidence level with 3 degrees of freedom is 11.34. Clearly, the calculated value for the test statistic exceeds the tabulated value, so the null hypothesis of homoscedasticity is rejected. Once again, the evidence points to a heteroscedasticity problem.

Given that a heteroscedasticity problem has been identified, the Breusch-Pagan approach was used to correct for it. The first step in applying the Breusch-Pagan method is to use the squared residuals from the original model as the dependent variable in a regression where the explanatory variables are those thought to cause the heteroscedasticity. Sometimes there might be a theoretical rationale for identifying these variables (as in the case of income discussed above), but for many social policy research questions this will not be the case. Instead, researchers

Table 5.3

Weighted Least Squares Model of Total Household Expenditures, 1984 (Breusch-Pagan Approach)

Variable	B	SE B	Beta	T	Sig T
Inverse Error	−410.646203	48.771729	−.200508	−8.420	.0000
Family Income before Tax	.016052	8.1440E-04	.121203	19.710	.0000
Northeast	40.328555	31.987405	.008741	1.261	.2074
College	901.762496	31.770400	.205687	28.384	.0000
South	253.994474	32.192737	.054564	7.890	.0000
Female	−105.832499	24.085209	−.033282	−4.394	.0000
West	371.332432	30.347431	.093657	12.236	.0000
High School	345.195908	26.073438	.106754	13.239	.0000
Family Size	233.315904	9.436419	.254318	24.725	.0000
Age	7.595042	.597888	.168366	12.703	.0000
White	318.551557	31.299332	.141331	10.178	.0000

Source: Estimates based on 1984 Consumer Expenditure Survey.

sometimes use the results of rank correlation tests to identify the variables to be included.

The specific regression results from the squared residuals model are not of interest. The motivation for estimating this equation is to save the predicted values of the squared residuals that it generates. The square root of these predictions is then used to estimate the variation in the estimated errors due to the heteroscedastic variables. Finally, the dependent variable and each of the explanatory variables are divided by the estimated errors. In addition, a variable equal to the inverse of the estimated errors $(1/\hat{e}_i)$ is included in the regression and *the model is estimated without a constant term*. The parameter estimate for the additional variable, $1/\hat{e}_i$, becomes the corrected estimate of the constant term. The weighted least squares version of the initial model is shown in Table 5.3. It is apparent that the results are very similar to the original model (Table 5.2). The coefficient signs are the same in both models. This would be expected, given that heteroscedasticity does not introduce bias into the coefficient estimates. Also as expected, the t-statistics for the explanatory variables are different in the two models. Presumably, the t-statistics for the weighted least squares model are the more reliable of the two; that is the motivation for estimating the model with weighted least squares.

Figure 5.5
Autocorrelation

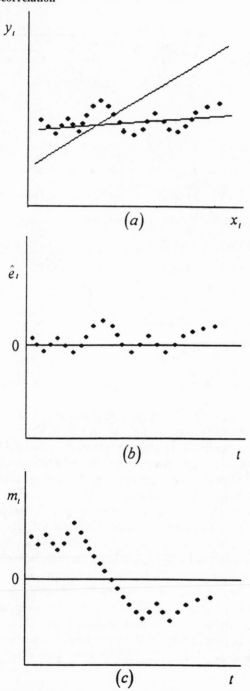

$$y = b_0 + b_1 x$$

$$\hat{y} = \grave{b}_0 + \hat{b}_1 x$$

AUTOCORRELATION

The problem of autocorrelation arises if the residuals from an estimated regression are correlated. This situation is most likely to occur with time-series data. Figure 5.5 illustrates the effects of autocorrelation on the estimated standard error of the regression.

Suppose a regression is estimated using a collection of sample points over a particular time period as shown in Figure 5.5a. Suppose also that the true population relationship is quite different from the one which has been estimated (Figure 5.5a). Then the estimated residuals would be as shown in Figure 5.5b. However, the true residuals (the differences between the sample observations and the predicted values from the population regression) would be much larger (Figure 5.3c). This implies that the estimated standard error from the sample regression will underestimate the true standard error; as a consequence the *t*-statistics will be overestimated. Nevertheless, the coefficient estimates will be unbiased because samples drawn from some periods will tend to overestimate the true regression parameters, while samples drawn from other periods will tend to underestimate the true regression parameters. From a policy perspective, autocorrelation is a serious problem because it undermines the reliability of the *t*-statistics. Policy makers may be led to pursue a policy that actually has a much weaker effect than estimated—or no effect at all!

THE DURBIN-WATSON TEST

The standard test for autocorrelation is the Durbin-Watson Test (Durbin and Watson, 1950, 1951, 1971). In time-series analysis the observations are ordered by time. Consequently, the residual for the first observation corresponds to the first time period in the sample; the second residual corresponds to the second time period; and so on. Let the residual at time t be denoted by $\hat{e}_t$; then the residual in the previous period would be $\hat{e}_{t-1}$.

$$DW = \frac{\sum_{t=2}^{T}(\hat{e}_t - \hat{e}_{t-1})^2}{\sum_{t=1}^{T}\hat{e}_t^2}$$

The summation takes place from the second time period on because of the need to calculate the difference between $\hat{e}_t$ and $\hat{e}_{t-1}$ and there is no $\hat{e}_{t-1}$ corresponding to the first time period:

$$\hat{e}_t \quad \hat{e}_{t-1} \quad \hat{e}_t - \hat{e}_{t-1}$$

$$\hat{e}_1 \quad - \quad -$$

$$\hat{e}_2 \quad \hat{e}_1 \quad \hat{e}_2 - \hat{e}_1$$

$$\hat{e}_3 \quad \hat{e}_2 \quad \hat{e}_3 - \hat{e}_2$$

$$\vdots \quad \vdots \quad \vdots$$

$$\hat{e}_t \quad \hat{e}_{t-1} \quad \hat{e}_t - \hat{e}_{t-1}$$

Unfortunately, the Durbin-Watson test is often inconclusive. Its statistical significance is a function of the number of independent variables and the number of observations used to estimate the equation. For each level of statistical significance, number of variables, and number of observations, upper and lower bounds for the statistic are tabulated. These values must be substituted along with the calculated value of the Durbin-Watson statistic into one of the following mutually exclusive categories:

1. $4 - d_l < DW < 4$ negative autocorrelation
2. $4 - D_u < DW < 4 - d_l$ indeterminate
3. $2 < DW < 4 - d_u$ no autocorrelation
4. $d_u < DW < 2$ no autocorrelation
5. $d_l < DW < d_u$ indeterminate
6. $0 < DW < d_l$ positive autocorrelation

The Durbin-Watson statistic varies between 0 and 4. In general, a Durbin-Watson close to 2 indicates that there is no evidence of autocorrelation. Values close to 0 are indicative of positive autocorrelation, and values close to 4 indicate negative auto-correlation.

Note that the Durbin-Watson statistic can be a valuable diagnostic tool even when one is not using time-series data. A statistically significant Durbin-Watson statistic when one is estimating a model based on cross-sectional data can be an indication of specification error (such as omitted variables or incorrect functional form).

The calculations necessary to compute the Durbin-Watson statistic for the federal deficit model discussed in Chapter 3 (Table 3.1) are shown in Table 5.4. Substituting the relevant values from Table 5.4 into the formula for the Durbin-Watson statistic yields

$$DW = \frac{10{,}148.55}{9{,}716.49}$$

$$= 1.044$$

At the 95 percent confidence level, the tabulated Durbin-Watson statistic for one variable and 10 observations has a lower bound of 0.879 and an upper bound of 1.32. Since the calculated value for the Durbin-Watson statistic falls within the

Table 5.4
Durbin-Watson Calculations for Deficit Model in Table 3.1

y_t	$\hat{y}_t$	$\hat{e}_t$	$\hat{e}_{t-1}$	$(e_t - e_{t-1})^2$	$\hat{e}_t^2$
73.5	23.7	49.8			2480
53.6	46.62	6.98	49.8	1833.55	48.72
59.2	63.52	–4.32	6.98	127.69	18.66
40.2	83.42	–43.22	–4.32	1513.21	1867.97
73.8	103.31	–29.51	–43.22	187.96	870.84
78.9	119.89	–40.99	-29.51	131.79	1680.18
127.9	139.79	–11.89	–40.99	846.81	141.37
207.8	159.68	48.12	–11.89	3601.20	2315.53
185.3	179.58	5.72	48.12	1797.76	32.72
212.3	196.16	16.14	5.72	108.58	260.50

$$\sum_{t=2}^{n} = 10,148.55 \qquad \sum_{t=1}^{n} = 9,716.49$$

range of the upper and lower bounds, the evidence of autocorrelation is indeterminate.

TIME-SERIES MODELS

There is a large literature concerning the estimation of time-series models. Prior to the 1980s the phrase "time-series models" usually referred to estimation procedures used when autocorrelation was present in the residuals of a regression model. More recently, the phrase "time-series models" has come to refer to autoregressive and/or moving average models (e.g., McLeary and Hay, 1980; Gottman, 1981). Autoregressive and moving average models, however, are most useful when forecasting is the primary objective; such models are less useful for estimating structural relationships. For this reason, autoregressive and moving average models will not be discussed in this book. Readers interested in these models can refer to a number of excellent texts.[8] Instead, we will briefly discuss time-series models that arise in the context of correcting autocorrelation in the residuals of a regression model.

Assume for the moment that the residual at time t is a linear function of the residual in the previous period, plus a random disturbance term meeting all of the assumptions of the OLS regression model:

$$\hat{e}_t = \rho\hat{e}_{t-1} + v_t \qquad\qquad \text{where } |e| < 1$$

Rearranging terms:

$$v_t = \hat{e}_t - \rho\hat{e}_{t-1}$$

Because

$$\hat{e}_t = y_t - \hat{y}_t$$

$$\hat{e}_t = y_t - (\hat{b}_0 + \hat{b}_1\, x_{1t} + ... + \hat{b}_k\, x_{xt})$$

it follows that

$$\hat{e}_t - \rho\hat{e}_{t-1} = [y_t - (\hat{b}_0 + \hat{b}_1\, x_{1t} + ... + \hat{b}_k\, x_{kt})] - \rho[y_{t-1} - (\hat{b}_0 + \hat{b}_1 x_{1t-1} + ... + \hat{b}_k\, x_{kt-1})]$$

Again rearranging terms:

$$(y_t - \rho y_{t-1}) = \hat{b}_0\,(1-\rho) + \hat{b}_1(x_{1t} - \rho x_{1t-1}) + ... + \hat{b}_k\,(x_{kt} - \rho x_{kt-1}) + v_t$$

In other words, if each period were a linear function of the errors in the previous period, and new variables were created of the form:

$$y^* = (y_t - \rho y_{t-1})$$
$$x_1^* = (x_{1t} - \rho x_{1t-1})$$
$$\vdots$$
$$x_k^* = (x_{kt} - \rho x_{kt-1})$$

the coefficients using these new variables would be unbiased and the residuals of the regression would be uncorrelated. In its simplest form, this estimation approach is known as first differences (where ρ is equal to 1). Versions of this approach that account for more complex relationships among the residuals are known as Cochrane-Orcutt or Prais-Winsten procedures.[9]

A simple estimate of the linear relationship between the error in two time periods, ρ, is

$$\hat{\rho} = 1 - \tfrac{1}{2}(DW)$$

where DW is the Durbin-Watson statistic. Or, using the lag function available in most statistics packages, one could use the $\hat{e}_t$ from the original regression to calculate a new variable, $\hat{e}_{t-1}$, and then run a regression between $\hat{e}_t$ and $\hat{e}_{t-1}$ to estimate ρ. The lag function can also be used to create the new variables $y_{t-1}, x_{1t-1} \cdots x_{kt-1}$. In any event, the estimate of ρ, along with the lagged variables, is used to create the new variables $y^*, x^*, \ldots x_k^*$. Finally, the regression is rerun using these new variables.

In the above discussion, the error term in each period was assumed to be a linear function of the error term in the previous period. This appears to be an extremely restrictive assumption. For example, using monthly data it is possible that the pattern of errors might follow a lag of 12 periods (i.e., the errors in the corresponding months of different years might be correlated). In fact, the Cochrane-Orcutt procedure generalizes to handle more complex autocorrelation problems—one simply keeps reapplying the procedure until the autocorrelation disappears.

Unfortunately, there is a catch; the lag variables cannot be calculated for the first observation. Consequently, an observation is lost each time the procedure is applied. To avoid this loss of cases the first observation for each variable can be estimated as follows:

$$Y_1^* = \sqrt{1-\rho^2} Y_1$$
$$X_{11}^* = \sqrt{1-\rho^2} X_{11}$$
$$\vdots$$
$$X_{kI}^* = \sqrt{1-\rho^2} X_{kI}$$

If this is done, the procedure is known as the Prais-Winsten approach.

MEASUREMENT ERROR

The regression model assumes that the variables have been measured without error.[10] The consequences of violating this assumption vary depending upon the extent of the error, whether the measurement error occurs in the dependent or explanatory variables, and whether the measurement error is nonrandom or random.

Nonrandom measurement errors occur when systematic errors are made in measuring the value of a variable. Intuitively, nonrandom measurement errors would be expected to result in biased coefficients. But even random errors can result in biased estimates. In this section some aspects of the measurement error problem are illustrated by considering the case of random measurement errors.[11]

Random Errors in Measuring the Dependent Variable

Suppose that the dependent variable is measured with random error so that instead of measuring Y we measure

$$Y^* = Y + u$$

where u is a random error term. The estimated regression equation is therefore:

$$Y = \hat{b}_0 + \hat{b}_1 x_1 + \hat{b}_2 x_2 + \ldots + \hat{b}_k x_k + (e + u)$$

In practice, it is not possible to distinguish the different error terms e and u, but the variance of the composite error $(e + u)$ will be larger than that for e alone. As a consequence, the standard error of the regression is increased by random errors in the measurement of the dependent variable. The underestimated standard error for the regression, in turn, implies that the adjusted R^2 will be higher, and the standard errors of the coefficients will be smaller, than they would be if measurement error were accounted for. As a result, the t-tests for the statistical significance of the coefficients and the F-test for the significance of the regression as a whole will be overestimated. The estimates of the coefficients themselves, however, will be unbiased even though they will no longer be efficient.

Random Errors in Measuring the Explanatory Variables

The effects of errors in measuring the explanatory variables are more complicated than those associated with the dependent variable. As with the dependent variable Y, assume that X is measured with some random error u:

$$X^* = X + u$$

Now suppose we estimate

$$Y = \hat{b}_0 + \hat{b}_1 X_1 + e$$

It can be shown that the expected value of $\hat{b}_1$ is

$$E(\hat{b}_1) = b_1 \frac{S_x^2}{S_x^2 + S_u^2}$$

In other words, the expected value of $\hat{b}_1$ is equal to the true population parameter b_1 times a ratio of the variance of X to the sum of the variance of X plus the variance of the measurement error u. Thus, to the extent that the variance of u differs from zero, the expected value of $\hat{b}_1$ will underestimate the true population parameter b_1. Of course, when S_u^2 is equal to zero there is no measurement error and $E(\hat{b}_1) = b_1$. For this reason the ratio of variances:

$$r_{xx} = \frac{S_x^2}{S_x^2 + S_u^2}$$

is known as the reliability of the measured variable X. Berry and Feldman (1985) point out that a reliability score in the range of 0.8 is considered good when measuring variables in the social sciences. Thus, the expected value for even a relatively well measured variable is apt to underestimate the true population parameter by 20 percent. The coefficients for less well measured variables will be even more badly biased.

When measurement error occurs in more than one of the explanatory variables, the nature of the bias becomes much more complex. This is because the estimation bias for each coefficient is a function of the reliabilities of all the variables and the correlations among them. Moreover, unlike the simple regression model with measurement error in the one explanatory variable, it is not possible to derive the direction of the bias in the multivariate case unless the reliabilities of all of the variables are known (Johnson, 1972, pp. 281–291). Even when this is possible, it is necessary to adjust the standard errors of the coefficients, which is also a complex task.

Minimizing the Effects of Measurement Error

The most effective way to reduce the effects of measurement error is to minimize the error at its source. A major goal of modern survey theory is the design of questionnaires and sampling frames so as to maximize the reliability of the information to be collected. Most researchers, however, do not collect their own data; for them the reliability of the data has already been determined (although it may not be easy, or even possible, to identify).

Several approaches have been suggested to correct for measurement error at the analysis stage. As mentioned above, it may be possible to adjust the coefficient estimates and standard errors if reliability measures are available for all of the variables (McIver and Carmines, 1981; Sullivan and Feldman, 1979; Long, 1983). It may also be possible to obtain unbiased and efficient estimates in the presence of measurement error by using the technique of instrumental variables. An instrumental variable is a reliable variable that is highly correlated with the variable that has been measured with error, but which is uncorrelated with the error term. For example, Wald (1940) suggested the method of group averages. In this method an instrumental variable Z is defined as follows:

$$Z=1 \quad if \; X > median$$
$$Z=0 \quad if \; X < median$$

(If N is even, the middle observation is omitted.) Similarly, Durbin (1954) suggested using the rankings of X, rather than the actual X values, as an instrumental variable. This approach assumes that the rankings are not affected by the size of the measurement error. Summaries of these and other instrumental variable methods are provided in Greene (1993, pp. 284–287) and Fomby, Hill, and Johnson (1984, pp. 268–276).[12]

Given that the reliability of one's data is generally not known, and the problems associated with correcting measurement errors are great, in most policy research measurement error is not given a great deal of attention.[13] At the very least, however, researchers need to recognize that measurement error can, and probably often does, introduce statistical bias into regression coefficient estimates and undermines the reliability of the model's standard errors.

IMPUTATION OF MISSING VALUES

A special case of measurement error is that of missing values. There are a variety of methods for dealing with missing values. In conducting multivariate analyses, the default of most statistical programs is to drop observations with missing values. This approach, commonly known as listwise deletion, implicitly assumes that nonrespondents are similar to respondents. If nonrespondents, however, are systematically different from respondents, the result will be biased parameter estimates.

The simplest method for imputing missing values is to substitute the mean value of a variable for each missing observation. This method assumes that the sample respondents are similar to nonrespondents. To the extent that sample respondents differ from nonrespondents, estimates of population parameters will be biased. Moreover, estimates of standard errors will be biased—in turn, biasing statistical tests of statistical significance.

A more sophisticated alternative to substituting the mean is to use multiple regression to estimate missing values. The regression approach utilizes data on explanatory variables for which observations are available for all cases; it is probably the most commonly used approach to the missing value problem. Like mean substitution, the multiple regression method fails to deal with the bias introduced if nonrespondents are different from respondents. In fact, the regression approach is really just a more elaborate form of mean substitution because it results in the same imputed value for all observations having a given set of values for the explanatory variables. For example, in a regression model of personal income using race, gender, and age as explanatory variables, every 45-year-old black woman would have the same imputed income value.

The "hot deck" method of the U.S. Census Bureau deals with the problem of imputing identical values for all persons with the same characteristics. The hot deck approach imputes missing values using nonmissing responses for other variables. For example, suppose data were missing for certain responses on household income. It would be possible to match cases with missing and nonmissing income values by using categorical variables that these cases had in common, such as race, marital status, and education. Using the observations for which income data were available, a categorical version of the income variable would first be constructed and then cross tabulated with race, marital status, and education. This cross tabulation yields a joint probability distribution of income by race, marital status, and education. Finally, missing income values are imputed by selecting them probabilistically from the estimated joint probability distribution. In contrast to the regression imputation method, the hot deck approach results in a distribution of income values for each combination of demographic characteristics.

CONCLUSION

This chapter has discussed a number of tests and corrective measures for violations of the assumptions underlying the regression model. Some of these procedures should be used whenever one estimates a regression model; others are more specialized and should be used when the need arises.

In general, when estimating regression models, it is good practice to (1) print out the tolerances and covariance/correlation matrix of the coefficients, (2) ask for a histogram plot of the residuals, and (3) plot the residuals against the predicted values of the dependent variable. Most statistical packages provide all of this information as optional output. The tolerances and coefficient covariance/correlation matrix are extremely useful in diagnosing whether multicollinearity is a problem; the plot of the residuals against the predicted values is a good indicator of whether heteroscedasticity is a problem. If time-series data are being used, the Durbin-Watson statistic should also be requested. In fact, it is a good idea to request the Durbin-Watson statistic even if the data are cross-sectional, because a statistically significant Durbin-Watson statistic for a cross-sectional model is an indicator of possible specification bias.

NOTES

1. Most econometrics texts describe the derivation of the standard errors in the OLS regression model. See, for example, Pindyck and Rubinfeld (1991), Berndt (1991), or Fomby, Hill, and Johnson (1984).

2. Note that "automatic" regression procedures such as stepwise regression drop variables in the presence of multicollinearity. The violation of the underlying theoretical model implied by the use of such procedures is one of the strongest criticisms of these procedures.

3. Hamilton (1992) provides an accessible introduction to principal components.

4. This section presents several tests for heteroscedasticity. However, there are a variety of additional tests that are not discussed. In particular, readers with a working knowledge of matrix algebra may wish to consult White (1980) for a general test of the homoscedasticity assumption.

5. See Fomby, Hill, and Johnson (1984) and Godfrey (1988) for concise summaries of this literature.

6. See Harvey and Phillips (1973).

7. Other forms of this equation can also be estimated (e.g., exponential or double log models) for the purposes of carrying out the weighted least squares procedure. However, the test for heteroscedasticity is based on the simple linear model.

8. Pindyck and Rubinfeld (1991), Gottman (1981), and McLeary and Hay (1980).

9. Cochrane and Orcutt (1949) and Prais and Winsten (1954).

10. The discussion in this section draws heavily from Carmines and Zellner (1979). See also, Greene (1993, pp. 279–287).

11. For a more detailed discussion of measurement errors see Carmines and Zellner (1979).

12. See also Hausman (1978) for an errors in variables test.

13. Structural equation models estimated by sociologists and researchers in other disciplines explicitly model measurement error. See, for example, Bollen (1989), Goldberger and Duncan (1973), and Duncan (1975).

6
Linear Probability, Logit, and Probit Models

Chapter 4 discussed the use of dummy *explanatory* variables to estimate the effects of qualitative variables in regression analysis. But when the *dependent* variable is a dummy variable, there are several problems with using ordinary least squares (OLS) regression to estimate the model. To see this, consider the simple example shown in Figure 6.1.

Let Y be equal to 1 if an individual is a widow and 0 otherwise, and let X be the age of the individual. Because the observed values for Y are either 1 or 0, the predicted values for Y are expected to fall within the interval [0,1]. Consequently, $\hat{Y}_i$ can be interpreted as an individual's predicted probability of widowhood, given his/her age. The ages of widows tend to be high while those of nonwidows tend to be lower. However, there is nothing to constrain the regression model from predicting $\hat{Y}_i > 1$ or $\hat{Y}_i < 0$. Such predictions clearly violate the rules of probability, which require that the probability of an event lie between 0 and 1. Thus, one criticism of using regression with a dummy dependent variable is that some of the predicted values may fall outside of the [0,1] interval, invalidating the interpretation of the predicted values as probabilities.

LINEAR PROBABILITY MODEL

An arbitrary rule can be established that sets the predicted value equal to 0 for those cases where the model generates negative predictions and equal to 1 for predicted values greater than 1. This results in the linear probability model:

$$\hat{Y} = \begin{cases} \hat{b}_0 + \hat{b}_1 X_{1i} & when\ 0 < \hat{b}_0 + \hat{b}_1 X_{1i} < 1 \\ 1 & when\ \hat{b}_0 + \hat{b}_1\ X_{1i} \geq 1 \\ 0 & when\ \hat{b}_0 + \hat{b}_1\ X_{1i} \leq 0 \end{cases}$$

Figure 6.1
Regression Analysis on a Binary Dependent Variable

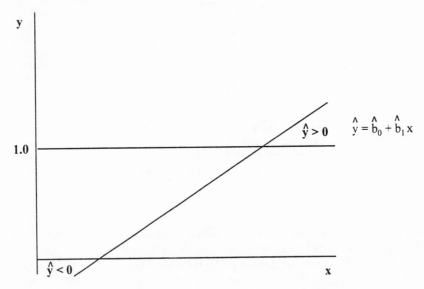

If predictions outside the [0,1] interval were the only problem with using regression with a dummy dependent variable, the linear probability model might work quite well—especially if not many of the observations had such troublesome predictions. In fact, it is often the case in empirical work that predictions outside the [0,1] interval are relatively few in number.

Unfortunately, predictions outside the [0,1] interval are not the only problem with using OLS regression when the dependent variable is binary. Observations that predict $\hat{Y}_i$ close to 1 when the actual values are 1 or close to 0 when the actual values are 0 will have relatively small errors, but those predicting $\hat{Y}_i$ close to 0.5 will have relatively large errors. This means that the regression model is inherently heteroscedastic when the dependent variable is binary.

In Chapter 5 the use of weighted least squares (WLS) was discussed for estimating heteroscedastic regression models. Goldberger (1964) proposed a three-step WLS procedure to correct for heteroscedasticity when estimating the linear probability model:[1]

1. Estimate the linear probability (regression) model in the usual fashion to obtain the $\hat{Y}_i$:

$$\hat{Y} = \hat{b}_0 + \hat{b}_1 X_{i1} + \hat{b}_2 X_{i2} + \dots + \hat{b}_k X_{ik}$$

2. Calculate a weight variable:

$$W_i = \frac{1}{[\hat{Y}_i(1-\hat{Y}_i)]^{\frac{1}{2}}}$$

3. Construct a set of weighted variables $W_i Y_i$, W_i, $W_i X_{1i}, W_i X_{2i} \ldots W_i X_{ki}$, and estimate the equation:

$$W_i Y_i = W_i \hat{b}_0 + \hat{b}_1 W_i X_{1i} + \hat{b}_2 W_i X_{2i} + \ldots + \hat{b}_k W_i X_{ki} + W_i \hat{e}_i$$

Note the equation in step 3 is estimated without an intercept because the coefficient for W_i is the constant term. The coefficient estimates will be unbiased and the standard errors will be reliable because the variance of the transformed error term $(w_i \hat{e}_i)$ will be a constant. The R^2 should not be used because it refers to the variance of the transformed dependent variable explained by the model. To obtain the correct R^2, the estimated coefficients from the WLS model need to be substituted into the original equation (with the untransformed data values); the R^2 is then calculated in the usual fashion.

Goldberger's WLS procedure, however, still does not guarantee that the $\hat{Y}_i$ will fall in the [0,1] interval. As discussed earlier, it would be possible to handle such troublesome predictions by arbitrarily setting them equal to 1 or 0. But, as will be discussed shortly, there are other (nonlinear) procedures that are more efficient than using WLS to estimate the linear probability model.

A final limitation of OLS regression models is that they assume that the marginal effect on the dependent variable of a one-unit change in an explanatory variable is constant over the entire range of the explanatory variable. Figure 6.2 illustrates the problem with this assumption by using the widowhood example once again. Below some age level, say 65, the probability of widowhood is very low. In this range the regression model would predict negative values, so these predictions would be constrained to 0. At ages greater than 70, however, the probability of widowhood begins to rise. Beyond some age (e.g., 95) the model predicts probabilities of widowhood greater than 1, so these predictions would need to be constrained to 1. This all seems pretty reasonable until it is recognized that the

Figure 6.2
Errors in Assuming a Constant Relationship between Age and the Probability of Widowhood

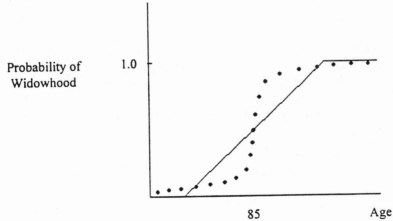

model also implies that an increase from age 71 to age 72 has the same effect on the change in the probability of widowhood as an increase from age 85 to 86. Clearly, this isn't true. There is an age range where the probability of widowhood rises rapidly. At some point in the age distribution, however, most members of the population are already widows, so the probability of widowhood changes very little with age. This nonlinear association between the probability of widowhood and age is shown by the S-shaped curve in Figure 6.2.

MAXIMUM LIKELIHOOD

In the remainder of this book a variety of estimation techniques are considered which are based on the maximum likelihood approach. Maximum likelihood is an alternative statistical approach to estimating population parameters that turns the theory of classical statistical inference on its head. In classical statistical inference it is assumed that there is one population from which many samples may be drawn. In contrast, maximum likelihood assumes that there are many different populations; its goal is to find estimates of population parameters that maximize the likelihood that the observed sample was drawn from the population of interest.

Formally, maximum likelihood estimators are defined as follows:

If a random variable x has a probability distribution $f(x)$ characterized by parameters $\Theta_1, \Theta_2, \ldots \Theta_k$ and if we observe a sample $x_1, x_2, \ldots x_n$ then the maximum likelihood estimates of $\Theta_1, \Theta_2, \ldots \Theta_k$ are the values of these parameters that would generate the observed sample most often. (Kmenta, 1971, p. 175)

The maximum likelihood approach can be illustrated with a simple example. Suppose x is a binary variable measuring school dropout which has a probability π of being 1 and a probability $1-\pi$ of being 0.[2] Then:

$$f(1) = \pi$$
$$f(0) = 1-\pi$$

Now consider the sample

$$\{0\ 0\ 0\ 1\ 0\ 0\}$$

What is the maximum likelihood estimate (MLE) of π? The value of π that would generate the observed sample most often can be found by trying different values for π and observing which value generates the highest probability of drawing the sample. For example, if one assumes that the probability of a high school dropout is 0, then the probability of remaining in school must be 1. The likelihood of observing the given sample of 1s and 0s is formed as the product of the probability of observing each of the sample members

$$\begin{aligned}
L(0\ 0\ 0\ 1\ 0\ 0) &= f(0) \times f(0) \times f(0) \times f(1) \times f(0) \times f(0) \\
&= 1 \times 1 \times 1 \times 0 \times 1 \times 1 \\
&= 0
\end{aligned}$$

Thus, if $\pi = 0$ the likelihood of observing the sample would be 0.

If π were equal to some other value, say 1/10, the likelihood function would be

$$L\,(0\,0\,0\,1\,0\,0) = 9/10 \times 9/10 \times 9/10 \times 1/10 \times 9/10 \times 9/10$$
$$= .059049$$

In other words, if π were equal to 0.1, the likelihood of observing the sample would be about 6 in 100.

Table 6.1 shows the values of the likelihood function corresponding to increments of π by 1/10. In terms of these increments of 0.1, the likelihood function appears to be maximized at $\pi = 0.2$. With the aid of a computer, it would be possible to explore smaller increments of π to refine the estimate of the value that maximizes the likelihood function.

Alternatively, it would be possible to solve for the value of π that maximizes the likelihood function analytically. In general, maximum likelihood estimators are found by forming the likelihood function and maximizing it with respect to the parameters of the probability distribution. The likelihood function is equal to the product of the probabilities associated with the observations in the sample. In the current example,

$$L(0\,0\,0\,1\,0\,0) = \pi(1-\pi)^5$$

The value of π that maximizes the likelihood function L can be found by taking the derivative of L with respect to π and setting it equal to 0.

Table 6.1
Finding the Value of π That Maximizes the Likelihood Function

π	L
0.0	0
0.1	.059049
0.2	.065536
0.3	.050421
0.4	.031104
0.5	.016525
0.6	.006144
0.7	.001701
0.8	.000256
0.9	.000009
1.0	0

$$\frac{\partial L}{\partial \pi} = (1-\pi)^5 - 5\pi(1-\pi)^4 = 0$$

Solving for π yields $\pi = 1/6$.

Of course, this is the same result that would have been obtained by using the relative frequency approach to estimate π based on the sample (i.e., one value of 1 divided by a sample size of six). It clearly was more complicated to arrive at the estimate of π using the maximum likelihood approach than it would have been using the relative frequency approach.

Suppose, however, that a researcher was interested in identifying the factors that influence the probability of being a high school dropout. Then the values for π in Table 6.1 would need to be estimated as a function of a set of explanatory variables. These estimates would differ, depending on the variables that were included in the model. The estimates of π would also be influenced by the form of the probability distribution that was chosen for relating the explanatory variables to π. In such cases, researchers may be less interested in the estimate of π, per se, but more interested in how π changes in response to changes in the explanatory variables. This is the type of problem at which maximum likelihood methods excel.

LOGIT AND PROBIT MODELS

One problem with the linear probability model discussed earlier in this chapter is that the $\hat{Y}_i$ values do not necessarily lie in the [0,1] interval as required by probability theory. However, suppose a different dependent variable, $P_i/(1-P_i)$, is used instead. This ratio is the odds of an event occurring. It is a function of the probability of interest but it has no upper bound. This means that the regression model would no longer have the potential problem of predicting values for the dependent variable that exceed 1. Moreover, if the logarithm of the odds ratio is calculated, the resulting quantity has no upper bound or lower bound. Now, *none* of the predicted values will be theoretically implausible.

Next, assume that this "log of the odds" is a linear function of a set of explanatory variables:

$$\ln(\frac{P_i}{1-P_i}) = \hat{b}_0 + \hat{b}_1 X_{1i} + \hat{b}_2 X_{2i} + ... + \hat{b}_k X_{ki} \tag{1}$$

For notational convenience, refer to this linear function collectively as z:

$$z = \hat{b}_0 + \hat{b}_1 X_1 + \hat{b}_2 X_2 + ... + \hat{b}_k x_k$$

Working backwards, equation (1) can be solved for P_i as a function of the explanatory variables. First, eliminate the logarithms by exponentiating both sides:

$$\frac{P_i}{1-P_i} = e^{\hat{b}_0 + \hat{b}_1 X_{1i} + \hat{b}_2 X_{2i} + ... + \hat{b}_k X_{ki}} = e^{z_i}$$

Then solve for P_i in the usual fashion. With a little algebra, it follows that:

$$P_i = \frac{e^{z_i}}{1+e^{z_i}}$$

and

$$(1-P_i) = \frac{1}{1+e^{z_i}}$$

The equation for P_i is known as the cumulative logistic probability distribution. To denote that it is a cumulative probability distribution, rather than a density function, P_i is often referred to as $F(z)$. The cumulative logistic probability distribution has a value close to 1 when z approaches positive infinity; it has a value close to 0 when z approaches negative infinity. Thus, unlike the linear probability model, the cumulative logistic probability distribution satisfies the [0,1] constraint without having to constrain z.

The cumulative logistic distribution may also help to reduce the heteroscedasticity problem inherent in the regression model that is caused by the flatness of the tails of the distribution. This flatness implies that the error variance will tend to be fairly constant in the tails. Consequently, if most people have predicted values in the appropriate tails (relatively high predicted probabilities for observed Y_i values of 1 and relatively low predicted probabilities for observed Y_i values of 0), heteroscedasticity may no longer be a problem. On the other hand, observations that have a predicted probability in the neighborhood of 0.5 will have higher error variances than those in the tails, just as in the regression model. Thus, heteroscedasticity is not necessarily eliminated by the estimation of logit models.

Unfortunately, it is not possible to estimate equation (1) with ordinary least squares regression directly. This is because the observed values for the dependent variable are not the probabilities P_i, but 0s and 1s. We can, however, estimate equation (1) using maximum likelihood methods.

MAXIMUM LIKELIHOOD ESTIMATION

Let P_i and $1-P_i$ be the probabilities that the dependent variable equals 1 and 0, respectively, given the values of the explanatory variables. Then a general expression for the probability of observing y_i (regardless of whether y equals 1 or 0) is given by:

$$P(y_i|x_i) = P_i^{y_i}(1-P_i)^{1-y_i}$$

When $y_i = 1$, the above equation simplifies to P_i; when $y_i = 0$, it simplifies to $1-P_i$. The probability of observing all N values for the dependent variable y in the sample, given the values of the explanatory variables X_{ik}, is

$$L = \Pi P_i^{y_i}(1-P_i)^{1-Y_i} \tag{2}$$

One of the most powerful features of maximum likelihood is its extraordinary generality. In particular, it is possible to substitute for P_i any probability distribution that is desired. Substituting the cumulative logistic function for P_i in the above equation yields:

$$L = \Pi \left[\frac{e^{\hat{b}_0 + \Sigma \hat{b}_k X_{ki}}}{1 + e^{\hat{b}_0 + \Sigma \hat{b}_k X_{ki}}} \right]^{Y_i} \left[\frac{1}{1 + e^{\hat{b}_0 + \Sigma \hat{b}_k X_{ki}}} \right]^{1 - Y_i} \tag{3}$$

The objective of the maximum likelihood approach is to find the parameter estimates that maximize L. Taking logarithms of the likelihood function makes it easier to use differential calculus to find the coefficient values that maximize the likelihood function because the logarithms transform the likelihood function from a series of products to a series of sums. It is fortuitous that the coefficient values which maximize the logarithm of the likelihood function are the same values that maximize the original likelihood function. Taking logarithms of equation (3) yields:

$$\ln L = \Sigma Y_i \ln \frac{e^{\hat{b}_0 + \Sigma \hat{b}_k X_{ki}}}{1 + e^{\hat{b}_0 + \Sigma \hat{b}_k X_{ki}}} + (1 - Y_i) \ln \frac{1}{1 + e^{\hat{b}_0 + \hat{b}_k x_{ki}}} \tag{4}$$

Taking the derivative of *ln L* with respect to b_0 and each b_k, and setting each of these derivatives equal to zero, one gets:

$$\frac{\partial \ln L}{\partial \hat{b}_0} = 0$$

$$\frac{\partial \ln L}{\partial \hat{b}_1} = 0$$

$$\frac{\partial \ln L}{\partial \hat{b}_2} = 0 \tag{5}$$

$$\vdots$$

$$\frac{\partial \ln L}{\partial \hat{b}_k} = 0$$

This results in a set of $k + 1$ equations in $k + 1$ unknowns. These equations can be solved to obtain estimates of the coefficients in terms of the explanatory variables. Because these equations are highly nonlinear, however, it is not possible to solve for the coefficients analytically; the solution must be approximated with numerical methods.

There are several numerical techniques for solving systems of nonlinear equations.[3] In finding solutions for the maximum likelihood coefficients, it is common to begin with the corresponding coefficient estimates from the linear probability model. The solution procedure involves making small changes in the coefficient values and observing the effects on the value of the likelihood function. The rules for making these changes are given by the derivatives of the log likelihood function in equation (5). The maximum likelihood coefficient estimates have been found when the value of the likelihood function cannot be increased by any further changes to the coefficients.

The difficulty of finding solutions to the system of nonlinear equations in (5) varies greatly, depending on which probability distribution is assumed for P_i in equation (2). The two most widely used distributions are the cumulative logistic distribution (which results in the logit model) and the cumulative multivariate normal distribution (which results in the probit model).[4] As shown in Figure 6.3, logit and probit models yield very similar estimates of the probability of an event occurring (e.g., that an individual will be a high school dropout, retire, or enter a nursing home). The two distributions differ mainly in the tails—with the probit model approaching the zero and one axes more rapidly than the logit model. This means that if the values of the explanatory variables predict a very low probability, the probability estimate from the probit model will tend to be somewhat closer to zero than will that from the logit model. Similarly, if a given set of values of the explanatory variables predict a very high probability, the prediction from the probit model will be somewhat closer to one than will that from the logit model. Comparisons of logit and probit models will be discussed in more detail later in the chapter.

INTERPRETING LOGIT OUTPUT

Coefficients

Logit coefficients are interpreted much like regression coefficients.[5] The only complication is introduced by the rather cumbersome dependent variable—the logarithm of the odds of an event. Each slope coefficient is interpreted as the change in the "log of the odds" associated with a one-unit increase in an

Figure 6.3
Predicted Probabilities from the Logit and Probit Models

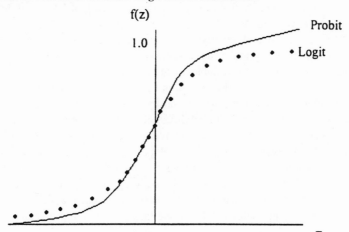

explanatory variable, controlling for the effects of the other variables in the equation. The intercept is the expected value of the log of the odds if all of the explanatory variables are set equal to zero.

The rather cumbersome interpretation of the logit coefficients is mitigated when it is recognized that the probability of an event moves in the same direction as the log of the odds (i.e., variables that increase the log of the odds will also increase the probability of an event). Therefore, if the specific numerical value of a coefficient is not of concern, the direction and significance of the effects of a variable on the probability of an event can be inferred directly from the sign and significance of that variable's coefficient.

Partial Derivatives

Analysts who wish to estimate the numerical change in the probability resulting from a one-unit increase in an explanatory variable must calculate the partial derivative. In the case of the linear probability (regression) model, the partial derivative of each variable is just its regression coefficient. In the logit model the partial derivative is a function of both the coefficient for the variable and the probabilities themselves:

$$\frac{\partial P_i}{\partial X_k} = \hat{b}_k P_i (1 - P_i) \tag{6}$$

In the logit model, therefore, the partial derivative is a function, not just a single value as in the linear probability model. This means that the change in the probability of an event resulting from a one-unit increase in an explanatory variable will be different for each individual in the sample.

The fact that the derivative is different for each individual suggests that the derivatives must be summarized in some way to be useful. An obvious summary measure is the mean of the derivative. The mean derivative for a particular variable is the average change in the probability of an event as a result of a one-unit increase in an explanatory variable. Note that the average derivative is *not* the same thing as the derivative evaluated at the mean of an explanatory variable (Train, 1986).

Researchers commonly make the mistake of evaluating the derivative at the mean values of the explanatory variables. The problem with doing so is illustrated in Figure 6.4, which compares the change in the probabilities implied by the two approaches. Suppose the sample was primarily composed of persons associated with either very low or very high probabilities, with few people in the middle. The average derivative method described above would generate relatively small estimates of the derivative because the slope of the cumulative probability distribution would be low at both extremes. On the other hand, the slope of the cumulative probability distribution would be very steep at the mean of the explanatory variables. Consequently, if a derivative is evaluated at the mean of the explanatory variables, the estimated derivative may be much higher than it should be.

Figure 6.4
Interpretation of Average Derivatives

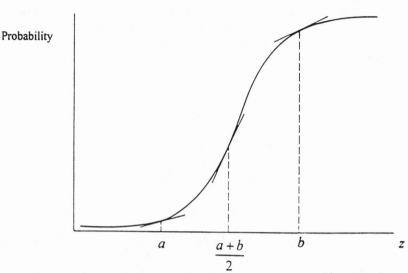

Source: Adapted from Train (1986, 43).

It is also important to recognize a limitation associated with calculating the mean derivative over the full range of the explanatory variable. The limitation arises because it is possible that the derivative may change substantially over the range of the explanatory variable. Consider, for example, the relationship between age and the probability of entering a nursing home by age. For ages 65 to 79 the probability of entering a nursing home might change very little. Between the ages of 80 and 90, however, the probability might climb steeply. Finally, after age 90 the probability of entering a nursing home might level off. Because a relatively high percentage of persons aged 90 and over are already in a nursing home, additional years of age would not contribute much to the probability of entering one.

The above example illustrates that calculating the mean derivative over the full range of the age variable may obscure the steep rise in the probability of entering a nursing home for those aged 80 to 90. To handle this problem, it is useful to calculate the average derivatives for different ranges of the explanatory variable (e.g., for persons aged 65 to 79, 80 to 90, and 91 years and older).

Calculating the average derivatives for different age ranges enables the derivatives to vary in magnitude, but it still does not allow them to vary in sign. The only way to enable the sign to change is to estimate separate coefficients by creating dummy variables from the original interval variable. In the above example, separate dummy variables could be created for persons aged 65 to 79, 80 to 90, and 91 years and older (one of these would be left out of the equation as the reference group).

Derivatives are defined only for interval variables. This is because derivatives measure the change in one variable with respect to a very small change in another variable. It clearly is not possible to talk about very small changes in a dummy variable—an individual either has a characteristic or doesn't. Consequently, rather than calculating derivatives for dummy variables, researchers generally calculate an alternative measure known as the odds ratio.

Odds Ratios

A common approach for measuring the effects of a dummy variable on the probability of an event is to calculate odds ratios. Odds ratios represent the ratio of the probabilities of the outcome occurring for sample members who have a value of one for the dummy variable versus those in the reference group. They are found simply by exponentiating dummy variable coefficients:

$$odds\ ratio_k = e^{b_k} \tag{7}$$

For example, an odds ratio of 2.31 for the Female dummy variable in the widowhood model considered earlier would mean that the probability of widowhood is 2.31 times higher for females than for males. Odds ratios are simple to calculate and provide useful information about the effects of dummy variables on the dependent variable. Nevertheless, it should be noted that they provide information only on the relative odds of the event occurring for the two categories of the dummy variable. This gives no indication of how *large* or *small* the underlying probabilities may be. For example, a ratio of probabilities of 8 percent to 2 percent gives an odds ratio of 4—indicating that those with a value of one for the dummy variable have a probability of 4 times that of those in the reference group—but the absolute difference in the probability level is only 6 percent. Moreover, the odds ratio is not calculated for each case in the sample. As a result, it is not possible to examine how it might vary for subgroups within the sample. For these reasons, odds ratios provide considerably less information than derivatives calculated for continuous variables.

Representative Cases

Finally, it is often useful to present the probabilities corresponding to cases with particular characteristics. Once the coefficients of the model have been estimated, one can substitute various representative values for the explanatory variables and calculate the associated probabilities. For example, a logistic model of nursing home placement might include explanatory variables for the age of the individual, extent of formal and informal supports, and health scales measuring physical and cognitive limitations. Substituting a high value for age, low values for formal and informal supports, and high numbers of physical and cognitive limitations would generate relatively high probabilities of nursing home placement. The opposite range for these variables would predict a much lower probability of nursing home placement. Choosing a set of values for the explanatory variables that generate a range of predicted probabilities from the lowest to the highest is a very useful way of interpreting the results of the model that is almost like a series of case studies.

A LOGIT MODEL OF POVERTY STATUS

Table 6.2 presents a simple logit model of poverty status. In the example, poverty status is a binary variable equal to one if a person has an income below the poverty level and zero otherwise. As in ordinary least squares regression analysis, the *t*-statistics are calculated by dividing the coefficient values by their respective standard errors. Technically, these are asymptotic *t*-statistics because, using maximum likelihood estimation, the ratios of the estimated coefficients to their standard errors approach the *t*-distribution only asymptotically (in large samples). The critical values for the *t*-statistics are the same as with regression—for large samples, 1.96 at the 95 percent confidence level and 2.57 at the 99 percent confidence level (assuming two-tailed tests). The precise critical value is found by looking up the tabulated *t*-statistic for $N-(k+1)$ degrees of freedom at the desired confidence level, where N is the sample size and k is the number of explanatory variables in the equation.

As with regression analysis, analysts are generally much more interested in the slope coefficients than in the constant term. The constant represents the expected value for the natural log of the odds of being in poverty versus not being in poverty when all of the values of the explanatory variables are set equal to zero. In Table 6.2, the *t*-statistic of 4.94 for the constant term is statistically significant at the 99 percent confidence level.

Each slope coefficient represents the change in the log of the odds of being in poverty with respect to a unit increase in a particular variable, controlling for the effects of the other variables in the equation. For example, the coefficient for the education variable in Table 6.2 means that the log of the odds of being in poverty decreases by 0.1809 for each one-year increase in education. The education variable is significant at the 99 percent confidence level. Similarly, each one-year increase in age decreases the log of the odds of poverty by 0.0317. The age variable is also highly significant.

All of the remaining variables in the equation are dummy variables. Dummy variables in logit models, as in multiple regression, cannot meaningfully be interpreted in terms of unit changes—dummy variables are equal to either zero or one. Instead, the coefficients for dummy variables are interpreted in terms of the expected value of the log of the odds of poverty status for individuals having particular characteristics. For example, the coefficient for the Female dummy variable indicates that being female increases the log of the odds of being in poverty by 0.3140 (relative to being male), controlling for the other variables in the equation. The expected log of the odds of being in poverty is also increased by being black, being single, and living in the South. Working decreases the expected log of the odds of being in poverty. All of these coefficients are statistically

Table 6.2
Logit Model of Poverty Status

Variable	Coefficient	*t*-statistic	Odds Ratio	Average Derivative
Constant	1.4119	4.94		
Female	0.3140	3.07	1.3689	
Black	0.6687	4.79	1.9517	
Central City	0.1200	1.05		
Single	1.0078	10.01	2.7396	
South	0.3166	3.08	1.3725	
Work	−1.5881	−13.74	0.2043	
Education	−0.1809	−11.30		
less than 12 years				−0.0237
12 or more years				−0.0118
Age	− 0.0317	− 10.83		
18–24				−0.0040
25–54				−0.0021
55–64				−0.0021
65+				−0.0032

$\ln L_o = -3,656.4$
$\ln L_{max} = -1,450.9$
$X^2 = -2(\ln L_o - \ln_{max}) = 4,411$

Source: Author's calculations based on 1989 Current Population Survey.

significant at the 99 percent confidence level. The coefficient for living in a central city is not statistically significant after controlling for the other variables in the equation.

The above discussion illustrates that the specific numerical interpretation of the coefficients in the logit model is exactly the same as in the regression model. The log of the odds interpretation of the dependent variable in logit analysis, however, is very cumbersome. For this reason, most analysts do not emphasize the specific numerical values of the coefficients. Instead, they note which variables are (and are not) statistically significant and discuss the signs of the significant variables. As already noted, variables with positive signs will increase the log of the odds of the dependent variable occurring; the converse is true for variables with negative signs. It is also true, however, that the log of the odds moves in the same direction as the probability itself. This means that if a variable has a positive (negative) sign, higher values for the variable will increase (decrease) the probability of the dependent variable. Therefore, although it is not possible to say anything about the magnitude of the impact of a variable on the probability directly from the variable's coefficient, it is possible to infer the sign of the relationship.

To measure the magnitude of the relationship between an interval explanatory variable and the probability of the event, it is necessary to calculate the derivative. The partial derivative for each variable relates how the probability changes for arbitrarily small increases in the explanatory variable. These derivatives, however, are a function not only of the coefficients, but also of the probabilities themselves. Consequently, the magnitude of the derivative will tend to differ for each value of the explanatory variable and the values of the other explanatory variables as well. Because of this, it is necessary to summarize the derivatives by calculating their means.

The last column in Table 6.2 shows the average derivatives for Age and Education corresponding to various ages and education levels. To arrive at these average derivatives, the derivatives for Age and Education were first calculated using equation (6).

The average derivatives for the age ranges in Table 6.2 were estimated by selecting the cases in the age categories 18–24, 25–54, 55–64, and 65+ and calculating the average of the age derivative for each of these categories. The average derivatives for the education categories were calculated in the same manner.

The results indicate a pattern of a declining probability of poverty with increases in years of education within both education categories reported in the table. Similarly, the results indicate that the probability of poverty declines with increases in age within each of the age categories. Specifically, the probability of poverty declines by an average of 2.4 percent for each additional year of education prior to high school graduation. Each additional year of education including high school graduation and higher reduces the probability of poverty by 1.2 percent on average. The average derivatives for each of the age ranges are interpreted in a like manner.

Unfortunately, derivatives do not make a great deal of sense when it comes to dummy variables. Derivatives measure the changes in one variable that result from small changes in another. As discussed above, however, dummy variables are like a switch—the observation either has the characteristic represented by the dummy variable or it does not. Consequently, it is not meaningful to think about changes in the probability of the dependent variable occurring (e.g., being in poverty) with respect to small changes in a dummy variable.

However, it is possible to calculate odds ratios for dummy variables as in equation (7). The odds ratio of 1.3689 for Female in Table 6.2 indicates that, controlling for the effects of the other explanatory variables, females are 37 percent more likely to be in poverty than males. Stated differently, the probability of being in poverty is 1.37 times greater for females than for males. Similarly, the odds ratio of 1.9517 for Black indicates that the probability of blacks being in poverty is 1.95 times that for other races. No odds ratio is calculated for Central city because the coefficient is not significantly different from zero.

The odds ratio for Single indicates that the probability for unmarried people of being in poverty is 2.74 times that for married persons; it is 1.37 times higher for those living in the South than for those living in other regions; and the probability of poverty for working persons is only 20 percent that for nonworking persons.

Odds ratios can also be helpful for investigating switches in coefficient signs over different ranges of an explanatory variable. A problem with the average derivative formula in equation (6) is that the sign of the derivative is determined by the variable's coefficient. With only one coefficient it is not possible for derivatives to change sign over different levels of the explanatory variables (e.g., over different age levels or education levels).

With odds ratios, however, it is possible to detect such sign switches. Table 6.3 illustrates this point by reestimating the poverty model in Table 6.2, replacing the interval age and education variables with dummy variables for age and education categories.

Note that the slope coefficients and significance levels for all of the other variables are very similar to the original values shown in Table 6.2, which are repeated here as those for Model 1. The coefficient for the constant changes sign, but this is a plausible result given the addition of dummy variables to the model (recall from Chapter 4 that noninteractive dummy variables have the effect of shifting the constant term up or down).

The biggest difference between the models in Tables 6.2 and 6.3 is the positive coefficient for having less than 12 years of education. This translates to an odds ratio of 2.49—meaning that the probability of being in poverty for those lacking a high school education is 2.49 times that of being in poverty for those having a high school education. The signs on the remaining educational categories are negative, as were the derivatives for these categories reported in Table 6.2. Similarly, the signs on the dummy variables for age are consistent with the derivatives in Table 6.2. Finally, there is very little change in the calculated χ^2 between the two models.

The final point to discuss with respect to the logit models presented in Tables 6.2 and 6.3 is the overall goodness-of-fit measure. As discussed above, logit models are estimated using the maximum likelihood technique. This estimation method finds the values for the coefficients that maximize the likelihood of observing the given sample. The maximum likelihood approach, therefore, is very different from ordinary least squares, which finds the coefficients that minimize the sum of the squared errors.

As a consequence of differences in the estimation approaches embodied in maximum likelihood and ordinary least squares, goodness-of-fit measures from the latter make no theoretical sense in a maximum likelihood context. Yet even so,

Table 6.3
Alternative Specifications of Age and Education in a Logit Model of Poverty

Variable	Model 1		Model 2	
	Coefficient	*t*-statistics	Coefficient	*t*-statistics
Constant	1.4119	4.94	−1.5027	−8.01
Female	0.3140	3.07	0.2942	2.87
Black	0.6687	4.79	0.6680	4.77
Central City	0.1200	1.05	0.1260	1.10
Single	1.0078	10.01	1.0557	9.80
South	0.3166	3.08	0.3430	3.34
Work	−1.5881	−13.74	−1.5772	−13.40
Education	−0.1809	−11.30		
under 12 years			0.9142	7.72
13–15 years			−0.4400	−2.90
16+ years			−0.8904	−4.69
Age	−0.0317	−10.83		
25–54 years			−0.4861	−3.53
55–64 years			−1.1431	−5.74
65+ years			−1.7493	−9.92
χ^2	4,411		4,414.6	

Source: Author's calculations based on 1989 Current Population Survey.

there are some broad similarities in hypothesis testing between the two types of models.

Goodness of fit for maximum likelihood models is based on improvements in the likelihood of observing the given sample that arise from changes in the model coefficients. When the likelihood of observing the sample cannot be increased by any further changes in the coefficients, the value of the likelihood function has been maximized.[6] A logical measure of goodness of fit, therefore, would be to compare the initial value of the likelihood function (assuming that all of the slope coefficients were equal to zero) to the maximum value.

It can be shown that $-2 \ln (L_0/L_{max})$ has a χ^2 distribution. One must be careful, however, in interpreting the values produced for these statistics by different software packages. This is the case for several reasons. First, the initial value of the likelihood function is commonly calculated in at least two major ways. In the simplest case, it is assumed that the probability of observing a value of 1 for the dependent variable is 50 percent for each observation. Therefore, the initial likelihood of observing the entire sample is 0.5^N. The χ^2 based on this initial likelihood function has $k+1$ degrees of freedom (the number of slope coefficients plus the constant term to be estimated). The software used to estimate all of the logit models presented in this chapter used this definition for calculating the initial log likelihood.

An alternative approach is to use the relative frequencies of the values of the dependent variable to calculate the initial value of the likelihood function. Suppose that, of our sample of N observations, p had a value of 1 and q had a value of 0. If the relative frequency of observing a value of 1 was f, then the initial value of the likelihood function would be $(f)^p(1-f)^q$. The χ^2 based on this initial likelihood function has k degrees of freedom (the total number of coefficients to be estimated minus 1).

Note that the values for the log of the initial and maximum likelihood functions are negative. This is because the likelihood of observing a sample is the product of the probabilities of observing each case. The product of probabilities typically is a very small number close to 0. The reader may recall from Chapter 4 that the natural logarithms of values between 0 and 1 are negative; logarithms of values close to 0 are large negative numbers.

The χ^2 values calculated from the log likelihood statistics share a characteristic with F-statistics in regression—the basic null hypothesis that all of the slope coefficients are jointly equal to zero is nearly always rejected. In the model reported in Table 6.2, for example, the calculated χ^2 value is 4,411 with 9 degrees of freedom. In contrast, the tabulated critical value of χ^2 with 9 degrees of freedom at the 99 percent confidence level is 21.67. Since the calculated value for the χ^2 is greater than the tabulated value, the null hypothesis that all of the slope coefficients are jointly equal to zero is rejected. In other words, the model as a whole is statistically significant.

In addition to the issue of how the initial likelihood function is constructed, there is the issue of how statistical packages report assessments of goodness of fit. Some packages report the initial and maximum log likelihood values. Others report the χ^2 value. Still others report a series of related statistics. Most of these other statistics are of dubious value. Aldrich and Nelson (1984) and Train (1986) discuss the limitations of these other statistics. Two basic types are particularly worthy of comment: (1) the percentage of cases "correctly" predicted by the model and (2) R^2 proxies.

What does it mean for a case to be correctly predicted by a logit or probit model? Most packages that produce this statistic begin by calculating the predicted value of the probability for each case. If the predicted probability is greater than 0.5, the individual is predicted to be a 1; otherwise, the individual is predicted to be a 0. A cross tabulation between the predicted distribution and actual distribution of [1,0] values is then constructed and used to ascertain the percentage of cases correctly predicted.

Train (1986) points out that this statistic is flawed because it ignores the basic notion of probability. That is, an individual with a predicted probability of 0.45 would always be classified as a 0 value by this procedure. But probabilistically, the individual has a 45 percent chance of being a 1. Because the "percentage correctly predicted" statistic always classifies such individuals as choosing the alternative 0, it provides a misleading assessment of model fit. Often samples that are unbalanced (e.g., 95 percent 0s and 5 percent 1s) will result in models that generate correspondingly unbalanced predictions (e.g., all 0s). In the example, the "percentage correctly classified" criterion would indicate that the model correctly predicted 95 percent of the cases, even though it predicted 0 percent of the ones correctly.

Aldrich and Nelson (1984) raise a similar set of issues with respect to the various R^2 proxies that are produced by many statistical packages. R^2 proxies are an attempt to provide researchers who are comfortable with multiple regression with a goodness-of-fit measure similar to the one they are familiar with. Several R^2 proxies have been proposed.[7] All of these measures share the common drawback of lacking a theoretical justification. This being the case, researchers who wish to have a sense of the proportion of variation in the dependent variable that is explained by their models should estimate the model using ordinary least squares regression. This will provide them with the intuitive value that they seek. Formal hypothesis testing, however, should be based on the maximum likelihood model.

HYPOTHESIS TESTING

The *F*-test is inappropriate for hypothesis testing with models that are nonlinear in the parameters or have non-normally distributed errors, or for testing nonlinear restrictions. Hypothesis testing with discrete-choice models always involves at least one of these characteristics. Consequently, an alternative test statistic is needed. Three alternatives are available: the likelihood ratio test, the Wald test, and the Lagrange multiplier test. All three of these tests have a χ^2 distribution with degrees of freedom equal to the number of restrictions being tested. This text focuses on the likelihood ratio test. In certain circumstances, however, the Wald and Lagrange multiplier tests can have computational advantages.[8]

Hypothesis testing with maximum likelihood models has many similarities with regression analysis. As already noted, the basic test of the null hypothesis that each coefficient is equal to zero (or some other value) is provided by the asymptotic *t*-statistics. Similarly, evaluation of the null hypothesis that all of the slope coefficients are jointly equal to zero is provided by the log likelihood test. But the similarity does not end there. The log likelihood test can be used just like the *F*-statistic to evaluate a wide range of specialized hypotheses.

Testing the Contribution of a Subset of Variables

Suppose that an analyst wishes to test whether a group of variables makes a contribution to a model. The null hypothesis is that the slope coefficients for the variables to be tested are equal to zero. As in multiple regression, testing this null hypothesis involves estimating a restricted model where the coefficients for these variables have been restricted to zero by omitting them from the equation. A corresponding unrestricted model containing these variables is also estimated. Using the log likelihood values from these models, the relevant likelihood ratio test is:

$$\chi^2 = -2\ln(\frac{L_R}{L_U})$$

This statistic has a χ^2 distribution with degrees of freedom equal to the number of restrictions in the restricted model.

Table 6.4 illustrates an application of this test to the poverty example. Model 1 is the unrestricted model. Several of the estimated coefficients in the model are not statistically significant (i.e., the coefficients for Central city, South, and West). In such an instance, a researcher might be interested in testing whether these variables contribute anything to the model as a group. To do so, the coefficients for these variables are restricted to zero. This is accomplished by dropping these variables from the equation; this is Model 2 in Table 6.4. Using the log of the maximum likelihoods for these two models, the χ^2 is -2(-1,430.9 + 1,429.4)=3. It has 3 degrees of freedom because three variables were dropped from the model. The tabulated χ^2 at a 95 percent confidence level with 3 degrees of freedom is 7.82. Since the tabulated χ^2 exceeds the calculated value, the null hypothesis that the slope coefficients of the tested variables are jointly equal to zero cannot be rejected. In other words, the three variables do not make a statistically significant contribution to the model.

Testing the Equivalence of Submodels

Chapter 3 discussed the use of the Chow test in regression models for checking the feasibility of pooling data from different time periods and for testing the merits of splitting a sample into subgroups (e.g., by race, gender, marital status, or region) and estimating separate models for each group. Analogous tests can be performed with logit or probit models using a likelihood ratio test.

The test is illustrated in Table 6.5. Separate poverty models have been estimated for blacks, whites, and the total sample. Is it useful to split the sample by race in this manner? The basic issue is whether the slope coefficients differ enough by race to warrant the estimation of separate models. The total model, by pooling blacks and whites, restricts the slope coefficients to be equal for both races. The separate models allow the coefficients to vary by race; consequently, these are the unrestricted estimates.

The χ^2 test is formed by adding the maximum likelihoods of the submodels (-198.58 and -1,236.9), subtracting the result from the maximum likelihood of the restricted model, and multiplying the result by -2. For the models in Table 6.5, this yields a calculated χ^2 of 48.84. It has $[q*(k+1)]-(k+1)]$ degrees of freedom, where

Table 6.4
Testing the Contribution of a Subset of Variables

Variable	Model 1 Coefficient	Model 1 t-statistics	Model 2 Coefficient	Model 2 t-statistics
Constant	−1.3868	−6.13	−1.2609	−6.09
Age 25–54	−0.6593	−4.14	−0.6654	−4.18
Age 55–64	−1.2312	−5.51	−1.2368	−5.54
Age 65+	−1.7371	−7.79	−1.7438	−7.82
Female	.3183	3.01	0.3215	3.05
Central City	0.0424	0.36	—	—
Divorced/Separated	1.4294	9.77	1.4343	9.82
Widowed	0.9197	4.99	0.9123	4.95
Never Married	0.9037	5.97	0.9012	5.97
Northeast	−0.3324	−2.10	−0.4592	−3.58
South	0.2240	1.66	—	—
West	0.0446	0.60	—	—
Work	−1.5947	−13.38	−1.6018	−13.45
Education under 12 years	0.8529	7.07	0.8727	7.26
Education 13–15 years	−0.4403	−2.89	−0.4359	−2.86
Education 16+ years	−0.8254	−4.32	−0.8083	−4.24
Black	0.8019	5.59	0.8554	6.29
Latino	0.6438	4.40	0.6738	4.74
χ^2	4,454.0		4,451.0	
L_{max}	−1,429.4		−1,430.9	

Source: Author's calculations based on 1989 Current Population Survey.

k is the number of explanatory variables in each of the restricted models, and q is the number of models compared. In the example, $k+1$ is equal to 12, so $2*(k+1)$ is equal to 24. At the 95 percent confidence level, the tabulated χ^2 for 24 degrees of freedom is 36.42. Since the calculated value of the χ^2 exceeds the tabulated value, the null hypothesis that there is no difference between the poverty models for blacks and whites is rejected. Consequently, it is useful to split the sample by race to obtain race-specific coefficient estimates.

COMPARISON OF LINEAR PROBABILITY, LOGIT, AND PROBIT MODELS

Logit analysis is popular because of its comparative simplicity relative to the probit model. The logit and probit models both use the maximum likelihood technique to estimate the coefficients, standard errors, and log likelihood statistics. But the probit model requires the use of integral calculus to calculate the cumulative normal probabilities, whereas the logit model has a "closed form" that enables these probabilities to be calculated without integration. Of course, being nonlinear, both models are computationally burdensome in comparison with the linear probability model.

Given these considerations, it is useful to compare the results obtained from the linear probability, logit, and probit models. Table 6.6 provides such a comparison for a model of poverty status. One apparent difference between the models is the numerical values of the coefficients. This difference is due to the measurement of the dependent variables in each model. In the case of the linear probability model, the slope coefficients represent the change in the probability of poverty resulting from a one-unit increase in each explanatory variable, controlling for the effects of the other explanatory variables. That is, the coefficients are the partial derivatives of the probability of poverty with respect to each variable. The constant term is the expected probability of poverty, setting all of the explanatory variables equal to zero.

The interpretation of the coefficients in the logit and probit models, however, is more complex. In both models, the coefficients refer to changes in a latent variable, Z, with respect to a unit change in each explanatory variable, controlling for the effects of the other variables in the equation. The logit and probit probabilities are, in turn, a function of the latent variable Z. Because of the comparatively simple form of the cumulative logistic probability distribution, it can also be shown that the logit coefficients represent the change in the log of the odds of the dependent variable with respect to a one-unit change in the explanatory variables, controlling for the effects of the other variables in the model. In the probit model, however, it is not possible to easily relate the coefficients to the probability of the outcome variable without calculating the partial derivative.[9]

Nevertheless, in all three models the signs of the slope coefficients indicate the direction of the change in the probability with respect to changes in the explanatory variable. Given the sensitivity of coefficient values to model specification, analysts

Table 6.5
Testing for Differences in the Determinants of Poverty by Race

Variable	Total		Black		White	
	Coefficient	*t*-statistics	Coefficient	*t*-statistics	Coefficient	*t*-statistics
Constant	−1.4881	−7.95	−0.5405	−1.09	−1.5511	−7.48
Age 25–54	−0.4832	−3.52	−0.7843	−2.33	−0.4278	−2.81
Age 55–64	−1.1276	−5.71	−1.5153	−3.04	−1.0203	−4.69
Age 65+	−1.7802	−10.17	−0.9430	−2.15	−1.8845	−9.54
Female	0.2891	2.83	0.6415	2.42	0.2392	2.13
Central City	0.2467	2.23	−0.1772	−0.66	0.2270	1.78
Single	1.1112	10.40	0.9719	3.41	1.0899	9.26
South	0.4357	4.36	0.7091	2.49	0.2572	2.2770
Work	−1.5951	−13.60	−1.8992	−6.36	−1.5533	−12.01
Educ. < 12 yrs	0.9234	7.88	0.1582	0.48	1.0108	7.83
Educ. 13–15 yrs	−0.4570	−3.02	−0.5470	−1.40	−0.4195	−2.52
Educ. 16+ yrs	−0.9359	−4.94	−1.6032	−2.42	−0.8251	−4.13
L_{max}	−1,459.9		−198.58		−1,236.9	

Source: Author's calculations based on 1989 Current Population Survey.

are often content (quite rightly) to constrain their policy observations to the signs and statistical significance of the coefficients. Note that the three models are very similar in this regard. The slope coefficients have the same signs in all three models and the same variables are statistically significant.

Although the constant term for the logit model in Table 6.6 is positive, it should be noted that it is fairly common to get a negative and statistically significant coefficient estimate for the constant term in logit models. This result is perfectly plausible when one recalls that the dependent variable of the logit model is the log of the odds. A negative expected value for the log of the odds when all of the explanatory variables are held to zero simply means that the expected odds are less than one.

Several authors have evaluated the results of logit, probit, and linear probability models and related techniques with similar conclusions.[10] What are the implications

Table 6.6
Comparison of Linear Probability, Logit, and Probit Models of Poverty Status

Variable	Linear Probability Coefficient	t	Logit Coefficient	t	Probit Coefficient	t
Constant	0.4938	19.34	1.4119	4.94	0.7364	4.75
Female	0.0197	2.45	0.3140	3.07	0.1410	2.66
Black	0.0976	6.70	0.6687	4.79	0.3618	4.61
Central City	0.0127	1.29	0.1200	1.05	0.0672	1.10
Single	0.0842	10.08	1.0078	10.01	0.5138	9.79
South	0.0288	3.36	0.3166	3.08	0.1749	3.21
Work	−0.1602	−15.45	−1.5881	−13.74	−0.8488	−13.67
Education	−0.0165	−12.15	−0.1809	−11.30	−0.0982	−11.47
Age	−0.0030	−11.41	−0.0317	−10.83	−0.0172	−10.78
$\bar{R}^2$	0.134		—		—	
χ^2	—		4,411.0		4,408.4	

Source: Author's calculations based on 1989 Current Population Survey.

of these studies for the use of the alternative estimators? First, empirical studies indicate that despite the theoretical limitations of using regression with a [0,1] dependent variable, ordinary least squares regression is a useful exploratory technique. Because of its lower computational costs and superior diagnostics for identifying problems such as multicollinearity, it is reasonable to use regression analysis to help develop a model specification to be subsequently estimated by logit or probit analysis. In doing so, however, it is important to remember that the statistical tests of significance in the regression model are undermined by inherent heteroscedasticity when the dependent variable is [0,1]. For this reason, the researcher needs to be cautious about dropping insignificant variables from the model specification.

Logit and probit models are now available in virtually all of the major statistical packages. Given their widespread availability, there is little justification for not estimating a logit or probit model when the dependent variable is dichotomous. But what are the grounds for choosing between logit and probit?

Economists, in particular, tend to use probit more widely than logit. An important reason for this choice is that the probit model is based on the multivariate cumulative normal distribution. This is a highly attractive feature for all of the same reasons that the normal distribution is attractive in the linear regression model. That is, unless given specific evidence to the contrary, it is reasonable to assume that the probability distribution is multivariate normal—especially in large samples.

On the other hand, although the cumulative logistic and normal distributions are extremely similar, the logistic model generates parameter estimates at a lower computational cost. Moreover, the simpler functional form of the cumulative logistic distribution enables supplemental measures such as the partial derivatives and odds ratios to be easily calculated. The simpler functional form of the logit model also lends itself to estimation problems where the dependent variable has more than two categories. In Chapter 7 it will be demonstrated that for models involving more complex dependent variables, the use of the cumulative logistic versus the cumulative normal distribution will differ, depending on the nature of the estimation problem being confronted.

NOTES

1. For discussion of this and other procedures for estimating regression models with [0,1] dependent variables, see Aldrich and Nelson (1984).

2. This example is patterned after Kmenta (1971, pp. 175–176).

3. See, for example, Pindyck and Rubinfeld (1991, pp. 232–234).

4. Many other distributions have been considered as well. See, for example, Domencich and McFadden (1975).

5. The discussion in this section is in specific reference to the logit model. Aside from the numerical interpretation of the coefficients, however, the discussion is completely transferable to other models such as probit. The interpretation of probit coefficients is discussed later in the chapter.

6. For descriptions of the computational strategies used in maximum likelihood estimation see Maddala (1977), Fomby, Hill, and Johnson (1984), and Ben-Akiva and Lerman (1987).

7. See, for example, Zavoina and McElvey (1975) and Pindyck and Rubinfeld (1991).

8. A good introductory discussion of likelihood ratio, Wald, and Lagrange multiplier tests is provided in Kennedy (1992).

9. The partial derivative in the probit model for the change in probability of the dependent variable with respect to a change in variable k is given by:

$$\frac{\partial P_i}{\partial X_{ik}} = \frac{1}{\sqrt{2\pi}} e^{\frac{-(\Sigma B_k X_{ik})^2 B_k}{2}}$$

10. See, for example, Aldrich and Cnudde (1975), Amemiya and Powell (1983), Cleary and Angel (1984), and Gunderson (1974).

7
Extensions to the Binary Dependent Variable Model

Many models in the social and behavioral sciences can be estimated using either multiple regression or binary logit or probit models. Often, however, the nature of the dependent variable is such that the models cannot be estimated using these techniques. An occupational choice model, for example, might have a dependent variable that has several categories. Because type of occupation is a categorical variable, it cannot be treated as though it were an interval variable and, consequently, regression analysis is not an appropriate estimation technique. Nor can binary logit or probit analysis be used to estimate such a model because the dependent variable contains more than two categories.

In other instances, some values of the dependent variable may be censored or not observable. For instance, in models of individual labor supply, hours worked are observed only for those individuals participating in the labor market; hours are zero for everyone else. At first glance, this would not seem to be a problem. However, if the relationship between the explanatory variables and hours worked is systematically different for people who are in the labor force versus those who are not, then using information only for those in the labor force may result in biased parameter estimates. In particular, there may be *unobservable* variables whose relationships with hours supplied differ for labor force participants and nonparticipants. The omission of unobservable variables results in biased parameter estimates just as the omission of observable variables does.

In this chapter, a variety of methodologies are discussed which are useful for estimating models when the dependent variable is neither interval nor binary. All of these methodologies utilize the maximum likelihood approach introduced in Chapter 6.

MULTINOMIAL LOGIT

The multinomial logit (MNL) model is a particularly useful technique which is an extension of the binary logit model to handle instances where the dependent variable takes on more than two categorical values. (In fact, the binary logit model is a special case of the MNL model, in which the dependent variable has only two possible values.) In the multinomial case, the probability of alternative k is given by:

$$P_k = \frac{e^{z_k}}{1 + \Sigma e^{z_k}}$$

As in the binary case, it is possible to estimate multinomial models using a variety of probability distributions. The computational advantages of the cumulative logistic distribution are especially pronounced, however, in the multinomial case. This is partly because of the "closed form" of the cumulative logistic distribution and partly because of a property known as independence from irrelevant alternatives (IIA).[1] The widespread availability of MNL estimation procedures, coupled with the computational advantages of these models, has led to a large number of empirical applications over the years. McFadden (1984, p. 1411) notes that MNL models are the most widely used techniques for estimation problems involving a multinomial response.[2]

Independence from Irrelevant Alternatives

The computational advantages of the MNL model relative to other multinomial response models such as multinomial probit stem from an underlying assumption known as the IIA property. The IIA property states that the ratio of the probabilities for any two alternatives is independent of any other alternatives. This follows directly from the functional form of the probabilities in the multinomial logit model. For example, the ratio of the probabilities for alternatives one and two is given by:

$$\frac{P_1}{P_2} = \frac{\dfrac{e^{z_1}}{\Sigma e^{z_k}}}{\dfrac{e^{z_2}}{\Sigma e^{z_k}}}$$

$$\frac{P_1}{P_2} = \frac{e^{z_1}}{e^{z_2}}$$

This enables the effects of any variable on the relative odds of any two alternatives to be compared without considering the remaining alternatives:

$$\frac{P_j}{P_{j'}} = \frac{e^{\hat{b}_0 + \Sigma \hat{b}_k X_k}}{e^{\hat{c}_0 + \Sigma \hat{c}_k X_k}}$$

$$\frac{P_j}{P_{j'}} = e^{(\hat{b}_0 - \hat{c}_0) + \Sigma(\hat{b}_k - \hat{c}_k)X_k}$$

For example, if $(b_k - c_k)$ is positive for a particular variable, then an increase in X_k will increase P_j relative to $P_{j'}$.

Although the IIA property is useful for reducing the computational cost of MNL models, as well as comparing the variables influencing the relative probabilities of two alternatives, the assumption that one can ignore the other alternatives is not always realistic.

The potential limitations of the IIA property are often illustrated using the red bus/blue bus example (e.g., Ben-Akiva and Lerman, 1987, pp. 51–52). Suppose an individual has a choice of traveling by automobile or taking a blue bus and does not prefer either alternative to the other. Then:

$$P(auto) = P(blue\ bus) = 0.5$$

and

$$\frac{P(auto)}{P(blue\ bus)} = 1$$

Now suppose a red bus is introduced which the traveler considers to be exactly like the blue bus. Then:

$$\frac{P(blue\ bus)}{P(red\ bus)} = 1$$

But the only probabilities where

$$\frac{P(auto)}{P(blue\ bus)} = 1$$

and

$$\frac{P(blue\ bus)}{P(red\ bus)} = 1$$

are P(auto) = P(blue bus) = P(red bus) = 0.33. This is what the MNL model predicts. In real life, however, the probability of taking a bus would be split between the two types of buses:

$$P(auto) = 0.50$$
$$P(blue\ bus) = 0.25$$
$$P(red\ bus) = 0.25$$

Thus, in situations where the alternatives are not really distinct, the MNL model will lead to biased estimates of the predicted probabilities.

Interpreting MNL Output

To understand MNL output, it is useful to reconsider the linear probability model for a moment.[3] Assume a dependent variable Y has the values 1, 2, 3 (e.g., 1 represents not working; 2 represents working part-time, and 3 represents working full-time). Define three dummy variables based on the possible values of Y:

$$P_1 = 1 \text{ if } Y = 1; 0 \text{ otherwise}$$
$$P_2 = 1 \text{ if } Y = 2; 0 \text{ otherwise}$$
$$P_3 = 1 \text{ if } Y = 3; 0 \text{ otherwise}$$

Now suppose that the only determinant of labor force participation is age, X. Then it would be possible to estimate the three models:

$$P_{1i} = \hat{a}_0 + \hat{a}_1 X_{1i}$$
$$P_{2i} = \hat{b}_0 + \hat{b}_1 X_{2i}$$
$$P_{3i} = \hat{c}_0 + \hat{c}_1 x_{3i}$$

But since the probabilities must sum to one, $P_1 + P_2 + P_3 = 1$, one of these equations is redundant. To see this, rewrite $P_1 + P_2 + P_3 = 1$ as:

$$(\hat{a}_0 + \hat{a}_1 X_{1i}) + (\hat{b}_0 + \hat{b}_1 X_{1i}) + (\hat{c}_0 + \hat{c}_1 X_{1i}) = 1$$

and rearrange the terms:

$$(\hat{a}_0 + \hat{b}_0 + \hat{c}_0) + (\hat{a}_1 + \hat{b}_1 + \hat{c}_1) X_{1i} = 1$$

The previous equation will always be true when

$$(\hat{a}_0 + \hat{b}_0 + \hat{c}_0) = 1$$

and

$$(\hat{a}_1 + \hat{b}_1 + \hat{c}_1) = 0$$

This implies that if a_0 and b_0 have been estimated, then $c_0 = 1 - (a_0 + b_0)$. Similarly, if a_1 and b_1 have been estimated, then $c_1 = -(a_1 + b_1)$.

The same logic holds for the MNL model because the predicted probabilities summed across all of the alternatives must equal one for each individual. Consequently, MNL models contain $k-1$ sets of coefficients where k is the number of categories in the dependent variable. Each equation relates the explanatory variables to $ln(P_k/P_0)$, where P_k is the probability of alternative k and P_0 is the probability of the reference group.

The fact that the probabilities must sum to one across the alternative categories of the dependent variable means that inferences based on the estimated coefficients must be made with caution. In the binary logit model, the sign of a coefficient on a particular variable indicates whether that variable increases or decreases the log of the odds of the dependent variable. This association with the log of the odds moves in the same direction as the probability of the outcome. But this is not necessarily true in the MNL model. The signs of statistically significant parameter estimates are reliable indicators for the direction of effects only relative to the reference group. For example, it is possible for a variable to have a positive parameter estimate, indicating a positive association between the variable and the log of the odds of that outcome relative to the reference group, but the same explanatory variable may be negatively associated with the probability of the outcome itself. This can be seen by examining the partial derivatives of the explanatory variables in an MNL model.

Partial Derivatives in the MNL Model

Partial derivatives enable the effects of a particular variable on the probability of an event to be examined without the inconvenience and confusion introduced by the log of the odds formulation. Suppose that in the labor force example just considered, not working was the reference group. Then the two estimated equations would be:

$$\ln\frac{(P_{1i})}{P_{0i}} = \hat{b}_{10} + \Sigma b_{1k} X_{ki}$$

$$\ln\frac{(P_{2i})}{P_{01}} = \hat{b}_{20} + \Sigma b_{2k} x_{ki}$$

After some algebra, it follows that:

$$P_{0i} = \frac{1}{1 + e^{\hat{b}_{10} + \Sigma \hat{b}_{1k} X_{ki}} + e^{\hat{b}_{20} + \Sigma \hat{b}_{2k} X_{ki}}}$$

$$P_{1i} = \frac{e^{\hat{b}_{10} + \Sigma \hat{b}_{1k} X_{ki}}}{1 + e^{\hat{b}_{10} + \Sigma \hat{b}_{1k} X_{ki}} + e^{\hat{b}_{20} + \Sigma \hat{b}_{2k} X_{ki}}}$$

$$P_{2i} = \frac{e^{\hat{b}_{20} + \Sigma \hat{b}_{2k} X_{ki}}}{1 + e^{\hat{b}_{10} + \Sigma \hat{b}_{1k} X_{ki}} + e^{\hat{b}_{20} + \Sigma \hat{b}_{2k} X_{ki}}}$$

Taking the partial derivatives of any of these probabilities with respect to an independent variable X_{jk} within a particular equation (e.g., the effect of part-time wages on the probability of working part-time) yields the following:

$$\frac{\partial P_j}{\partial X_{jk}} = P_j(1 - P_j)\hat{b}_{jk}$$

The partial derivative of the probability of a particular outcome (e.g., part-time work) with respect to an independent variable X_{lk} in another equation (e.g., full-time wages) is given by:

$$\frac{\partial P_j}{\partial X_{lk}} = -P_j P_l \hat{b}_{lk}$$

Not surprisingly, partial derivatives of the MNL model present the same reporting problems of those of the binary logit model. The same methods can be used to facilitate reporting of the partial derivatives in the MNL model as can be used with the binary logit model. Average partial derivatives for each outcome can be reported for various subsamples.

Odds Ratios

Chapter 6 discussed the problems associated with attempting to calculate partial derivatives when the explanatory variables are dummy variables. In such cases, the derivative is technically not defined because derivatives measure the change in one variable with respect to extremely small changes in another variable. Clearly, it is not possible to examine fine gradations of changes in dummy variables.

The main approach for dealing with this problem in MNL models, just as in simple logit models, is to calculate odds ratios. Odds ratios in MNL models are defined exactly as they are in simple logit models; the odds ratios refer to the ratio of the dependent variable probabilities for the two categories in the dummy variable. For example, an odds ratio of 3.1 for a dummy variable in a particular equation of an MNL model would mean that the probability of the event is 3.1 times higher for those with the characteristic (dummy variable = 1) than for those without it (dummy variable = 0).

It is also often useful to calculate the probabilities associated with representative cases. For example, using the estimated coefficients for each equation, it would be possible to calculate the probabilities for hypothetical persons who have characteristics positively associated with the event occurring; for another group of persons who have characteristics that reduce the probability of the event occurring; and for other groups that have a mixture of characteristics. Calculating illustrative probabilities in this way enables the researcher to see the range of probabilities associated with having particular characteristics.

Example

Table 7.1 reports the results for an MNL model of labor force participation. The reference category is nonparticipation in the labor force. The coefficients in the model are interpreted in exactly the same way as in the binary logit model. Each coefficient represents the change in the log of the odds of the dependent variable resulting from a one-unit increase in the explanatory variable, controlling for the other variables in the equation. The dependent variable for the first set of coefficients is the log of the odds of working part-time versus not working; the

Table 7.1
Multinomial Logit Model of Work

Parameter	Coefficient	*t*-statistic
Equation 1		
Constant	−3.3183	−19.516
Age	0.0058	1.754
Female	−0.5795	−5.016
White	0.2428	1.617
Education	0.0517	6.905
Married	0.1308	1.108
Earnings	0.0042	31.238
Other Income	−0.0010	−4.840
Equation 2		
Constant	−5.3113	−14.274
Age	−0.0058	−0.88
Female	− 0.4362	−2.103
White	0.5885	1.877
Education	0.0678	4.906
Married	0.1506	0.705
Earnings	0.0035	20.284
Other Income	−0.0010	−2.4522

- 2 log likelihood = 7,745.92

second equation refers to the log of the odds of working full-time versus not working.

The model indicates that higher education levels and earnings are associated with an increased odds of working part-time versus not working; being female and having higher levels of unearned income are associated with a decreased log of the odds of working part-time.[4] Age, race, and marital status are not statistically significant at a 95 percent confidence level. Not surprisingly, the same pattern of association and significance was evident for the second set of coefficients predicting the log of the odds of working full-time versus not working.

Table 7.2
Average Derivatives

	Not Working	Working Full-Time	Working Part-Time
Age	−.0003	.0005	−.0002
Female	.0384	−.0368	−.0015
White	−.0195	.0095	.0100
Education	−.0037	.0029	.0008
Married	−.0091	.0076	.0015
Earnings	−.0003	.0003	.00002
Other Income	.00007	−.00006	−.0000008

These results appear to be very similar to what would have been obtained if two binary logits had been estimated. But there is a difference. In the binary case, there are only two outcomes, so the log of the odds moves in the same direction as the probability. In the multinomial case, however, there are three or more outcomes. The probabilities of these outcomes must sum to one for each case. This means that the sign of a coefficient measuring the association of a variable with the log of the odds of the dependent variable is an unreliable indicator of the sign of the variable's association with the probability of that particular outcome. To be confident about the sign of a variable's association with the probability of a particular outcome, it is necessary to calculate its average derivative.

The average derivatives for each of the variables in Table 7.1 are shown in Table 7.2. The average derivatives for the probability of full-time employment are shown in column 2; those for the part-time model are shown in column 3. In this example, the signs of these derivatives are consistent with the associated coefficients in the MNL model, but this need not be the case. Column 1 contains the average derivatives for the reference group—the probability of not working.

The goodness-of-fit measure for the MNL model is the now familiar χ^2 statistic of $-2 \ln (L_0/L_{Max})$. This statistic has $q*(K+1)$ degrees of freedom, where K is the number of explanatory variables in each of q sets of estimated coefficients. In the current example, the estimated χ^2 is 7,745.92 and it has 16 degrees of freedom. The tabulated χ^2 at the 95 percent confidence level and 16 degrees of freedom is 26.296. Consequently, the null hypothesis that all of the coefficients of the model are jointly equal to zero is rejected.

Other likelihood ratio tests with MNL models, such as restrictions on coefficients and comparisons of models across subsamples, can be carried out exactly as discussed in the previous chapter on logit models. Likelihood ratio tests can also be used to test hypotheses for the other maximum likelihood models discussed in the remainder of this chapter.

There are a number of models that are closely related to the MNL model. Although the MNL model is very flexible and computationally tractable, it is often criticized because of its IIA property. Two alternative models that attempt to deal with the IIA limitations of the MNL model are the nested logit model and the multinomial probit model.[5]

NESTED LOGIT MODELS

Nested logit models enable decision making to be modeled in stages. This is one way of dealing with the failure to satisfy the IIA assumption of MNL models in problems like the red bus/blue bus example discussed earlier. For example, suppose an analyst is interested in modeling the probability that someone works as a nurse. This might be thought of as consisting of several stages. First, an individual decides whether or not to participate in the labor force. Upon deciding to work, individuals decide whether to be a health care worker or not. Those that decide to be health care workers decide between being nurses versus other sorts of health care workers. This decision-making process is represented schematically in Figure 7.1.

Nested logit models can be estimated in two primary ways. The first way is to explicitly specify all branches of the model in the log likelihood function and then maximize it. This approach has the advantage of producing the correct standard errors for the estimated parameters. However, the software for maximizing user-specified likelihood functions (not to mention software for nested logit models) is not as widely available as for specific maximum likelihood models such as logit, probit, and multinomial logit. Consequently, researchers often estimate nested logit models sequentially. Estimation of the sequential model is carried out by estimating the submodels at the left of Figure 7.1 first and working forward. That is, the analyst would begin by estimating a logit model of working versus not working. Next, the analyst would calculate:

$$I_k = \ln(e^{z_{Work}} + e^{z_{Nowork}})$$

This is the log of the denominator of the submodel for each case (or submodels if there is more than one). The I_k is a new variable that is entered into the estimation of the model or models at the next level (working forward). The coefficient for this variable indicates how the z index varies over the components of a submodel.

The sequential approach just described is fairly straightforward and yields consistent estimates of the coefficients in the submodel. Unfortunately, the estimates of the standard errors are biased—the t-statistics will appear to be more significant than they really are (Train, 1986, p. 75). In addition, the variables included in the submodel at one level often overlap with those at the next level. This can result in strong covariance between I_k and the other variables in an equation. For both of these reasons it is theoretically preferable to estimate nested

Figure 7.1
A Nested Logit Model of Nursing Occupational Choice

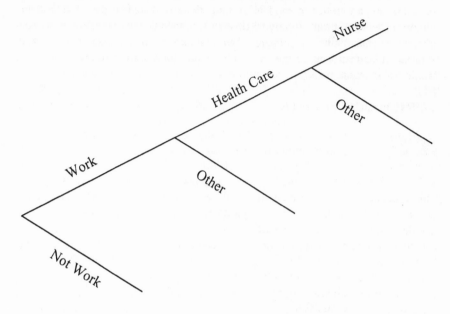

logit models through explicit maximization of the likelihood function when it is feasible to do so.

To estimate the parameters for all branches of the nested model simultaneously, the generalized extreme value (GEV) distribution is often used. The GEV distribution is a generalization of the extreme value distribution used in the logit model. It does, however, generate a convenient form for the marginal and conditional probabilities in the likelihood function to be maximized. These are, respectively:

$$P^k{}_i = \frac{e^{z^k{}_i + \lambda_k I_{ik}}}{\Sigma e^{z^k{}_i + \lambda_k I_{il}}}$$

$$P_i | w^k{}_i = \frac{e^{w^k{}_i}}{\Sigma e^{w^k{}_i}}$$

where

$$I_k = \ln\Sigma e^{z^k{}_i}$$

The conditional probability of making a particular choice is a logit model with variables that vary over the subsets of different choices (e.g., characteristics of different occupations). The "inclusive value term" I_{ik} can also be interpreted as the average utility that the person can expect from the alternatives within the subset (Train, 1986, p. 69).

MULTINOMIAL PROBIT MODELS

As with binary logit and probit models, multinomial logit and probit models differ in the probability distributions that they assume. Multinomial probit models assume a multivariate cumulative normal distribution; multinomial logit models assume a multivariate cumulative logistic distribution. Unlike the case of binary logit and probit models, however, the computational differences between multinomial logit and probit models are substantial. In fact, multinomial probit models tend to be computationally intractable if the dependent variable contains more than three categories. For this reason, multinomial logit models are much more commonly used than multinomial probit models. When the use of multinomial logit is questioned because of the unreasonableness of its IIA assumption, it is often possible to estimate the model using nested logit. Therefore, it is important to have a specification test to evaluate the validity of the IIA assumption.

SPECIFICATION TESTS FOR THE IIA PROPERTY

Several tests for the validity of the IIA property are available.[6] Such tests are useful because when the IIA assumption is valid, it is possible to estimate a multinomial logit model rather than a computationally more complex nested logit model or multinomial probit model.

Hausman and McFadden (1984) present a test for assessing the IIA assumption which involves comparisons of the coefficients for an equation estimated with all alternatives in the model to the same coefficients estimated with a subset of the alternatives in the model. For example, suppose the full set of alternatives was not working, working as a health care worker, and working as some other type of worker. First, the researcher would estimate an MNL model with all of these alternatives. This is the unrestricted choice set.

Next, a logit model would be estimated with just health care workers and other workers as the dependent variable. This is the restricted choice set. The idea is to compare the similarity of the coefficients for the health care worker equation in the two models.

Let the coefficients for the health care worker equation from the unrestricted model be denoted by $\hat{B}_U$ and the coefficients from the restricted model by $\hat{B}_R$. Similarly, define the covariance matrix for $\hat{B}_U$ by $COV(\hat{B}_U)$ and the covariance matrix for $\hat{B}_R$ by $COV(\hat{B}_R)$. Hausman and McFadden showed that:

$$(\hat{B}_R - \hat{B}_U)' \; [COV(\hat{B}_R) - COV(\hat{B}_U)]^{-1} (\hat{B}_R \; \hat{B}_u)$$

has an asymptotic χ^2 distribution with k degrees of freedom, where k is the number of coefficients in the restricted model. If the calculated value of the χ^2 is greater than the tabulated value at the specified level of significance and degrees of freedom, the null hypothesis that the coefficients are equal in the two equations,

$\hat{B}_U = \hat{B}_R$, is rejected. In other words, the null hypothesis of IIA is rejected and the model must be reestimated using a nested logit or multinomial probit model.

CENSORING, TRUNCATION, AND SAMPLE SELECTION

There are many instances in which a dependent variable has interval values for some observations but the remaining observations are either concentrated at a particular value or are missing. For example, the values for certain variables such as income or caregiver stress may be topcoded in some surveys. In other instances, data may be available for only part of the population of interest (e.g., hours supplied are available only for those participating in the labor force). Although it is not always obvious, the use of ordinary least squares (OLS) regression in such cases is generally not justified. The appropriate estimation procedure to use, however, will vary depending upon several considerations that are discussed below.

Censoring versus Truncation

First, it is useful to make the distinction between censoring and truncation (Maddala, 1990). Censoring occurs when information is available for the explanatory variables, but the values for the dependent variable below some threshold are not observed.[7] This would be the case, for example, if income were the dependent variable and negative income values (e.g., from business losses) were coded as zero in the sample.

Truncation is a more serious problem. In this case, no information is available on either the dependent or explanatory variables when the values of the dependent variable fall above or below some threshold. To see why truncation is a problem, consider Figure 7.2. If observations were available for all of the variables when Y was less than c, the estimated equation would be $Y^* = b_0^* + b_1^* X_1$; if observations for Y less than c were not available, the estimated equation would be $Y = b_0 + b_1 X_1$. The coefficients for the second equation are clearly different from those for the first equation. This is because the coefficients for the second equation are biased.

Figure 7.2 illustrates the bias introduced by truncation. However, if the dependent variable were censored (e.g., negative income values were coded as zero), the extent of bias would be similar. Figure 7.3 represents a less obvious case. This is the type of situation that arises when the dependent variable takes on a seemingly plausible value (e.g., zero expenditures). One would be tempted to use OLS regression in such a case. In his study of durable goods expenditures, however, Tobin (1958) pointed out that the failure to consider the concentration of observations at a particular value of the dependent variable introduces bias into the estimates. The reason for the bias stems from the assumption of OLS regression that the distribution of errors is normal with constant variance σ^2 for each X. It is apparent from Figure 7.3 that the distribution of the residuals will not be normal for each value of X because the residuals will be censored at zero (where they cross the X-axis). The lack of a normal distribution of residuals with constant variance undermines the statistical tests commonly carried out with the regression model.

Figure 7.2
Bias Resulting from a Truncated Sample

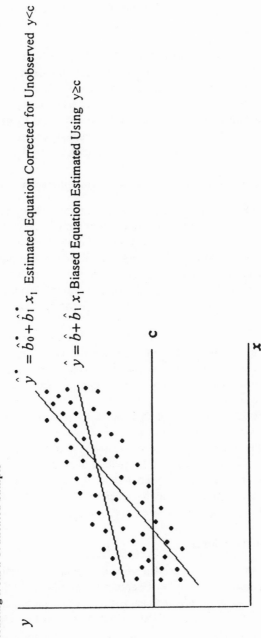

In addition, the concentration of Y values at the threshold c introduces a correlation between the explanatory variables and the residuals which results in biased parameter estimates.

Censoring or truncation of samples does not always result in biased estimates, however. Figure 7.4 illustrates the instance where the sample is truncated based on an explanatory variable. This might be the case, for example, if people of all income levels but only those with high school educations or less were sampled (Berk, 1983). If the relationships between income and education were really linear, the estimated regression coefficients would be unbiased. Even so, however, the efficiency of the estimates would be decreased because of the smaller sample size and perhaps less variation in the education variable.

Implications of Censoring or Truncation for Internal and External Validity

The bias introduced by truncated or censored samples has implications for both the internal and external validity of statistical inferences. External validity refers to the ability to extend inferences to groups other than those analyzed. It is clear from Figure 7.2 that external validity is threatened by truncating or censoring the dependent variable. For example, if negative income values were coded as zero, a regression using only non-negative income values would produce biased coefficient estimates of the factors that determine income levels in the population as a whole.

As Berk (1983) points out, however, truncation and censoring also affect the internal validity of the coefficient estimates. That is, the estimates of the coefficients of explanatory variables that determine income levels will be invalid *even for those with incomes greater than or equal to zero*. To see this, consider Figure 7.2 once again.

From the figure it is apparent that for each value of X, the expected value (mean) of Y is systematically overestimated or underestimated by the regression equation. For low values of X, the regression equation overestimates the mean of Y; for high values of X, the regression equation underestimates the mean of Y. As a result, negative residuals will predominate for low values of X and positive residuals will predominate for high values of X. Thus, the error term will be correlated with X—leading to biased regression coefficient estimates.

Estimation Procedures

The estimation procedures needed when the dependent variable is censored or truncated are a combination of binary choice techniques and OLS regression. On reflection, this is not surprising. If an analyst only wanted to predict the probability that the value of the dependent variable was above or below some limit, logit or probit analysis could be used but some available information would be ignored. On the other hand, if the dependent variable were interval and not censored or truncated, OLS regression could be used to estimate the model. Consequently, a hybrid technique is needed for estimating models when the dependent variable is

Figure 7.3
Bias Resulting from a Concentration of Values in the Dependent Variable at a Particular Point

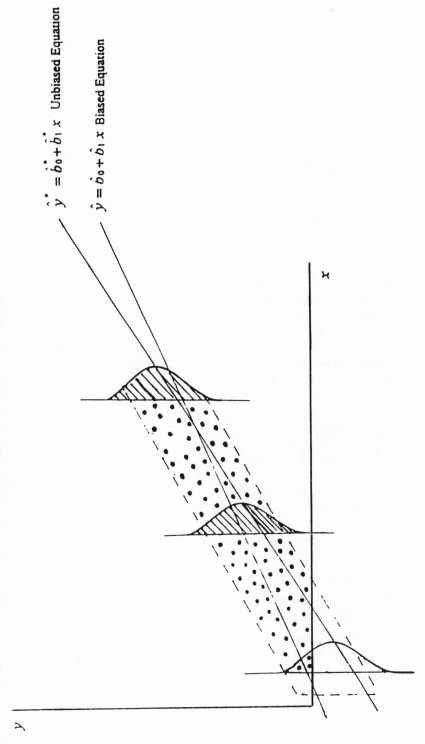

$\hat{y}^{*} = \hat{b}_0^{*} + \hat{b}_1^{*} x$ Unbiased Equation

$\hat{y} = \hat{b}_0 + \hat{b}_1 x$ Biased Equation

Figure 7.4
Example of No Bias as a Result of Censoring on the Explanatory Variable

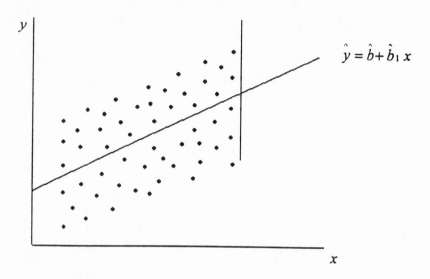

$$\hat{y} = \hat{b} + \hat{b}_1 x$$

censored or truncated. Three such techniques are widely used—Tobit analysis, two-part models, and sample selection models.

TOBIT ANALYSIS

An interesting example of censoring is provided by hospital length of stay. For those not admitted to a hospital, length of stay is equal to zero. Let Y^* denote the observed length of stay. A new length of stay variable, Y, can be defined as:

$$Y=0 \quad if \ Y^* \le 0$$

$$Y=Y^* \quad if \ Y^* > 0$$

Our desire is to estimate the model:

$$Y=\hat{b}_0+\hat{b}_1 X_{i1}+\hat{b}_2 X_{i2}+...+\hat{b}_k X_{ik}+\hat{e}_i$$

where the $\hat{e}_i$ are normally distributed with mean 0 and variance $\hat{\sigma}^2$. Our task is to estimate the $\hat{b}_k$ and $\hat{\sigma}^2$.

The first step in estimating the desired equation is to form the likelihood function:

$$L=\Pi F(B,\sigma^2)\Pi f(B,\sigma^2)$$

where $F(B,\sigma^2)$ is the cumulative probability that the dependent variable is less than or equal to 0 and $f(B,\sigma^2)$ is the probability of a particular length of stay, Y_j, given that $Y_j > 0$. The object is to find values of the coefficients $\hat{b}_k$ and $\hat{\sigma}^2$ that maximize this likelihood function. As with the logit and probit procedures discussed in Chapter 6, this is done by taking the derivatives of the likelihood function with respect to the $\hat{b}_k$ and $\hat{\sigma}^2$, setting the coefficients equal to zero, and iteratively solving the resulting system of nonlinear equations for $\hat{b}_k$ and $\hat{\sigma}^2$.

$$\frac{\partial L}{\partial B_0} = 0$$

$$\frac{\partial L}{\partial B_1} = 0$$

$$\vdots$$

$$\frac{\partial L}{\partial B_k} = 0$$

$$\frac{\partial L}{\partial \sigma^2} = 0$$

The resulting slope coefficients of the Tobit model represent the change in Y with respect to a one-unit increase in X, holding the effects of the other variables constant. Thus, they are interpreted in exactly the same manner as OLS regression coefficients.

Note that the Tobit estimates refer to the entire population, not just members of the population above or below the censored values. Often, however, the conditional estimates are also of interest. McDonald and Moffit (1980) point out that the expected value of Y is equal to the expected value of Y^* given that Y^* is greater than 0, weighted by the probability that Y^* is less than or equal to 0:[8]

$$E(Y) = E(Y^*)F(B,\sigma^2)$$

Using this relationship, they show that the total change in Y with respect to a change in X can be disaggregated into two parts: (1) the change in Y^* with respect to X for those above the limit, weighted by the probability of being above the limit; and (2) the change in the probability of being above the limit, weighted by the expected value of Y^* if above:

$$\frac{\partial E(Y)}{\partial X_i} = \frac{\partial E(Y^*)}{\partial X_i}F(B,\sigma^2) + E(Y^*)\frac{\partial F(B,\sigma^2)}{\partial X_i}$$

Example

Table 7.3 reports the results for an OLS regression model and a Tobit model of hospital length of stay using the 1984 Survey of Income and Program Participation (SIPP). In this sample, about 8 percent of the cases had a hospital stay in 1984. For those who had a hospital stay, a hospital length of stay is also observed—some

Table 7.3
OLSQ and Tobit Models of Hospital Length of Stay

	OLSQ		Tobit	
Variable	Coefficient	*t*-statistic	Coefficient	*t*-statistic
Constant	0.147	0.504	−58.409	−11.872
Age	0.021	3.293	0.311	5.208
Female	−0.278	−1.216	4.175	1.837
White	0.277	0.983	0.149	0.051
Married	0.027	0.116	6.010	2.615
Total Net Worth	−0.119E-05	−1.071	−0.957E-05	−0.934
Total Personal Income	−0.111E-03	−0.934	−0.247E-03	−0.246
Private Insurance	−0.119	−0.405	3.031	1.139
Medicare	1.967	3.562	6.971	1.696
Sigma	—	—	27.814	16.835

patients stayed one night, others two nights, and so forth. Hospital length of stay for these individuals is an interval variable. On the other hand, for those who did not have a hospital stay, the length of stay is zero. Theoretically, Tobit analysis corrects for the bias that would otherwise be introduced by the clustering of so many observations at zero.

The OLS regression results based on all of the cases (including the zeros) indicate that expected hospital length of stay is higher for older persons and those with Medicare coverage. None of the other variables is statistically significant using a two-tailed test at a 95 percent confidence level. The adjusted R^2 is only 1.5 percent.

The Tobit results are quite different from the OLS results. Although the parameter estimate for Age is also positive and statistically significant, Medicare is not statistically significant in the Tobit model. Moreover, the constant term is negative and statistically significant and the coefficient for Married is positive and statistically significant.

The coefficient values of Tobit models are interpreted exactly as if they were regression coefficients. Thus, for example, the coefficient for the Age variable indicates that each year's increase in age increases hospital length of stay by 0.311 days, controlling for the effects of the other variables in the model.

Dummy variables are also interpreted just as in regression analysis. The model reported in Table 7.3 contains five dummy variables—of which only Married is statistically significant at a 95 percent confidence level (two-tailed test). Expected length of stay is 2.6 days longer for married persons than nonmarried persons. The coefficient for Sigma is an estimate of the standard error of the regression, after adjusting for the zero responses.

Because Tobit models are estimated using maximum likelihood methods, the goodness-of-fit measure is the χ^2 measuring the change between the initial and maximum log likelihood functions. Like the F-statistic in regression analysis, the χ^2 tests the null hypothesis that all of the slope coefficients are jointly equal to zero. The χ^2 has degrees of freedom equal to the number of explanatory variables (or slope coefficients) in the model. The calculated value of the χ^2 for the model in Table 7.3 (3,543.4) has 8 degrees of freedom and greatly exceeds the tabulated value of 20.09 at a 99 percent confidence level. Thus, the null hypothesis that the slope coefficients are jointly equal to zero is rejected. Of course, this result could be anticipated because the t-statistics for Age and Married were statistically significant.

It should be recognized that the Tobit model places an extremely strong restriction on the parameter estimates. This restriction is that the probability of having a particular length of stay is a function of the same parameter estimates as the probability of having any length of stay at all. This restriction arises because the Tobit model involves only one set of coefficients.

At one level, this makes sense because the cumulative probability that the value of the dependent variable is above, or below, a particular threshold is found by adding up the individual probabilities above or below the threshold. Yet, intuitively, one might expect the *variables* that influence admission to a hospital to be quite different from those affecting length of stay. That is, there may be a selection process for patients that are admitted to the hospital. Moreover, people that have a hospital stay may differ in both observable and unobservable ways from those that do not have a hospital stay. Failure to account for these unobservable variables introduces the possibility of sample selection bias. It is to this type of problem that we now turn.

SAMPLE SELECTION MODELS

The problem of sample selection bias can be very subtle and is best understood with an example. In the 1960s and 1970s labor economists were struggling with how to best estimate labor supply equations. At first, they estimated hours of labor supplied using hours and wage data only for workers. Gradually, however, labor economists came to realize that using data only on workers might not represent the relationship between the determinants of labor supply and hours worked for all people. In particular, nonworkers might be out of the labor force because the wages offered were not high enough. As a consequence, the determinants of labor supply might be fundamentally different for those currently working and those not in the labor force. Using data only on workers, therefore, could lead to biased coefficient estimates for the variables that are the determinants of labor supply.

To handle this problem, labor economists came to view labor supply as a two-step process. First, persons are hypothesized to decide whether to participate in the labor force or not. Second, those who decide to participate in the labor force decide how many hours of labor to supply. Such "second generation" labor supply models (Killingsworth, 1983) are estimated in two steps. In the first step, a probit model of the probability of participating in the labor force is estimated. The estimated probabilities are used to calculate a quantity known as the inverse mills ratio, which is a measure of unobserved variables in the participation decision. In the second equation, the estimated inverse mills ratio from the first equation is entered as an additional explanatory variable in the hours equation using observations for workers only.

The two-step procedure just described was developed by James Heckman (1976, 1979). It provides an alternative to the Tobit model for problems involving censored dependent variables when it is assumed that there is a selection process that determines whether the dependent variable is observed. Formally, the problem can be stated as follows:

$$Y = \hat{b}_0 + \hat{b}_1 X_1 + \hat{b}_2 X_2 + ... + \hat{b}_k X_k + \hat{e}_i$$
$$Z^* = \hat{a}_0 + \hat{a}_1 V_1 + \hat{a}_2 V_2 + ... + \hat{a}_l V_l + u_i$$

where Z^* is a variable that determines the selection of observations on Y. Unfortunately, Z^* is not observed. Instead, a related variable Z is observed, where:

$$Z = 1 \ if \ Z^* > 0$$

and

$$Z = 0 \ if \ Z^* \leq 0$$

If it is further assumed that individuals participate in the labor force when $Z^* > 0$ and do not if $Z^* \leq 0$ (this is an arbitrary normalization that does not affect the results), it follows that individuals will participate in the labor force when

$$\mu_i > -AV$$

where A is a vector of parameter estimates and V is a vector of variables involved in the labor force selection process, Z^*.

Johnson and Kotz (1972) show that the expected value for the residuals of the hours equation is given by:

$$E(e_i | \mu_i > -AV) = -\frac{\sigma_{12}}{(\sigma_{22})^{\frac{1}{2}}} \lambda$$

where σ_{22} is the variance of the selection equation, σ_{12} is the covariance of the two sets of residuals, and

$$\lambda_i = \frac{f(-AV)}{1-F(-AV)} \qquad I=1$$

$$\lambda_i = \frac{-f(-AV)}{F(-AV)} \qquad I=0$$

λ is known as the inverse Mills ratio (IMR) and is a strictly decreasing function of the probability of participating in the labor force, $F(-AV)$. In particular, as the probability of participating in the labor force approaches one, λ approaches zero. This implies that the expected value of e_i is zero in these cases. That is, for people that participate in the labor force, if the predicted probability of participating in the labor force is high based upon observable factors, the influence of unobservable factors must be small; consequently, the bias is small. Conversely, as the probability of participating in the labor force approaches zero, λ approaches infinity. In this instance, the expected value of e_i becomes very large. As a result, the potential for bias is large for individuals who participate in the labor force, but who are predicted *not* to participate in the labor force based upon observable factors. Conceptually, this means that unobservable variables which are responsible for deciding to participate in the labor force are omitted from the equation and the risk of bias is high.

Estimation Method

The estimation method for controlling the effects of sample selection bias involves two steps. In the first step, a probit model of the selection process (e.g., participating in the labor force) is generally estimated. The estimated probabilities from the probit model, which are a function of observable variables, are used to calculate an estimate of the IMR, λ. All individuals have a value for the IMR as a result of their observable characteristics, whether they are actually in the selected sample or not. The outcome (e.g., hours) equation is estimated in the second step with the estimated IMR from the first equation entered as an additional explanatory variable using the observations for the selected sample (e.g., labor force participants) only.[9] The IMR captures the effects of unobserved variables on the outcome variable, enabling unbiased estimates to be obtained for the parameters associated with the observed variables. The estimated coefficient for λ is the ratio:

$$-\frac{\sigma_{12}}{(\sigma_{22})^{\frac{1}{2}}}$$

That is, if the estimated λ is included in the hours equation, the bias from unobserved variables is explicitly modeled and the expected value of e_i is zero. Theoretically, this means that the estimated parameters for the observed variables in the outcome equation are unbiased.

The standard sample selection model just described can be easily extended to the situation where the outcome variable is observed for both groups (e.g., household incomes of workers and non-workers). The values of the IMR for the zero cases are easily obtained by reversing the (1,0) coding of the dependent variable, reestimating the probit model, and recalculating the IMR for the "new" cases that have the value of one (the original zero cases). The IMR used in this type of analysis "stacks" the IMR values corresponding to the "ones" in the two probit models. This approach is often very useful. For example, it is useful for estimating treatment effects in medical outcomes or for evaluating program outcomes because the analysis can be conducted on the pooled sample of outcomes, enabling the treatment effect or program variable to be included in the equation.

Adjusting the Standard Errors in Sample Selection Models

Heckman pointed out that the two-step estimation approach just noted results in biased estimates of the standard errors because it does not account for the correlation between the residuals of the probit and OLS regression equations. Consequently, it is necessary to correct the standard errors in such models before reliable statistical inferences can be drawn from the results. Some econometric programs (e.g., LIMDEP) do this automatically, but most do not (e.g., SAS).

A second approach for obtaining unbiased estimates of parameters and their standard errors in the presence of sample selection is to jointly estimate the probit and OLS equations using full information maximum likelihood. This can be done by maximizing a likelihood function that contains both the probit sample selection equation and the OLS outcome equation. These models involve the estimation of an adjusted standard error for the regression equation (as in a Tobit model), as well as the estimation of the correlation between the residuals of the probit and OLS equations. Several econometric packages contain sample selection procedures that allow joint estimation of the selection and outcome equations (e.g., LIMDEP and TSP).

Although this approach provides unbiased estimates of the parameter estimates and standard errors, maximizing the likelihood function is often problematic because of nonconvergence. In addition, unlike the two-step Heckman model, joint estimation of the probit and OLS equations does not provide a parameter estimate for λ, measuring the bias introduced by unobserved variables.

Example

A sample selection model of hospital length of stay is presented in Table 7.4. The upper portion of the table contains the estimated coefficients and t-statistics for the probit component of the model. Being married, having higher education, poor self-reported health, and higher numbers of doctor visits are all associated with an increased probability of having a hospital stay. In the Heckman model approach, this portion of the model is used to calculate the inverse mills ratio, which measures the effects of unobserved variables on the probability of having a hospitalization.

The lower portion of the table contains the regression coefficients and t-statistics for hospital length of stay. The coefficients for the second portion of a

Table 7.4
Sample Selection Model of Hospital Length of Stay

Variable	Coefficient	t-statistic
Probit Model		
Constant	–2.376	–18.230
Age	0.415E-02	1.874
Female	0.121	1.435
Married	0.239	2.701
Education	0.029	3.064
Poor Health	0.798	7.043
See Doctor	0.041	10.128
Regression Model		
Constant	23.770	3.370
Age	–0.025	–0.382
Female	–7.340	–2.789
White	5.171	1.543
Married	–6.451	–2.403
Totworth	–0.486E-05	–0.524
Income	–0.769E-03	–0.870
Private	–4.379	–1.495
Medicare	5.767	1.380
IMR	–3.656	–1.315

sample selection model are interpreted in the same manner as the coefficients in OLS and Tobit models—as the change in the dependent variable due to a unit increase in an explanatory variable, controlling for the other variables in the equation. A comparison of the lower portion of Table 7.4 with the OLS regression and Tobit results in Table 7.3 indicates that they are quite different from the former. These differences might have been ascribed to the presence of sample selection bias if the IMR variable in Table 7.4 had been statistically significant.

The parameter estimate for the IMR, however, is not statistically significant. Assuming that the model is properly specified (a very *big* assumption), this suggests that there is no significant bias introduced by the omission of unobserved variables in the selection process describing entry into the sample of hospitalized persons. Before making this conclusion, however, it is important to rule out multicollinearity as a possible reason for the statistical insignificance of the IMR. None of the tolerances for the OLS parameter estimates in the second part of the selection model were lower than 0.61 (not shown). The tolerance for the IMR was 0.75—indicating that the statistical insignificance of the IMR was not due to multicollinearity; consequently, it appears that there is no selection bias introduced by unobserved variables.

The statistical insignificance of the IMR indicates that a sample selection model is not necessary. Nevertheless, it is clear from the probit results that several observable variables, which were excluded from the models in Table 7.3, are related to the probability of having a hospitalization. These variables—education, poor health, and doctor visits—should be added to the models in Table 7.3.

OTHER SELECTION BIAS MODELS

Separate Models for Each Group

It is also possible to estimate separate equations for each group, including the relevant IMR in each (e.g., Murnane, Newstead, and Olsen, 1985). This approach has been widely used in the program evaluation literature. The model is as follows:

$$Y^1 = XB^1 + \lambda^1 \Gamma^1 + \sigma_1$$
$$Y^2 = XB^2 + \lambda^2 \Gamma^2 + \sigma_2$$
$$I = ZA + \sigma_3$$

Program effects with this model are assessed as the difference in the expected values:

$$E[Y^1 - Y^B] = [XB^1 - XB^2]$$

This expected value of differences in outcomes has a standard error of:

$$[X'(V^1 + V^2)X]^{\frac{1}{2}}$$

where V^1 and V^2 are the variance-covariance matrices of B^1 and B^2, respectively.

Switching-regime models are a further extension of the model just described. The following set of equations describe a switching-regime model for interstate migration in response to state wage differentials:

$$I = Z\alpha + \epsilon_1$$
$$Wages_{Stayers} = XB_{Stayers} + \epsilon_2$$
$$Wages_{Movers} = XB_{Movers} + \epsilon_3$$
$$I^* = Wages_{Stayers} - Wages_{Movers}$$
$$Wages = Wages_{Stayer} \quad if \ I^* \leq I$$
$$Wages = Wages_{Mover} \quad if \ I^* > I$$

where X and Z are matrices of relevant explanatory variables, α and B are vectors of estimated coefficients, and ϵ_1, ϵ_2, and ϵ_3 are the residuals associated with the three equations.

In the above model, it is assumed that individuals will move only if the wage gap between states is sufficiently large. The unobserved wage threshold, I, is a function of the individual's characteristics. Thus, the wage gap between states is compared to the individual's unobserved wage threshold. If the wage gap is greater than the threshold, the individual will be a mover; if not, the individual will be a stayer (Nakosteen and Zimmer, 1980; Robinson and Tomes, 1982).

Multinomial Logit Selection Models

The sample selection models described to this point have considered only two groups. Lee (1983) presents a sample selection model using a multinomial logit (MNL) model as the first stage selection equation. His approach enables selection effects to be examined for more than two groups (when the IIA assumption is valid). The outcome equation for alternative k is given by:

$$Y_k = XB_k + \Gamma_k \lambda_k + \eta_k$$

where

$$\lambda_k = \frac{f(-ZA_k)}{1 - F(-ZA_k)}$$

This is a straightforward generalization of the standard sample selection model.

Bivariate Probit

A methodological approach to handling selection bias when the dependent variable of interest is a binary variable is provided by the bivariate probit model. Following Wynand and van Praag (1981), the specification of the bivariate probit model is as follows:

$$z_{i1} = B_1 X_{i1} + \epsilon_{i1}, \quad y_{i1} = 1 \ \text{if} \ z_{i1} > 0, \ y_{i1} = 0 \ \text{otherwise}$$

$$z_{i2} = B_2 X_{i2} + \epsilon_{i2}, \quad y_{i2} = 1 \ \text{if} \ z_{i2} > 0, \ y_{i2} = 0 \ \text{otherwise}$$

where ϵ_{i1} and ϵ_{i2} are jointly distributed with a bivariate normal distribution whose marginal distributions have means of zero, variances of one, and a covariance of ρ.

In the bivariate probit model, the first equation describes a binary outcome of interest. The second equation describes the sample selection process. This process is assumed to be a function of the unobserved latent variable z_{i2}, which, in turn, is assumed to be a linear function, $B_2 X_{i2}$, of a set of explanatory variables X_2. When z_{i2} is greater than zero, individuals are assumed to be selected into the sample;

otherwise they are not. This equation is estimated using all of the cases in the sample.

For example, suppose a researcher is interested in estimating a model of elderly migration, but some individuals die before their migration behavior can be observed. In this case, the first equation would model the factors associated with migration behavior for individuals still alive at the time the migration variable is measured. The probability of migration would be assumed to be a function of an unobserved latent variable z_{il}, which, in turn, would be a linear function $B_l X_{il}$ of a set of explanatory variables X_l. This equation would be estimated using only those cases in the second period. In contrast, the survival equation would be estimated using all observations in the first period. The advantage of the bivariate probit procedure is that the two set of coefficients B_l and B_2 are estimated jointly, along with ρ, which corrects the standard errors of the estimated parameters to account for the covariance between ϵ_{il} and ϵ_{i2}.

SPECIFICATION ISSUES IN SELECTION MODELS

A key issue with sample selection models is the need to carry out extensive specification testing to determine, as completely as possible, how well the models correct for selection bias introduced by unobserved variables. In general, it is never possible to be fully confident that the effects of all unobserved variables have been captured, just as it is never possible to be absolutely sure about any other aspects of the model specification. However, by extensive specification testing of the outcome equation in the selection model, as described in Chapter 5, it is possible to gain significant insights into the effectiveness of sample selection methods.

The problem of sample selection models is basically the problem of omitted variables—it is just that the omitted variables are unobservable. If sample selection bias is a problem, therefore, it should be indicated by such factors as autocorrelation in the residuals, correlations between the residuals and the explanatory variables, heteroscedasticity, or other deviations of the residuals from a normal distribution. Consequently, if the original outcome model exhibits one or more of these problems and the "corrected" model does not, a measure of confidence has been gained with regard to the effectiveness of the sample selection methods. In short, testing for proper specification with sample selection models is no different from the usual specification tests in OLS regression models. Bias from the omission of unobserved variables is just a particular type of specification error.

A variety of factors influence how well sample selection models work in practice. For example, if the observed variables used to model the probability of being selected into the sample are exactly the same as those used to model the outcome variable in the second equation, λ will be highly correlated with the observed variables in the second equation, leading to a severe multicollinearity problem. The only thing that prevents the occurrence of perfect multicollinearity in such a case is the fact that λ is a nonlinear function of the observed variables. In these types of situations, it is not possible to properly specify the selection process. In practice, at least one variable should appear in the selection equation that is not included in the outcome equation, and vice versa.

It is important to emphasize that estimating sample selection models is often difficult. Several authors have noted the sensitivity of sample selection models to the specification of the first-stage model. Sample selection models are most often estimated using a first-stage probit model, but other specifications, such as logit, can lead to very different results (Goldberger, 1983). Recent research has attempted to develop estimators that are less sensitive to the normality assumption, but these tend to be restrictive in terms of the number of variables they allow the researcher to include in the model (Manski, 1990; Heckman, 1990). Heckman and Smith (1995), however, have argued convincingly that carefully specified sample selection models yield the same policy conclusions as fully randomized experimental designs using data from several program evaluations. Nevertheless, program evaluations using sample selection methods must be based on models that have been subjected to extensive specification testing before the results of these models can be used with confidence.

Finally, it should be emphasized that Tobit models and sample selection models provide *unconditional* estimates of outcomes for the entire population, not only those with nonzero outcomes alone. Duan et al. (1983) argue that *conditional* models are sometimes more appropriate. Estimation approaches proposed by Duan et al. (1983, 1984) involve multi-part models that appear to be very similar to sample selection models, but are actually quite different.

LONGITUDINAL MODELS

Another extension of the binary dependent variable model occurs when the data are measured over time. Many data bases are longitudinal in nature—the Panel Study of Income Dynamics (PSID), the Survey of Income and Program Participation (SIPP), the National Long-Term Care Survey (NLTCS), and the Health Retirement Survey (HRS)—to name just a few. Longitudinal datasets such as these are extremely rich, but they also present some challenges to researchers.

To illustrate, suppose a sample contains N individuals in the base period who are approaching retirement age (e.g., 62), but none of whom are retired. These same individuals are resurveyed 6 months later and it is found that X_1 of them have retired. This leaves a sample of $N-X_1$ persons at risk of retiring during the next period. Next, the remaining individuals are resurveyed 6 months later and it is found that X_2 individuals have retired. This leaves a sample of $N - (X_1 + X_2)$ at risk of retiring during the next period, and so on. Because of changes in the sample composition as individuals retire, one might expect the risk of retirement for the remaining group to change over time. Moreover, the way this risk is influenced by explanatory variables might change as well. To make matters even more complicated, the risk of retirement at any point in time may also be influenced by sample attrition (individuals dying, moving away, etc.) or by the addition of new individuals to the sample. (New individuals might be added to help keep the sample adequate in size, or some of the individuals who had previously retired might reenter the labor force, thereby reentering the sample.) Finally, there is the problem of right censoring. Right censoring refers to the fact that the data collection has to stop at some point. Consequently, it is possible that the event being studied (e.g., retirement) might occur immediately following the last period observed. Failure to account for this introduces the possibility of right censoring bias.

Discrete-Time Methods

The simplest method for dealing with the issues just described is to estimate a discrete-time model. The most general form of the discrete-time model is as follows:

$$\ln(P(t)/1-P(t))=a(t)+b_1x_1+b_2x_2(t)$$

where $p(t)/1-p(t)$ is the odds of an event occurring to a particular individual at time t, given that the individual is at risk of experiencing the event; $a(t)$ is a set of time-specific dummy variables; X_1 is a set of time-invariant variables (such as sex); and $X_2(t)$ is a set of time-variant variables (such as age).

Estimating discrete-time models generally involves some preliminary data preparation. In the retirement example discussed above, individuals who retired during the first 6 months would contribute one observation, those who retired during the second 6 months would contribute two observations, those who retired during the third 6-month period would contribute three observations, and so on. For each observation, the dependent variable is coded as one if the event occurs (retirement) and zero otherwise. The observations are then all pooled and the model estimated using logit analysis.

The Proportional Hazards Model

Cox (1972) proposed an approach to estimating binary choice models when the data are longitudinal which is known as the proportional hazards model. To understand the proportional hazards model, consider the following equation:

$$log\ h(t) = a(t) + b_1x_1 + b_2x_2 + ... + b_kx_k$$

where $h(t)$ is the hazard of an event, $a(t)$ can be any function of time, and the x_k are variables that do not change with time. In the simplest case, the proportional hazards model assumes that the ratio of the hazards for any two individuals does not change with time—hence the name "proportional hazards model." Actually, this assumption is not a critical feature of proportional hazard models, but it is frequently made because time-variant variables greatly increase the complexity of estimating hazard models. Allison (1995) describes several tests of the proportional hazards assumption for those concerned about its validity in specific situations. He also points out, however, that other problems, such as omitted variables or measurement error, are apt to be more serious.

Cox showed that the likelihood function for the proportional hazards model could be segmented into two components. One component is a function of $a(t)$ and b_k; the other component is a function of b_k alone. If one is willing to live with the loss of information resulting from ignoring the specific times that events occur, then Cox showed that asymptotically unbiased (and normally distributed) estimates of b_k could be obtained by maximizing the portion of the likelihood function containing b_k alone.

The proportional hazards model has been widely used in a variety of policy areas. A review of the use of hazards models in the economics literature prior to the mid-1980s is provided by Kiefer (1988). More-recent references, as well as other techniques for estimating longitudinal models, can be found in Allison (1995).

SUGGESTED READINGS

A number of texts are now available that discuss the theory and estimation of multinomial logit models, nested logit models, sample selection models, and related techniques. The presentations of the theory and estimation of these models, however, tend to be highly technical and are mainly confined to the econometrics literature.

Econometric presentations of multinomial and nested logit models can be found in Maddala (1990), Train (1986), Ben-Akiva and Lerman (1987), and Greene (1993). The book by Train (1986) is the most mathematically accessible of the four.

A good, nontechnical introduction to sample selection models is Berk (1983). Several econometrics texts also contain chapters on sample selection models. See, for example, Ghosh (1991) and Berndt (1991). Chapter 11 of Berndt (1991) is a particularly useful discussion of the use of sample selection models and related techniques in the estimation of labor supply equations. Maddala (1990), Train (1986), and Greene (1993) also contain chapters dealing with sample selection models.

NOTES

1. A closed form cumulative probability distribution generates the cumulative probability directly, rather than requiring summation of the area under the density function.

2. See, for example, McFadden (1973), Domencich and McFadden (1975), Schmidt and Strauss (1975), and Crown, MacAdam, and Ahlburg (1995). In the transportation literature, MNL models are often referred to as conditional logit models, because the models contain variables that are specific to transportation mode choice (such as mode-specific travel time and cost).

3. The example in this section is patterned after Pindyck and Rubinfeld (1991).

4. Note that this is undoubtedly an extremely poor specification because earnings are zero for all nonworkers. In addition, earnings are the product of hours worked and hourly

wages, so the explanatory variable is partly determined by the dependent variable—introducing the possibility of simultaneous equations bias.

5. See Maddala (1990) for a comprehensive discussion of econometric methods for estimating models with limited dependent variables. Maddala (1990) and Green (1993) also discuss ordinal logit and probit models which are not considered in this book.

6. See, for example, the discussion in Ben-Akiva and Lerman (1987, pp. 183–194).

7. Throughout the chapter, we will discuss the case when the values of the dependent variable fall below some threshold. The discussion is equally valid for cases where the dependent variable is censored or truncated above some limit, as well as for more complicated cases with more than one threshold.

8. The discussion of the clustering of observations in the Tobit model has focused on zero values because this is an extremely common value for censoring on the dependent variable. The results, however, are very general and easily extend to censoring at any other point. For example, we might wish to estimate a model of earnings, only to learn that earnings are topcoded at $99,999. In this case, we would observe Y^* for all earnings less than $100,000. But for earnings greater than or equal to $100,000, Y^* would be censored at $99,999. The Tobit model can also be used in this case. Partly because of its flexibility with respect to the threshold value, the Tobit model has been used to study everything from the determinants of the number of extramarital affairs to the number of hours of labor supplied (Amemiya, 1984).

9. See the seminal articles by Heckman (1976, 1979) on sample selection methods for the estimation of labor supply models.

8
Summary of Methods

A large number of multivariate models were presented in Chapters 3 through 7. Many readers may feel overwhelmed by the number of choices and wonder whether they would be able to select the appropriate method for a specific research question.

The choice of the appropriate model is largely determined by the form of the dependent variable. The possibilities are listed in Table 8.1. If the dependent variable is measured on an interval scale, and no sample selection, censoring, or truncation issues are involved, the appropriate method is multiple regression analysis. In applying multiple regression analysis to a particular problem, researchers must be very careful that all of the assumptions of the regression model are upheld. This requires testing for multicollinearity, autocorrelation, heteroscedasticity, and normality of the residuals. If assumptions of the regression model are found to be violated, corrective measures such as transformations of the variables, weighted least squares, time-series modeling, ridge regression, or factor analysis may be required.

It is important to remember, however, that when the assumptions of the regression model *are* met, ordinary least squares estimators are best linear unbiased estimators (BLUE). Moreover, the power of ordinary least squares (OLS) regression to provide useful estimates, even in the presence of fairly severe violations of its assumptions, helps to explain why OLS is so widely used by researchers.

One such violation occurs when the dependent variable is binary. In this instance, the residuals are inherently heteroscedastic and non-normal. Yet even in this case it was shown that OLS tends to provide results that are remarkably similar, in terms of their policy implications, to logit and probit models. On the other hand, with the widespread availability of logit and probit estimation procedures in statistical packages, there is little justification for using OLS when logit and probit are theoretically superior. The one exception to this is the use of OLS as an exploratory technique for model specification. The superior diagnostics

Table 8.1
Summary of Estimation Methods

Interval	Binary	Polychotomous	Interval with Clustered Data Points	Interval with Sample Selection
Ordinary least squares (OLS) regression. OLS estimates are BLUE when assumptions are valid.	Logit or probit analysis. Probit widely used by economists. Logit widely used by everyone else.	Multinomial logit (MNL) or nested logit. Use nested logit if test of IIA property fails.	Tobit analysis. Many problems involving a dependent variable with clustered observations can be treated as sample selection problems.	Heckman two-stage sample selection models.
Variants: Weighted least squares (WLS), ridge regression, Prais-Winston/Cochrane-Orcutt.		Alternatives: Multinomial probit, ordered logit, ordered probit. Multinomial probit computationally burdensome. Not widely used—especially if dependent variable has more than 3 categories. Ordered logit and probit models difficult to interpret.	Two-part models useful for problems with real zeros.	Variants: MNL selection models, switching-regime models, bivariate probit when second stage is also binary.

of OLS are particularly useful in identifying multicollinearity, which is much more difficult to diagnose in logit and probit models.

For most research questions involving a binary dependent variable, logit and probit models are equally valid. Probit models have the advantage of being based on the cumulative normal distribution, which, in the absence of information to the contrary, is a reasonable distribution to assume. On the other hand, the cumulative logistic distribution, which is the basis of the logit model, is very similar empirically to the cumulative normal except in the tails of the distribution. Moreover, the cumulative logistic distribution is computationally much easier to work with. With binary dependent variables, the computational edge of logit models is not of much consequence. When the dependent variable takes on more than two values, however, the computational edge of logit models becomes very important.

When the dependent variable takes on more than two categories, multinomial logit (MNL) models or nested logit models are usually the techniques of choice. The selection between MNL and nested logit models depends upon the statistical support for the independence of irrelevant alternatives (IIA) assumption of MNL models. If there is no statistical evidence for rejecting the IIA assumption, the MNL model should be used. If the IIA assumption is rejected, then a nested logit, ordered logit, ordered probit, or multinomial probit (MNP) model must be estimated.

In theory, MNP models provide an alternative specification to nested logit, order logit, or ordered probit models if tests of the IIA assumption indicate that the MNL model cannot be justified. Unfortunately, MNP models are *very* intensive computationally. For this reason, MNP models are rarely estimated when the dependent variable takes on more than three categories.

Logit models are also widely used in estimating models where a binary dependent variable is measured over time (e.g., in retirement models using longitudinal data). Proportional hazard models commonly use logistic (or closely related) distributions because of their computational advantages over more complicated probability distributions.

The final models discussed in this book were those that (1) involve observations clustered at a particular point (often zero) with an interval scale of measurement for the remaining observations or (2) models that involve an interval dependent variable and a sample selection process.

Both of these types of models involve a probit component and a regression component. Tobit models assume that the same variables and parameter estimates influence whether an observation is above (or below) a particular threshold, as well as what the level of the interval dependent variable is. Tobit models tend to be better behaved in terms of convergence than sample selection models, but they do not allow the researcher to specify separate sets of variables for the sample selection and outcome components of the model.

In contrast, sample selection models *do* allow the variables in the probit and regression components to be different. Sample selection models estimate a probit model of the probability of observing the interval dependent variable. The probit model is used to create an inverse mills ratio, which is entered into the regression model in the second stage as an additional explanatory variable. The addition of the inverse mills ratio results in unbiased coefficient estimates, but the standard errors of the coefficients in the regression model remain biased unless one takes account of the covariance between the residuals of the probit and regression models.

FUTURE DIRECTIONS

Many of the methods described in this book are continuing to develop extremely rapidly. Multiple regression models have now been used for several decades, so new developments involving OLS tend to be in the combination of OLS with other methods. Most commonly, these other methods deal with various types of sample selection. Bivariate probit and switching-regime models (described briefly in Chapter 7) are appearing with increasing frequency in the policy research literature, and further developments are surely just on the horizon.

A particularly exciting area for future developments is that of simultaneous equations in limited dependent variable models. The discussion in this book has focused on single-equation methods, but there are instances in which we might expect "dependent" and "explanatory" variables to be jointly determined and therefore to switch roles in different equations. The theory for simultaneous-equations techniques is well developed for OLS models, but far less so for limited dependent variable models. As survey data on individual behavior become increasingly available—especially longitudinal data on individuals—simultaneity among choices will increasingly occupy the attention of researchers. Readers interested in pursuing these topics further may consult Bowden (1978), Lee (1978), Lee, Maddala, and Trost (1980), Maddala (1986), Nelson and Olson (1978), and Smith and Blundell (1986).

Appendix A

Differential calculus is widely used in statistical modeling for two primary reasons. First, it provides a means of deriving how one variable changes with respect to changes in other variables. In regression analysis, the slope coefficients are the derivatives of the dependent variable with respect to each of the explanatory variables; the slope coefficients measure the change in the dependent variable with respect to a one-unit change in each of the explanatory variables. In nonlinear models such as logit or probit, however, the derivatives are somewhat more complex.

Second, calculus is widely used in statistical modeling because it provides a mechanism for finding the maximum or minimum of many functions. For example, in ordinary least squares regression, we are interested in finding the coefficients that minimize the sum of the squared errors associated with the model (Chapter 3). With maximum likelihood methods, we are interested in finding the values of the coefficients that maximize the likelihood that the sample comes from the population of interest (Chapter 6).

TOTAL FUNCTIONS AND MARGINAL FUNCTIONS

The basic thing to understand about derivatives is that they are functions which describe how some original function changes. To see this, consider the following simple example. Suppose you are operating a hospital on an isolated South Sea island. Suppose also that the hospital's profits are described by:

$$f(y) = 16X - X^2 \qquad (1)$$

where X is the number of hospital beds. We can calculate the total hospital profits associated with a given number of beds by substituting different values for X into the hospital profit function. For example, total hospital profits associated with one, two, and three beds are as follows:

$$f(1)=16-1^2$$
$$=15$$
$$f(2)=16(2)-2^2$$
$$=28$$
$$f(3)=16(3)-3^2$$
$$=39$$

Note, however, that even though total profits seem to increase with the number of beds this is not necessarily true of the marginal profits (i.e., the change in total profits from adding another bed). The marginal profit from adding the first bed is:

$$f(1)-f(0)=15$$

But the marginal profits from adding the second and third beds are:

$$f(2)-f(1)=28-15$$
$$=13$$
$$f(3)-f(2)=39-28$$
$$=11$$

It seems clear that the marginal profits are decreasing with increases in the number of beds. The hospital will maximize its profits if it increases the number of beds to the point where marginal profits (or the increment to profits) are equal to zero. If marginal profits are positive, the hospital can make more profits by adding another bed; if marginal profits are negative, profits are actually decreased by increasing the number of beds further.

How can we find the point of maximum profit other than by trial and error? We need to transform the total profit function into a marginal profit function and find the point where the marginal function is equal to zero.

LIMITS

Intuitively, the way to do this is to examine how total profits change with respect to small changes in the number of beds. Figure A.1 provides a schematic representation of the problem. With X beds, profits will be equal to $f(X)$. If we add ΔX beds, profits will now be a function of $X + \Delta X$ beds or $f(X + \Delta X)$. The change in profits with respect to a change in beds is given by

$$\frac{f(x+\Delta x)-f(x)}{\Delta x}$$

As we make ΔX smaller and smaller, we get a better and better estimate of the instantaneous change in profit with respect to a change in the number of beds. Mathematically, the limit as ΔX approaches zero is given by:

$$\lim_{\Delta x \to 0} \frac{f(x+\Delta x)-f(x)}{\Delta x} \qquad 2$$

Figure A.1
Hospital Profit Function

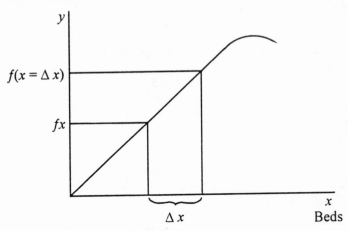

In our profit example, we form $f(x + \Delta X)$ by substituting $(X + \Delta X)$ for X in the profit function. Using equation (2):

$$\underset{\Delta \to 0}{Lim} \frac{[16(x+\Delta x)-(x+\Delta x)^2]-(16x-x^2)]}{\Delta x}$$

$$= \underset{\Delta x \to 0}{Lim} \frac{[16(x+\Delta x)-x^2-2x\Delta x-\Delta x^2]-16x+x^2}{\Delta x}$$

$$= \underset{\Delta x \to 0}{Lim} \frac{16\Delta x-2x\Delta x-\Delta x^2}{\Delta X}$$

$$= \underset{\Delta \to 0}{Lim} \ 16-2x-\Delta x$$

$$= 16-2x$$

Recall that we want to find the point where marginal profits are equal to zero. Setting the above result equal to zero we have:

$$16-2x=0$$

or

$$x=8$$

The profits are maximized with eight beds. The hospital loses money by adding a ninth bed; it fails to capture all possible profits with seven beds. This can be verified by substituting into the total profit function from equation (1). With seven beds, total profits are 63; total profits are 64 with eight beds and 63 with nine beds.

RULES OF DIFFERENTIATION

The process of differentiation using limits is extremely tedious. Fortunately, there are rules for differentiating different types of functions which greatly simplify the process.

1. If $f(X)$ is equal to some constant k, then the derivative $f'(X)=0$.
   Example

$$f(x)=5$$
$$f'(x)=0$$

2. If $f(X)=X^n$, then $f'(x)=nX^{n-1}$.
   Example

$$f(x)=x^3$$
$$f'(x)=3x^2$$

3. If $f(X)=kX^n$, then $f'(X)=nkX^{n-1}$
   Example

$$f(x)=5x^3$$
$$f'(x)=3 \cdot 5x^2$$
$$=15x^2$$

4. If $f(X)$ is the sum of two functions $g(X)$ and $h(X)$, then $f'(X)=g'(X) + h'(X)$.
   Example 1

$$f(x)=x^2+x^4$$
$$Let \ g(x)=x^2 \ and \ h(x)=x^4$$
$$f'(x)=2x+4x^3$$

Example 2 (the hospital example)

$$f(x)=(16x-x^2)$$

$$let \ g(x)=16x$$
$$h(x)=-x^2$$

$$then \ g'(x)=16$$
$$h'(x)=-2x$$

$$therefore \ f'(x)=16-2x$$

5. The product rule: If $f(X)$ is the product of two other functions $g(X)$ and $h(X)$, then

$$f'(x)=g'(x)h(x)+h'(x)g(x)$$

Example

$$f(x)=(2x+3)(3x^2)$$
$$Let \ g(x)=2x+3 \quad and \quad h(x)=3x^2$$
$$then \ g'(x)=2 \quad and \quad h'(x)=6x$$

Therefore:

$$f'(x)=2(3x^2)+6x(2x+3)$$
$$=18x^2+18x$$
$$=18x(x+1)$$

6. The quotient rule: If $f(X)$ is the quotient of two functions $g(X)$ and $h(X)$, then

$$f'(x)=\frac{g'(x)h(x)-g(x)h'(x)}{[h(x)]^2}$$

Example

$$f(x)=\frac{2x^3-1}{4x^2+2x+5}$$

$$g(x)=2x^3-1 \qquad h(x)=4x^2+2x+5$$
$$g'(x)=6x^2 \qquad h'(x)=8x+2$$

$$f'(x)=\frac{(6x^2)(4x^2+2x+5)-(2x^3-1)(8x+2)}{(4x^2+2x+5)^2}$$

7. The chain rule: Suppose one function is also a function of another:

$$y=f(u) \quad where \quad u=g(X)$$

Then the derivative of y with respect to x is equal to the derivative of y with respect to u times the derivative of u with respect to x:

$$\frac{dy}{dx}=\frac{dy}{d\mu}\cdot\frac{d\mu}{dx}$$

Example

$$y=4\mu^3$$
$$\mu=5x+3$$

$$\frac{dy}{dx}=12\mu^2(5)$$
$$=60\mu^2$$

Substituting for μ

$$=60(5x+3)^2$$

The chain rule is very convenient when one is faced with finding the derivatives of functions like

$$y=(x^3+3x^2-5)^{16}$$

Without the chain rule, we would need to expand this expression before we could calculate the derivative. Using the chain rule, however, we can define

$$\mu = (x^3 + 3x^2 - 5)$$

Therefore:

$$y = \mu^{16}$$

$$\frac{dy}{dx} = (16\mu^{15})(3x^2 + 6x)$$
$$= 16(x^3 + 3x^2 - 5)^{15}(3x^2 + 6x)$$

In addition to the general rules for derivatives just discussed, there are some special rules for exponential and logarithmic functions. Exponential functions are extremely important in statistics because exponents are so common in probability distributions. Similarly, logarithmic functions are important because logarithms can be used to linearize nonlinear functions (e.g., exponential expressions or products terms). Moreover, it can be shown that the maximum (or minimum) of a function and the maximum (or minimum) of the logarithm of that function are the same. Because it is generally easier to maximize a linear function, logarithms are widely used to first linearize functions with exponential or product terms before finding the derivative.

8. Exponential functions: If $f(X)=ae^{kx}$, then $f'(X)=ake^{kx}$.
   Example

$$f(x) = 3e^{-4x}$$
$$f'(x) = -12e^{-4x}$$

9. Logarithmic functions: If $f(X)=ln\ x$, then $f'(X)=1/x\ dx$.
   Example 1

$$f(x) = \ln(3x^2 - 4x)$$
$$f'(x) = \frac{1}{(3x^2 - 4x)}(6x - 4)$$

Example 2 (the hospital example again)

$$f(x)=(16x-x^2)$$

$$lnf(x)=\ln(16x-x^2)$$

$$\frac{d\ln f(x)}{dx}=\frac{1}{(16x-x^2)}(16-2x)$$

$$=\frac{16}{(16x-x^2)}-\frac{2x}{(16x-x^2)}$$

$$=16-2x$$

$$=8$$

PARTIAL DERIVATIVES

In estimating models to be used for policy analysis, we are generally interested in functions involving several variables. For example, the probability that a child is growing up in poverty is a function of the employment status of the household head, family type, residential location, and many other factors. It is possible to take the derivative of such a function with respect to individual variables by treating all other variables as though they were constants.

Example 1

$$f(p,y)=4p^2-9py+6y^3$$
$$\frac{\partial f}{\partial p}=8p-9y$$
$$\frac{\partial f}{\partial y}=-9p+18y^2$$

Example 2

$$f(t,g,r)=14t^3gr+12g^2t+7r^4$$
$$\frac{\partial f}{\partial t}=42t^2gr+12g^2$$
$$\frac{\partial f}{\partial g}=14t^3r+24gt$$
$$\frac{\partial f}{\partial r}=14t^3g+28r^3$$

Appendix B

Table B.1
Normal Curve Areas

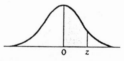

z	.00	.01	.02	.03	.04	.05	.06	.07	.08	.09
0.0	.0000	.0040	.0080	.0120	.0160	.0199	.0239	.0279	.0319	.0359
0.1	.0398	.0438	.0478	.0517	.0557	.0596	.0636	.0675	.0714	.0753
0.2	.0793	.0832	.0871	.0910	.0948	.0987	.1026	.1064	.1103	.1141
0.3	.1179	.1217	.1255	.1293	.1331	.1368	.1406	.1443	.1480	.1517
0.4	.1554	.1591	.1628	.1664	.1700	.1736	.1772	.1808	.1844	.1879
0.5	.1915	.1950	.1985	.2019	.2054	.2088	.2123	.2157	.2190	.2224
0.6	.2257	.2291	.2324	.2357	.2389	.2422	.2454	.2486	.2517	.2549
0.7	.2580	.2611	.2642	.2673	.2704	.2734	.2764	.2794	.2823	.2852
0.8	.2881	.2910	.2939	.2967	.2995	.3023	.3051	.3078	.3106	.3133
0.9	.3159	.3186	.3212	.3238	.3264	.3289	.3315	.3340	.3365	.3389
1.0	.3413	.3438	.3461	.3485	.3508	.3531	.3554	.3577	.3599	.3621
1.1	.3643	.3665	.3686	.3708	.3729	.3749	.3770	.3790	.3810	.3830
1.2	.3849	.3869	.3888	.3907	.3925	.3944	.3962	.3980	.3997	.4015
1.3	.4032	.4049	.4066	.4082	.4099	.4115	.4131	.4147	.4162	.4177
1.4	.4192	.4207	.4222	.4236	.4251	.4265	.4279	.4292	.4306	.4319
1.5	.4332	.4345	.4357	.4370	.4382	.4394	.4406	.4418	.4429	.4441
1.6	.4452	.4463	.4474	.4484	.4495	.4505	.4515	.4525	.4535	.4545
1.7	.4554	.4564	.4573	.4582	.4591	.4599	.4608	.4616	.4625	.4633
1.8	.4641	.4649	.4656	.4664	.4671	.4678	.4686	.4693	.4699	.4706
1.9	.4713	.4719	.4726	.4732	.4738	.4744	.4750	.4756	.4761	.4767
2.0	.4772	.4778	.4783	.4788	.4793	.4798	.4803	.4808	.4812	.4817
2.1	.4821	.4826	.4830	.4834	.4838	.4842	.4846	.4850	.4854	.4857
2.2	.4861	.4864	.4868	.4871	.4875	.4878	.4881	.4884	.4887	.4890
2.3	.4893	.4896	.4898	.4901	.4904	.4906	.4909	.4911	.4913	.4916
2.4	.4918	.4920	.4922	.4925	.4927	.4929	.4931	.4932	.4934	.4936
2.5	.4938	.4940	.4941	.4943	.4945	.4946	.4948	.4949	.4951	.4952
2.6	.4953	.4955	.4956	.4957	.4959	.4960	.4961	.4962	.4963	.4964
2.7	.4965	.4966	.4967	.4968	.4969	.4970	.4971	.4972	.4973	.4974
2.8	.4974	.4975	.4976	.4977	.4977	.4978	.4979	.4979	.4980	.4981
2.9	.4981	.4982	.4982	.4983	.4984	.4984	.4985	.4985	.4986	.4986
3.0	.4987	.4987	.4987	.4988	.4988	.4989	.4989	.4989	.4990	.4990

Table B.2
Percentage Points of the *t*-Distribution

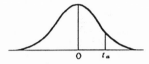

d.f	a = .10	a = .05	a = .025	a = .010	a = .005
1	3.078	6.314	12.706	31.821	63.657
2	1.886	2.920	4.303	6.965	9.925
3	1.638	2.353	3.182	4.541	5.841
4	1.533	2.132	2.776	3.747	4.604
5	1.476	2.015	2.571	3.365	4.032
6	1.440	1.943	2.447	3.143	3.707
7	1.415	1.895	2.365	2.998	3.499
8	1.397	1.860	2.306	2.896	3.355
9	1.383	1.833	2.262	2.821	3.250
10	1.372	1.812	2.228	2.764	3.169
11	1.363	1.796	2.201	2.718	3.106
12	1.356	1.782	2.179	2.681	3.055
13	1.350	1.771	2.160	2.650	3.012
14	1.345	1.761	2.145	2.624	2.977
15	1.341	1.753	2.131	2.602	2.947
16	1.337	1.746	2.120	2.583	2.921
17	1.333	1.740	2.110	2.567	2.898
18	1.330	1.734	2.101	2.552	2.878
19	1.328	1.729	2.093	2.539	2.861
20	1.325	1.725	2.086	2.528	2.845
21	1.323	1.721	2.080	2.518	2.831
22	1.321	1.717	2.074	2.508	2.819
23	1.319	1.714	2.069	2.500	2.807
24	1.318	1.711	2.064	2.492	2.797
25	1.316	1.708	2.060	2.485	2.787
26	1.315	1.706	2.056	2.479	2.779
27	1.314	1.703	2.052	2.473	2.771
28	1.313	1.701	2.048	2.467	2.763
29	1.311	1.699	2.045	2.462	2.756
inf.	1.282	1.645	1.960	2.326	2.576

Source: Based on Maxine Merrington, "Table of Percentage Points of the *t*-Distribution." *Biometrika.*
Vol. 32 (1942), p. 300. Reproduced by permission of the *Biometrika* Trustees.

Table B.3
Values of X² a, v

v	a = 0.995	a = 0.99	a = 0.975	a = 0.95	a = 0.05	a = 0.025	a = 0.01	a = 0.005	v
1	0.0000393	0.000157	0.00098	0.00393	3.841	5.024	6.635	7.879	1
2	0.0100	0.0201	0.0506	0.103	5.991	7.378	9.210	10.597	2
3	0.0717	0.115	0.216	0.352	7.815	9.348	11.345	12.838	3
4	0.207	0.297	0.484	0.711	9.488	11.143	13.277	14.860	4
5	0.412	0.554	0.831	1.145	11.070	12.832	15.086	16.750	5
6	0.676	0.872	1.237	1.635	12.592	14.449	16.812	18.548	6
7	0.989	1.239	1.690	2.167	14.067	16.013	18.475	20.278	7
8	1.344	1.646	2.180	2.733	15.507	17.535	20.090	21.955	8
9	1.735	2.088	2.700	3.325	16.919	19.023	21.666	23.589	9
10	2.156	2.558	3.247	3.940	18.307	20.483	23.209	25.188	10
11	2.603	3.053	3.816	4.575	19.675	21.920	24.725	26.757	11
12	3.074	3.571	4.404	5.226	21.026	23.337	26.217	28.300	12
13	3.565	4.107	5.009	5.892	22.362	24.736	27.688	29.819	13
14	4.075	4.660	5.629	6.571	23.685	26.119	29.141	31.319	14
15	4.601	5.229	6.262	7.261	24.996	27.488	30.578	32.801	15
16	5.142	5.812	6.908	7.962	26.296	28.845	32.000	34.267	16
17	5.697	6.408	7.564	8.672	27.587	30.191	33.409	35.718	17
18	6.265	7.015	8.231	9.390	28.869	31.526	34.805	37.156	18
19	6.844	7.633	8.907	10.117	30.144	32.852	36.191	38.582	19
20	7.434	8.260	9.591	10.851	31.410	34.170	37.566	39.997	20
21	8.034	8.897	10.283	11.591	32.671	35.479	38.932	41.401	21
22	8.643	9.542	10.982	12.338	33.924	36.781	40.289	42.796	22
23	9.260	10.196	11.689	13.091	35.172	38.076	41.638	44.181	23
24	9.886	10.856	12.401	13.848	36.415	39.364	42.980	45.558	24
25	10.520	11.524	13.120	14.611	37.652	40.646	44.314	46.928	25
26	11.160	12.198	13.844	15.379	38.885	41.923	45.642	48.290	26
27	11.808	12.879	14.573	16.151	40.113	43.194	46.963	49.645	27
28	12.461	13.565	15.308	16.928	41.337	44.461	48.278	50.993	28
29	13.121	14.256	16.047	17.708	42.557	45.722	49.588	52.336	29
30	13.787	14.953	16.791	18.493	43.773	46.979	50.892	53.672	30

Source: Abridged from Table 8, "Percentage Points of the X²-Distribution," pp. 136–137. *Biometrika Tables for Statisticians.* Vol. 1, 3rd. edition (1966), edited by E. S. Pearson and H. O. Hartley. Cambridge, England: Cambridge University Press. Reproduced by permission of the *Biometrika* Trustees.

Table B.4A
Values of $F_{0.05}, \nu_1, \nu_2$

ν_1 = degrees of freedom for numerator

ν_2	1	2	3	4	5	6	7	8	9	10	12	15	20	24	30	40	60	120	∞
1	161	200	216	225	230	234	237	239	241	242	244	246	248	249	250	251	252	253	254
2	18.5	19.0	19.2	19.2	19.3	19.3	19.4	19.4	19.4	19.4	19.4	19.4	19.4	19.5	19.5	19.5	19.5	19.5	19.5
3	10.1	9.55	9.28	9.12	9.01	8.94	8.89	8.85	8.81	8.79	8.74	8.70	8.66	8.64	8.62	8.59	8.57	8.55	8.53
4	7.71	6.94	6.59	6.39	6.26	6.16	6.09	6.04	6.00	5.96	5.91	5.86	5.80	5.77	5.75	5.72	5.69	5.66	5.63
5	6.61	5.79	5.41	5.19	5.05	4.95	4.88	4.82	4.77	4.74	4.68	4.62	4.56	4.53	4.50	4.46	4.43	4.40	4.37
6	5.99	5.14	4.76	4.53	4.39	4.28	4.21	4.15	4.10	4.06	4.00	3.94	3.87	3.84	3.81	3.77	3.74	3.70	3.67
7	5.59	4.74	4.35	4.12	3.97	3.87	3.79	3.73	3.68	3.64	3.57	3.51	3.44	3.41	3.38	3.34	3.30	3.27	3.23
8	5.32	4.46	4.07	3.84	3.69	3.58	3.50	3.44	3.39	3.35	3.28	3.22	3.15	3.12	3.08	3.04	3.01	2.97	2.93
9	5.12	4.26	3.86	3.63	3.48	3.37	3.29	3.23	3.18	3.14	3.07	3.01	2.94	2.90	2.86	2.83	2.79	2.75	2.71
10	4.96	4.10	3.71	3.48	3.33	3.22	3.14	3.07	3.02	2.98	2.91	2.85	2.77	2.74	2.70	2.66	2.62	2.58	2.54
11	4.84	3.98	3.59	3.36	3.20	3.09	3.01	2.95	2.90	2.85	2.79	2.72	2.65	2.61	2.57	2.53	2.49	2.45	2.40
12	4.75	3.89	3.49	3.26	3.11	3.00	2.91	2.85	2.80	2.75	2.69	2.62	2.54	2.51	2.47	2.43	2.38	2.34	2.30
13	4.67	3.81	3.41	3.18	3.03	2.92	2.83	2.77	2.71	2.67	2.60	2.53	2.46	2.42	2.38	2.34	2.30	2.25	2.21
14	4.60	3.74	3.34	3.11	2.96	2.85	2.76	2.70	2.65	2.60	2.53	2.46	2.39	2.35	2.31	2.27	2.22	2.18	2.13
15	4.54	3.68	3.29	3.06	2.90	2.79	2.71	2.64	2.59	2.54	2.48	2.40	2.33	2.29	2.25	2.20	2.16	2.11	2.07
16	4.49	3.63	3.24	3.01	2.85	2.74	2.66	2.59	2.54	2.49	2.42	2.35	2.28	2.24	2.19	2.15	2.11	2.06	2.01
17	4.45	3.59	3.20	2.96	2.81	2.70	2.61	2.55	2.49	2.45	2.38	2.31	2.23	2.19	2.15	2.10	2.06	2.01	1.96
18	4.41	3.55	3.16	2.93	2.77	2.66	2.58	2.51	2.46	2.41	2.34	2.27	2.19	2.15	2.11	2.06	2.02	1.97	1.92
19	4.38	3.52	3.13	2.90	2.74	2.63	2.54	2.48	2.42	2.38	2.31	2.23	2.16	2.11	2.07	2.03	1.98	1.93	1.88
20	4.35	3.49	3.10	2.87	2.71	2.60	2.51	2.45	2.39	2.35	2.28	2.20	2.12	2.08	2.04	1.99	1.95	1.90	1.84
21	4.32	3.47	3.07	2.84	2.68	2.57	2.49	2.42	2.37	2.32	2.25	2.18	2.10	2.05	2.01	1.96	1.92	1.87	1.81
22	4.30	3.44	3.05	2.82	2.66	2.55	2.46	2.40	2.34	2.30	2.23	2.15	2.07	2.03	1.98	1.94	1.89	1.84	1.78
23	4.28	3.42	3.03	2.80	2.64	2.53	2.44	2.37	2.32	2.27	2.20	2.13	2.05	2.01	1.96	1.91	1.86	1.81	1.76
24	4.26	3.40	3.01	2.78	2.62	2.51	2.42	2.36	2.30	2.25	2.18	2.11	2.03	1.98	1.94	1.89	1.84	1.79	1.73
25	4.24	3.39	2.99	2.76	2.60	2.49	2.40	2.34	2.28	2.24	2.16	2.09	2.01	1.96	1.92	1.87	1.82	1.77	1.71
30	4.17	3.32	2.92	2.69	2.53	2.42	2.33	2.27	2.21	2.16	2.09	2.01	1.93	1.89	1.84	1.79	1.74	1.68	1.62
40	4.08	3.23	2.84	2.61	2.45	2.34	2.25	2.18	2.12	2.08	2.00	1.92	1.84	1.79	1.74	1.69	1.64	1.58	1.51
60	4.00	3.15	2.76	2.53	2.37	2.25	2.17	2.10	2.04	1.99	1.92	1.84	1.75	1.70	1.65	1.59	1.53	1.47	1.39
120	3.92	3.07	2.68	2.45	2.29	2.18	2.09	2.02	1.96	1.91	1.83	1.75	1.66	1.61	1.55	1.50	1.43	1.35	1.25
∞	3.84	3.00	2.60	2.37	2.21	2.10	2.01	1.94	1.88	1.83	1.75	1.67	1.57	1.52	1.46	1.39	1.32	1.22	1.00

ν_2 = degrees of freedom for denominator

Source: Abridged from M. Merrington and C. M. Thompson, "Tables of Percentage Points of the Inverted Beta (*F*) Distribution." *Biometrika*, Vol. 33 (1943), p. 80–81. Reproduced by permission of the *Biometrika* Trustees.

Table B.4B
Values of $F_{0.01}$, ν_1, ν_2

ν_1 = degrees of freedom for numerator

ν_2	1	2	3	4	5	6	7	8	9	10	12	15	20	24	30	40	60	120	∞
1	4052	5000	5403	5625	5764	5859	5928	5982	6023	6056	6106	6157	6209	6235	6261	6287	6313	6339	6366
2	98.5	99.0	99.2	99.2	99.3	99.3	99.4	99.4	99.4	99.4	99.4	99.4	99.4	99.5	99.5	99.5	99.5	99.5	99.5
3	34.1	30.8	29.5	28.7	28.2	27.9	27.7	27.5	27.3	27.2	27.1	26.9	26.9	26.6	26.5	26.4	26.3	26.2	26.1
4	21.2	18.0	16.7	16.0	15.5	15.2	15.0	14.8	14.7	14.5	14.4	14.2	14.0	13.9	13.8	13.7	13.7	13.6	13.5
5	16.3	13.3	12.1	11.4	11.0	10.7	10.5	10.3	10.2	10.1	9.89	9.72	9.55	9.47	9.38	9.29	9.20	9.11	9.02
6	13.7	10.9	9.78	9.15	8.75	8.47	8.26	8.10	7.98	7.87	7.72	7.56	7.40	7.31	7.23	7.14	7.06	6.97	6.88
7	12.2	9.55	8.45	7.85	7.46	7.19	6.99	6.84	6.72	6.62	6.47	6.31	6.16	6.07	5.99	5.91	5.82	5.74	5.65
8	11.3	8.65	7.59	7.01	6.63	6.37	6.18	6.03	5.91	5.81	5.67	5.52	5.36	5.28	5.20	5.12	5.03	4.95	4.86
9	10.6	8.02	6.99	6.42	6.06	5.80	5.61	5.47	5.35	5.26	5.11	4.96	4.81	4.73	4.65	4.57	4.48	4.40	4.31
10	10.0	7.56	6.55	5.99	5.64	5.39	5.20	5.06	4.94	4.85	4.71	4.56	4.41	4.33	4.25	4.17	4.08	4.00	3.91
11	9.65	7.21	6.22	5.67	5.32	5.07	4.89	4.74	4.63	4.54	4.40	4.25	4.10	4.02	3.94	3.86	3.78	3.69	3.60
12	9.33	6.93	5.95	5.41	5.06	4.82	4.64	4.50	4.39	4.30	4.16	4.01	3.86	3.78	3.70	3.62	3.54	3.45	3.36
13	9.07	6.70	5.74	5.21	4.86	4.62	4.44	4.30	4.19	4.10	3.96	3.82	3.66	3.59	3.51	3.43	3.34	3.25	3.17
14	8.86	6.51	5.56	5.04	4.70	4.46	4.28	4.14	4.03	3.94	3.80	3.66	3.51	3.43	3.35	3.27	3.18	3.09	3.00
15	8.68	6.36	5.42	4.89	4.56	4.32	4.14	4.00	3.89	3.80	3.67	3.52	3.37	3.29	3.21	3.13	3.05	2.96	2.87
16	8.53	6.23	5.29	4.77	4.44	4.20	4.03	3.89	3.78	3.69	3.55	3.41	3.26	3.18	3.10	3.02	2.93	2.84	2.75
17	8.40	6.11	5.19	4.67	4.34	4.10	3.93	3.79	3.68	3.59	3.46	3.31	3.16	3.08	3.00	2.92	2.83	2.75	2.65
18	8.29	6.01	5.09	4.58	4.25	4.01	3.84	3.71	3.60	3.51	3.37	3.23	3.08	3.00	2.92	2.84	2.75	2.66	2.57
19	8.19	5.93	5.01	4.50	4.17	3.94	3.77	3.63	3.52	3.43	3.30	3.15	3.00	2.92	2.84	2.76	2.67	2.58	2.49
20	8.10	5.85	4.94	4.43	4.10	3.87	3.70	3.56	3.46	3.37	3.23	3.09	2.94	2.86	2.78	2.69	2.61	2.52	2.42
21	8.02	5.78	4.87	4.37	4.04	3.81	3.64	3.51	3.40	3.31	3.17	3.03	2.88	2.80	2.72	2.64	2.55	2.46	2.36
22	7.95	5.72	4.82	4.31	3.99	3.76	3.59	3.45	3.35	3.26	3.12	2.98	2.83	2.75	2.67	2.58	2.50	2.40	2.31
23	7.88	5.66	4.76	4.26	3.94	3.71	3.54	3.41	3.30	3.21	3.07	2.93	2.78	2.70	2.62	2.54	2.45	2.35	2.26
24	7.82	5.61	4.72	4.22	3.90	3.67	3.50	3.36	3.26	3.17	3.03	2.89	2.74	2.66	2.58	2.49	2.40	2.31	2.21
25	7.77	5.57	4.68	4.18	3.86	3.63	3.46	3.32	3.22	3.13	2.99	2.85	2.70	2.62	2.53	2.45	2.36	2.27	2.17
30	7.56	5.39	4.51	4.02	3.70	3.47	3.30	3.17	3.07	2.98	2.84	2.70	2.55	2.47	2.39	2.30	2.21	2.11	2.01
40	7.31	5.18	4.31	3.83	3.51	3.29	3.12	2.99	2.89	2.80	2.66	2.52	2.37	2.29	2.20	2.11	2.02	1.92	1.80
60	7.08	4.98	4.13	3.65	3.34	3.12	2.95	2.82	2.72	2.63	2.50	2.35	2.20	2.12	2.03	1.94	1.84	1.73	1.60
120	6.85	4.79	3.95	3.48	3.17	2.96	2.79	2.66	2.56	2.47	2.34	2.19	2.03	1.95	1.86	1.76	1.66	1.53	1.38
∞	6.63	4.61	3.78	3.32	3.02	2.80	2.64	2.51	2.41	2.32	2.18	2.04	1.88	1.79	1.70	1.59	1.47	1.32	1.00

ν_2 = degrees of freedom for denominator

Source: Abridged from M. Merrington and C. M. Thompson, "Tables of Percentage Points of the Inverted Beta (*F*) Distribution." *Biometrika*, Vol. 33 (1943), p. 84–85. Reproduced by permission of the *Biometrika* Trustees.

Table B.5A
Significance Points of d_L and d_U: 5%

n	k' = 1		k' = 2		k' = 3		k' = 4		k' = 5	
	d_L	d_U	d_L	d_U	d_L	d_U	d_L	d_U	d_L	d_U
15	1.08	1.36	0.95	1.54	0.82	1.75	0.69	1.97	0.56	2.21
16	1.10	1.37	0.98	1.54	0.86	1.73	0.74	1.93	0.62	2.15
17	1.13	1.38	1.02	1.54	0.90	1.71	0.78	1.90	0.67	2.10
18	1.16	1.39	1.05	1.53	0.93	1.69	0.82	1.87	0.71	2.06
19	1.18	1.40	1.08	1.53	0.97	1.68	0.86	1.85	0.75	2.02
20	1.20	1.41	1.10	1.54	1.00	1.68	0.90	1.83	0.79	1.99
21	1.22	1.42	1.13	1.54	1.03	1.67	0.93	1.81	0.83	1.96
22	1.24	1.43	1.15	1.54	1.05	1.66	0.96	1.80	0.86	1.94
23	1.26	1.44	1.17	1.54	1.08	1.66	0.99	1.79	0.90	1.92
24	1.27	1.45	1.19	1.55	1.10	1.66	1.01	1.78	0.93	1.90
25	1.29	1.45	1.21	1.55	1.12	1.66	1.04	1.77	0.95	1.89
26	1.30	1.46	1.22	1.55	1.14	1.65	1.06	1.76	0.98	1.88
27	1.32	1.47	1.24	1.56	1.16	1.65	1.08	1.76	1.01	1.86
28	1.33	1.48	1.26	1.56	1.18	1.65	1.10	1.75	1.03	1.85
29	1.34	1.48	1.27	1.56	1.20	1.65	1.12	1.74	1.05	1.84
30	1.35	1.49	1.28	1.57	1.21	1.65	1.14	1.74	1.07	1.83
31	1.36	1.50	1.30	1.57	1.23	1.65	1.16	1.74	1.09	1.83
32	1.37	1.50	1.31	1.57	1.24	1.65	1.18	1.73	1.11	1.82
33	1.38	1.51	1.32	1.58	1.26	1.65	1.19	1.73	1.13	1.81
34	1.39	1.51	1.33	1.58	1.27	1.65	1.21	1.73	1.15	1.81
35	1.40	1.52	1.34	1.58	1.28	1.65	1.22	1.73	1.16	1.80
36	1.41	1.52	1.35	1.59	1.29	1.65	1.24	1.73	1.18	1.80
37	1.42	1.53	1.36	1.59	1.31	1.66	1.25	1.72	1.19	1.80
38	1.43	1.54	1.37	1.59	1.32	1.66	1.26	1.72	1.21	1.79
39	1.43	1.54	1.38	1.60	1.33	1.66	1.27	1.72	1.22	1.79
40	1.44	1.54	1.39	1.60	1.34	1.66	1.29	1.72	1.23	1.79
45	1.48	1.57	1.43	1.62	1.38	1.67	1.34	1.72	1.29	1.78
50	1.50	1.59	1.46	1.63	1.42	1.67	1.38	1.72	1.34	1.77
55	1.53	1.60	1.49	1.64	1.45	1.68	1.41	1.72	1.38	1.77
60	1.55	1.62	1.51	1.65	1.48	1.69	1.44	1.73	1.41	1.77
65	1.57	1.63	1.54	1.66	1.50	1.70	1.47	1.73	1.44	1.77
70	1.58	1.64	1.55	1.67	1.52	1.70	1.49	1.74	1.46	1.77
75	1.60	1.65	1.57	1.68	1.54	1.71	1.51	1.74	1.49	1.77
80	1.61	1.66	1.59	1.69	1.56	1.72	1.53	1.74	1.51	1.77
85	1.62	1.67	1.60	1.70	1.57	1.72	1.55	1.75	1.52	1.77
90	1.63	1.68	1.61	1.70	1.59	1.73	1.57	1.75	1.54	1.78
95	1.64	1.69	1.62	1.71	1.60	1.73	1.58	1.75	1.56	1.78
100	1.65	1.69	1.63	1.72	1.61	1.74	1.59	1.76	1.57	1.78

Note: k' = number of explanatory variables excluding the constant term.

Source: J. Durbin and G. S. Watson, "Testing for Serial Correlation in Least Squares Regression—II." *Biometrika*, Vol. 38 (1951), Table 4, "Significance Points of d_l and d_u: 5%," p. 173. Reproduced by permission of the *Biometrika* Trustees.

Table B.5B
Significance Points of d$_L$ and d$_U$: 2.5%

n	k' = 1		k' = 2		k' = 3		k' = 4		k' = 5	
	d$_L$	d$_U$	d$_L$	d$_U$	d$_L$	d$_U$	d$_L$	d$_U$	d$_L$	d$_U$
15	0.95	1.23	0.83	1.40	0.71	1.61	0.59	1.84	0.48	2.09
16	0.98	1.24	0.86	1.40	0.75	1.59	0.64	1.80	0.53	2.03
17	1.01	1.25	0.90	1.40	0.79	1.58	0.68	1.77	0.57	1.98
18	1.03	1.26	0.93	1.40	0.82	1.56	0.72	1.74	0.62	1.93
19	1.06	1.28	0.96	1.41	0.86	1.55	0.76	1.72	0.66	1.90
20	1.08	1.28	0.99	1.41	0.89	1.55	0.79	1.70	0.70	1.87
21	1.10	1.30	1.01	1.41	0.92	1.54	0.83	1.69	0.73	1.84
22	1.12	1.31	1.04	1.42	0.95	1.54	0.86	1.68	0.77	1.82
23	1.14	1.32	1.06	1.42	0.97	1.54	0.89	1.67	0.80	1.80
24	1.16	1.33	1.08	1.43	1.00	1.54	0.91	1.66	0.83	1.79
25	1.18	1.34	1.10	1.43	1.02	1.54	0.94	1.65	0.86	1.77
26	1.19	1.35	1.12	1.44	1.04	1.54	0.96	1.65	0.88	1.76
27	1.21	1.36	1.13	1.44	1.06	1.54	0.99	1.64	0.91	1.75
28	1.22	1.37	1.15	1.45	1.08	1.54	1.01	1.64	0.93	1.74
29	1.24	1.38	1.17	1.45	1.10	1.54	1.03	1.63	0.96	1.73
30	1.25	1.38	1.18	1.46	1.12	1.54	1.05	1.63	0.98	1.73
31	1.26	1.39	1.20	1.47	1.13	1.55	1.07	1.63	1.00	1.72
32	1.27	1.40	1.21	1.47	1.15	1.55	1.08	1.63	1.02	1.71
33	1.28	1.41	1.22	1.48	1.16	1.55	1.10	1.63	1.04	1.71
34	1.29	1.41	1.24	1.48	1.17	1.55	1.12	1.63	1.06	1.70
35	1.30	1.42	1.25	1.48	1.19	1.55	1.13	1.63	1.07	1.70
36	1.31	1.43	1.26	1.49	1.20	1.56	1.15	1.63	1.09	1.70
37	1.32	1.43	1.27	1.49	1.21	1.56	1.16	1.62	1.10	1.70
38	1.33	1.44	1.28	1.50	1.23	1.56	1.17	1.62	1.12	1.70
39	1.34	1.44	1.29	1.50	1.24	1.56	1.19	1.63	1.13	1.69
40	1.35	1.45	1.30	1.51	1.25	1.57	1.20	1.63	1.15	1.69
45	1.39	1.48	1.34	1.53	1.30	1.58	1.25	1.63	1.21	1.69
50	1.42	1.50	1.38	1.54	1.34	1.59	1.30	1.64	1.26	1.69
55	1.45	1.52	1.41	1.56	1.37	1.60	1.33	1.64	1.30	1.69
60	1.47	1.54	1.44	1.57	1.40	1.61	1.37	1.65	1.33	1.69
65	1.49	1.55	1.46	1.59	1.43	1.62	1.40	1.66	1.36	1.69
70	1.51	1.57	1.48	1.60	1.45	1.63	1.42	1.66	1.39	1.70
75	1.53	1.58	1.50	1.61	1.47	1.64	1.45	1.67	1.42	1.70
80	1.54	1.59	1.52	1.62	1.49	1.65	1.47	1.67	1.44	1.70
85	1.56	1.60	1.53	1.63	1.51	1.65	1.49	1.68	1.46	1.71
90	1.57	1.61	1.55	1.64	1.53	1.66	1.50	1.69	1.48	1.71
95	1.58	1.62	1.56	1.65	1.54	1.67	1.52	1.69	1.50	1.71
100	1.59	1.63	1.57	1.65	1.55	1.67	1.53	1.70	1.51	1.72

Note: k' = number of explanatory variables excluding the constant term.

Source: J. Durbin and G. S. Watson, "Testing for Serial Correlation in Least Squares Regression—II." *Biometrika*, Vol. 38 (1951), Table 5, "Significance Points of d$_l$ and d$_u$: 2.5%," p. 174. Reproduced by permission of the *Biometrika* Trustees.

Table B.5C
Significance Points of d_L and d_U: 1%

n	k' = 1		k' = 2		k' = 3		k' = 4		k' = 5	
	d_L	d_U	d_L	d_U	d_L	d_U	d_L	d_U	d_L	d_U
15	0.81	1.07	0.70	1.25	0.59	1.46	0.49	1.70	0.39	1.96
16	0.84	1.09	0.74	1.25	0.63	1.44	0.53	1.66	0.44	1.90
17	0.87	1.10	0.77	1.25	0.67	1.43	0.57	1.63	0.48	1.85
18	0.90	1.12	0.80	1.26	0.71	1.42	0.61	1.60	0.52	1.80
19	0.93	1.13	0.83	1.26	0.74	1.41	0.65	1.58	0.56	1.77
20	0.95	1.15	0.86	1.27	0.77	1.41	0.68	1.57	0.60	1.74
21	0.97	1.16	0.89	1.27	0.80	1.41	0.72	1.55	0.63	1.71
22	1.00	1.17	0.91	1.28	0.83	1.40	0.75	1.54	0.66	1.69
23	1.02	1.19	0.94	1.29	0.86	1.40	0.77	1.53	0.70	1.67
24	1.04	1.20	0.96	1.30	0.88	1.41	0.80	1.53	0.72	1.66
25	1.05	1.21	0.98	1.30	0.90	1.41	0.83	1.52	0.75	1.65
26	1.07	1.22	1.00	1.31	0.93	1.41	0.85	1.52	0.78	1.64
27	1.09	1.23	1.02	1.32	0.95	1.41	0.88	1.51	0.81	1.63
28	1.10	1.24	1.04	1.32	0.97	1.41	0.90	1.51	0.83	1.62
29	1.12	1.25	1.05	1.33	0.99	1.42	0.92	1.51	0.85	1.61
30	1.13	1.26	1.07	1.34	1.01	1.42	0.94	1.51	0.88	1.61
31	1.15	1.27	1.08	1.34	1.02	1.42	0.96	1.51	0.90	1.60
32	1.16	1.28	1.10	1.35	1.04	1.43	0.98	1.51	0.92	1.60
33	1.17	1.29	1.11	1.36	1.05	1.43	1.00	1.51	0.94	1.59
34	1.18	1.30	1.13	1.36	1.07	1.43	1.01	1.51	0.95	1.59
35	1.19	1.31	1.14	1.37	1.08	1.44	1.03	1.51	0.97	1.59
36	1.21	1.32	1.15	1.38	1.10	1.44	1.04	1.51	0.99	1.59
37	1.22	1.32	1.16	1.38	1.11	1.45	1.06	1.51	1.00	1.59
38	1.23	1.33	1.18	1.39	1.12	1.45	1.07	1.52	1.02	1.58
39	1.24	1.34	1.19	1.39	1.14	1.45	1.09	1.52	1.03	1.58
40	1.25	1.34	1.20	1.40	1.15	1.46	1.10	1.52	1.05	1.58
45	1.29	1.38	1.24	1.42	1.20	1.48	1.16	1.53	1.11	1.58
50	1.32	1.40	1.28	1.45	1.24	1.49	1.20	1.54	1.16	1.59
55	1.36	1.43	1.32	1.47	1.28	1.51	1.25	1.55	1.21	1.59
60	1.38	1.45	1.35	1.48	1.32	1.52	1.28	1.56	1.25	1.60
65	1.41	1.47	1.38	1.50	1.35	1.53	1.31	1.57	1.28	1.61
70	1.43	1.49	1.40	1.52	1.37	1.55	1.34	1.58	1.31	1.61
75	1.45	1.50	1.42	1.53	1.39	1.56	1.37	1.59	1.34	1.62
80	1.47	1.52	1.44	1.54	1.42	1.57	1.39	1.60	1.36	1.62
85	1.48	1.53	1.46	1.55	1.43	1.58	1.41	1.60	1.39	1.63
90	1.50	1.54	1.47	1.56	1.45	1.59	1.43	1.61	1.41	1.64
95	1.51	1.55	1.49	1.57	1.47	1.60	1.45	1.62	1.42	1.64
100	1.52	1.56	1.50	1.58	1.48	1.60	1.46	1.63	1.44	1.65

Note: k' = number of explanatory variables excluding the constant term.

Source: J. Durbin and G. S. Watson, "Testing for Serial Correlation in Least Squares Regression—II." *Biometrika*, Vol. 38 (1951), Table 6, "Significance Points of d_l and d_u: 1%," p. 175. Reproduced by permission of the *Biometrika* Trustees.

References

Agresti, Alan. 1990. *Categorical Data Analysis*. New York: John Wiley & Sons.

Aldrich, John, and Charles Cnudde. 1975. "Probing the Bounds of Conventional Wisdom: A Comparison of Regression, Probit, and Discriminant Analysis." *American Journal of Political Science* 19 (3): 571–608.

Aldrich, John, and Forest Nelson. 1984. *Linear Probability, Logit, and Probit Models*. Beverly Hills, CA: Sage Publications.

Allison, Paul. 1995. *Survival Analysis Using the SAS System: A Practical Guide*. Gary, NC: The SAS Institute.

Amemiya, Takeshi. 1984. "Tobit Models: A Survey." *Journal of Econometrics* 24: 3–63.

Amemiya, Takeshi, and James Powell. 1983. "A Comparison of the Logit Model and Normal Discriminant Analysis When the Independent Variables Are Binary." In Samuel Karlin, Takeshi Amemiya, and Leo Goodman (eds.), *Studies in Econometrics, Time Series, and Multivariate Statistics*, pp. 3–30. New York: Academic Press.

Ben-Akiva, Moshe, and Steven Lerman. 1987. *Discrete Choice Analysis*. Cambridge, MA: MIT Press.

Berk, Richard. 1983. "An Introduction to Sample Selection Bias in Sociological Data." *American Sociological Review* 48 (June): 386–398.

Berndt, Ernst. 1991. *The Practice of Econometrics: Classic and Contemporary*. Reading, MA: Addison-Wesley Publishing Company.

Berry, William, and Stanley Feldman. 1985. *Multiple Regression in Practice*. Monograph no. 50. Beverly Hills, CA: Sage Publications.

Bollen, Kenneth. 1989. *Structural Equations with Latent Variables*. New York: Wiley.

Bowden, Roger. 1978. "Specification, Estimation and Inference for Models of Markets in Disequilibrium." *International Economic Review* 19 (3): 711–726.

Bradu, D., and Y. Mundlak. 1970. "Estimation in Lognormal Linear Models." *Journal of the American Statistical Association* 65: 198–211.

Breusch, T., and A. Pagan. 1979. "A Simple Test for Heteroscedasticity and Random Coefficient Variation." *Econometrica* 47: 1287–1294.

Carmines, E., and R. Zellner. 1979. *Reliability and Validity Assessment*. Beverly Hills, CA: Sage Publications.

Chow, G. 1960. "Tests of Equality between Sets of Coefficients in Two Linear Regressions." *Econometrica* 28: 591–605.

Cleary, Paul, and Ronald Angel. 1984. "The Analysis of Relationships Involving Dichotomous Dependent Variables." *Journal of Health and Social Behavior* 25 (September): 334–348.

Cochrane, D., and G. Orcutt. 1949. "Application of the Least Squares Regression to Relationships Containing Autocorrelated Error Terms." *Journal of the American Statistical Association* 44: 32–61.

Cox, David. 1972. "Regression Models and Life Tables." *Journal of the Royal Statistical Society*, series B, Vol. 34: 187–202.

Crown, W. 1991. "Migration and Regional Economic Growth: An Origin-Destination Model." *Economic Development Quarterly* 5 (1): 45–59.

Crown, W., M. MacAdam, and D. Ahlburg. 1995. "The Demographic and Employment Characteristics of Home Care Aides: A Comparison with Nursing Home Aides, Hospital Aides, and Other Workers." *The Gerontologist* 35 (2): 162–170.

Domencich, T., and D. McFadden. 1975. *Urban Travel Demand*. Amsterdam: North Holland.

Duan, N. 1983. "Smearing Estimate: A Nonparametric Retransformation Method." *Journal of the American Statistical Assocation* 78: 605–610.

Duan, N., W. Manning, C. Morris, and J. Newhouse. 1983. "A Comparison of Alternative Models for the Demand for Medical Care." *Journal of Business & Economic Statistics* 1 (2): 115–126.

Duan, N., W. Manning, C. Morris, and J. Newhouse. 1984. "Choosing Between the Sample-Selection Model and the Multi-Part Model." *Journal of Business & Economic Statistics* 2 (3): 283–289.

Dubin, Jeffrey, and Douglass Rivers. 1989/90. "Selection Bias in Linear Regression, Logit, and Probit Models." *Sociological Methods and Research* 18 (2&3): 360–390.

Duncan, O. D. 1975. *Introduction to Structural Equation Models*. New York: Academic Press.

Durbin, J. 1954. "Errors in Variables." *Review of the International Statistics Institute* (1): 23–32.

Durbin, J., and G. S. Watson. 1950. "Testing for Serial Correlation in Least Squares Regression—I." *Biometrica* 37: 409–428.

Durbin, J., and G. S. Watson. 1951. "Testing for Serial Correlation in Least Squares Regression—II." *Biometrica* 38: 159–178.

Durbin, J., and G. S. Watson. 1971. "Testing for Serial Correlation in Least Squares Regression—III." *Biometrica* 58: 1–42.

Ebbeler, D. 1973. "A Note on Large-Sample Approximation in Lognormal Linear Models." *Journal of the American Statistical Association* 68: 231.

Evans, I., and S. Shaban. 1974. "A Note on Estimation in Lognormal Models." *Journal of the American Statistical Association* 69: 779–781.

Fomby, Thomas, R. Carter Hill, and Stanley Johnson. 1984. *Advanced Econometric Methods*. New York: Springer-Verlag.

Fox, John. 1991. *Regression Diagnostics*. Newbury Park, CA: Sage Publications.

Ghosh, Sukesh. 1991. *Econometrics: Theory and Applications*. Englewood Cliffs, NJ: Prentice Hall.

Godfrey, L. 1988. *Misspecification Tests in Econometrics*. Cambridge: Cambridge University Press.

Goldberger, A. 1964. *Econometric Theory*. New York: Wiley.

Goldberger, A. 1983. "Abnormal Selection Bias." In S. Karlin, T. Amemiya, and L. Goodman (eds.), *Studies in Econometrics, Time Series, and Multivariate Statistics*. New York: Academic Press.

Goldberger, A. S., and O. D. Duncan, eds. 1973. *Structural Equation Models in the Social Sciences*. New York: Seminar Press.

Goldfeld, S., and R. Quandt. 1965. "Some Tests for Homoscedasticity." *Journal of the American Statistical Association* 60: 539–547.

Gottman, John. 1981. *Time-Series Analysis: A Comprehensive Introduction for Social Scientists*. Cambridge, England: Cambridge University Press.

Greene, William. 1993. *Econometric Analysis*. 2nd ed. Englewood Cliffs, NJ: Prentice Hall.

Gunderson, M. 1974. "Retention of Trainees: A Study with Dichotomous Dependent Variables." *Journal of Econometrics* 2: 79–93.

Hamilton, Lawrence. 1992. *Regression with Graphics: A Second Course in Applied Statistics*. Pacific Grove, CA: Brooks/Cole Publishing Company.

Harvey, A. C., and G. D. A. Phillips. 1973. "A Comparison of the Power of Some Tests of Heteroscedasticity in the General Linear Model." *Journal of Econometrics* (2): 312–316.

Hausman, J. 1978. "Specification Tests in Econometrics." *Econometrica* 46: 1251–1271.

Hausman, J., and D. McFadden. 1984. "Specification Tests for the Multinomial Logit Model." *Econometrica* 52: 1219–1240.

Heckman, J. 1976. "The Common Structure of Statistical Models of Truncation, Sample Selection, and Limited Dependent Variables and a Simple Estimator for Such Models." *Annals of Economic and Social Measurement* 5: 475–492.

Heckman, J. 1979. "Sample Selection Bias as a Specification Error." *Econometrica* 47: 153–161.

Heckman, J. 1990. "Varieties of Selection Bias." *American Economic Review* 80: 313–318.

Heckman, J., and J. Smith. 1995. "Assessing the Case for Social Experiments." *Journal of Economic Perspectives* 9 (2): 85–110.

Hoerl, A., and R. Kennard. 1970. "Ridge Regression: Biased Estimation for Nonorthogonal Problems." *Technometrics*, 12: 69–82.

Hosmer, D., and S. Lemeshow. 1989. *Applied Logistic Regression*. New York: John Wiley & Sons.

Johnson, A., M. Johnson, and R. Buse. 1987. *Econometrics: Basic and Applied*. New York: Macmillan Publishing Company.

Johnson, J. 1972. *Econometric Methods*. 2nd ed. New York: McGraw-Hill.

Johnson, N., and S. Kotz. 1972. *Distributions in Statistics—Continuous Multivariate Distributions*. New York: Wiley.

Judge, G., W. Griffiths, R. Hill, and T. Lee. 1980. *The Theory and Practice of Econometrics*. New York: Wiley.

Kennedy, Peter. 1992. *A Guide to Econometrics*. Cambridge, MA: MIT Press.

Kiefer, N., and M. Salmon. 1983. "Testing Normality in Econometric Models." *Economics Letters* 11: 123–128.

Kiefer, Nicholas. 1988. "Economic Duration Data and Hazard Functions." *Journal of Economic Literature* 26: 646–679.

Killingsworth, Mark. 1983. *Labor Supply*. Cambridge, England: Cambridge University Press.

Kmenta, J. 1971. *Elements of Econometrics*. New York: Macmillan.

Lee, L. 1983. "Generalized Econometric Models with Selectivity Bias." *Econometrica* 51: 507–512.

Lee, Lung-Fei. 1978. "Unionism and Wage Rates: A Simultaneous Equations Model with Qualitative and Limited Dependent Variables." *International Economic Review* 19 (2): 415–433.

Lee, Lung-Fei, G. S. Maddala, and R. P. Trost. 1980. "Asymptotic Covariance Matrices of Two-Stage Probit and Two-Stage Tobit Methods for Simultaneous Equations Models with Selectivity." *Econometrica* (March): 491–504.

Lewis-Beck, Michael. 1980. *Applied Regression: An Introduction.* Monograph no. 22. Beverly Hills, CA: Sage Publications.

Long, J. 1983. *Covariance Structure Models: An Introduction to LISREL.* Beverly Hills, CA: Sage Publications.

Maddala, G. S. 1977. *Econometrics.* New York: McGraw-Hill.

Maddala, G. S. 1986. "Disequilibrium, Self-Selection, and Switching Models." In Z. Griliches and M. D. Intriligator (eds.), *Handbook of Econometrics,* vol. 3, pp. 1634–1688. New York: North Holland.

Maddala, G. S. 1990. *Limited-Dependent and Qualitative Variables in Econometrics.* Cambridge, England: Cambridge University Press.

Malinvaud, E. 1966. *Statistical Methods of Econometrics.* Chicago: Rand McNally.

Manski, C. 1990. "Nonparametric Bounds on Treatment Effects." *American Economic Review* 80: 319–323.

Mauser, Elizabeth, and Nancy Miller. 1994. "A Profile of Home Health Users in 1992." *Health Care Financing Review* 16 (1): 17–33.

McDonald, J., and R. Moffit. 1980. "The Uses of Tobit Analysis." *The Review of Economics and Statistics* 62: 318–321.

McFadden, D. 1973. "Conditional Logit Analysis of Quantitative Choice Behavior." In P. Zarambka (ed.), *Frontiers in Econometrics.* New York: Academic Press.

McFadden, D. 1984. "Econometric Analysis of Qualitative Response Models." In Z. Griliches and M. Intriligator (eds.), *Handbook of Econometrics,* Vol. 2. Elsevier Science Publishers.

McIver, J., and E. Carmines. 1981. *Unidimensional Scaling.* Beverly Hills, CA: Sage Publications.

McLeary, Richard, and Richard A. Hay, Jr. 1980. *Applied Time Series Analysis for the Social Sciences.* Beverly Hills, CA: Sage Publications.

Mehran, F. 1973. "Variance of the MVUE for the Lognormal Mean." *Journal of the American Statistical Association* 68: 726–727.

Merrington, Maxine. 1942. "Table of Percentage Points of the *t*-Distribution." *Biometrika* 32: 300.

Merrington, M., and C. M. Thompson. 1943. "Tables of Percentage Points of the Inverted Beta (*F*) Distribution." *Biometrika* 33: 73–88.

Meulenberg, M. 1965. "On the Estimation of an Exponential Function." *Econometrica* 33: 863–868.

Morely, Gunderson. 1974. "Retention of Trainees: A Study with Dichotomous Dependent Variables." *Journal of Econometrics* 2: 79–93.

Murnane, Richard, Stuart Newstead, and Randall Olsen. 1985. "Comparing Public and Private Schools: The Puzzling Role of Selectivity Bias." *Journal of Business and Economic Statistics* 3 (1): 23–35.

Nakosteen, R., and M. Zimmer. 1980. "Migration and Income: The Question of Self-Selection." *Southern Economic Journal* 46: 840–851.

Nelson, Forest, and Lawrence Olson. 1978. "Specification and Estimation of a Simultaneous Equation Model with Limited Dependent Variables." *International Economic Review* 19 (3): 695–709.

Neter, J., W. Wasserman, and M. Kutner. 1990. *Applied Linear Statistical Models: Regression, Analysis of Variance, and Experimental Designs.* Boston: Richard D. Irwin.

Neyman, J., and E. Scott. 1960. "Correction for Bias Introduced by a Transformation of Variables." *Annals of Mathematical Statistics* 31: 643–655.

Pearson, E. S., and H. O. Hartley, eds. 1966. *Biometrika Tables for Statisticians.* Vol. 1, 3rd. ed. Cambridge, England: Cambridge University Press.

Pindyck, Robert, and Daniel Rubinfeld. 1991. *Econometric Models & Economic Forecasts.* 3rd ed. New York: McGraw-Hill.

Prais, S., and H. Houthakker. 1955. *The Analysis of Family Budgets.* New York: Cambridge University Press.

Prais, S., and C. Winsten. 1954. *Trend Estimation and Serial Correlation.* Discussion paper 383. Chicago: Cowles Commission.

Robinson, C., and N. Tomes. 1982. "Self Selection and Interprovincial Migration in Canada." *Canadian Journal of Economics* 15: 474–502.

Schmidt, Peter, and Robert Strauss. 1975. "The Prediction of Occupation Using Multiple Logit Models." *International Economic Review* 16 (2): 471–486.

Schroeder, Larry, David Sjoquist, and Paula Stephan. 1986. *Understanding Regression Analysis: An Introductory Guide.* Monograph no. 57. Beverly Hills, CA: Sage Publications.

Shimizu, K., and K. Iwase. 1981. "Uniformly Minimum Variance Unbiased Estimation in Lognormal and Related Distributions." *Communications in Statistics* A (11): 687–697.

Smith, Richard, and Richard Blundell. 1986. "An Exogeneity Test for a Simultaneous Equation Tobit Model with an Application to Labor Supply." *Econometrica* 54 (3): 679–685.

Sullivan, J., and S. Feldman. 1979. *Multiple Indicators: An Introduction.* Beverly Hills, CA: Sage Publications.

Tobin, J. 1958. "Estimation of Relationships for Limited Dependent Variables." *Econometrica* 26: 24–36.

Train, Kenneth. 1986. *Qualitative Choice Analysis.* Cambridge, MA: MIT Press.

Wald, A. 1940. "The Fitting of Straight Lines If Both Variables Are Subject to Errors." *Annals of Mathematical Statistics* 11: 284–300.

White, H. 1980. "A Heteroscedasticity-Consistent Covariance Matrix Estimator and a Direct Test for Heteroscedasticity." *Econometrica* 48: 817–838.

White, H., and G. MacDonald. 1980. "Some Large Sample Tests for Non-Normality in the Linear Regression Model." *Journal of the American Statistical Association* 75: 16–28.

Willis, Robert, and Sherwin Rosen. 1979. "Education and Self-Selection." *Journal of Political Economy* 87 (5), pt.2: S7–S36.

Wynand, P., and B. van Praag. 1981. "The Demand for Deductibles in Private Health Insurance: A Probit Model with Sample Selection." *Journal of Econometrics* 17: 229–252.

Zavoina, R., and W. McElvey. 1975. "A Statistical Model for the Analysis of Ordinal Level Dependent Variables." *Journal of Mathematical Sociology* (Summer): 103–120.

Index

About the Author

WILLIAM H. CROWN is Director of outcomes research and econometrics at The MEDSTAT Group. Dr. Crown's research focuses on the application of econometric methods to problems in outcomes research, the economics of aging, health policy, and regional economics. He has published numerous articles and is coauthor of *State Per-Capita Income Change Since 1950* (Greenwood, 1995) and *Economics of Population Aging* (Auburn House, 1990), and editor of *Handbook on Employment and the Elderly* (Greenwood, 1996).

ISBN 0-275-95316-5

EAN

9 780275 953164

90000>

HARDCOVER BAR CODE